The Korean War Novel

Edinburgh Critical Studies in War and Culture
Series Editors: Kate McLoughlin and Gill Plain

Available Titles:
Our Nazis: Representations of Fascism in Contemporary Literature and Film
Petra Rau

Writing the Radio War: Literature, Politics and the BBC, 1939–1945
Ian Whittington

The Korean War Novel: Rewriting History from the Civil War to the Post-Cold War
Suk Koo Rhee

Visit our website at: https://edinburghuniversitypress.com/series-edinburgh-critical-studies-in-war-and-culture

The Korean War Novel

Rewriting History from the Civil War to the
Post-Cold War

Suk Koo Rhee

EDINBURGH
University Press

Edinburgh University Press is one of the leading university presses in the UK. We publish academic books and journals in our selected subject areas across the humanities and social sciences, combining cutting-edge scholarship with high editorial and production values to produce academic works of lasting importance. For more information visit our website: edinburghuniversitypress.com

© Suk Koo Rhee, 2024

This work was supported by the Ministry of Education of the Republic of Korea and the National Research Foundation of Korea (NRF-2020S1A6A4041254).

Edinburgh University Press Ltd
13 Infirmary Street
Edinburgh EH1 1LT

Typeset in 10.5/13 pt Sabon by
Cheshire Typesetting Ltd, Cuddington, Cheshire, and
printed and bound in Great Britain.

A CIP record for this book is available from the British Library

ISBN 978 1 3995 2452 0 (hardback)
ISBN 978 1 3995 2454 4 (webready PDF)
ISBN 978 1 3995 2455 1 (epub)

The right of Suk Koo Rhee to be identified as the author of this work has been asserted in accordance with the Copyright, Designs and Patents Act 1988, and the Copyright and Related Rights Regulations 2003 (SI No. 2498).

Contents

List of Figures	vi
Acknowledgements	vii
Series Editors' Preface	ix
Romanisation and Abbreviations	x
Introduction: The War That Is Not One	1
1 The Metaphysical War	32
2 The UN Ladies' War	58
3 Orientalism and the Cold War	91
4 The Politics of Neutrality	114
5 Beyond the Cold War?	149
6 A Postcolonial War in Reverse	179
Conclusion: Living the Cold War Legacy	212
Bibliography	233
Index	246

Figures

0.1	An anti-communist rally on 23 September 1948 in a stadium in Seoul. (Source: National Archives photo no. 111-SC-308846)	13
0.2	North Korean attack, June to September 1950, and UN offensive, late September to November 1950. (Source: © Lee Wol-sun)	21
1.1	Pyongyang Central Marshalling Yards on 25 October 1950 after a raid by US B-29 bombers. (Source: National Archives photo no. 342-FH-4A38936-B87162ac)	40
3.1	A right-wing protest against trusteeship on 23 June 1947. (Source: National Archives photo no. 111-SC-288649)	101
4.1	A North Korean prisoner forced to undergo tattooing in a photo taken on 18 July 1952. (Source: National Archives photo no. 111-C-9290)	122
4.2	Anti-communist slogans tattooed on the arms of pro-Nationalist prisoners. (Source: National Archives photo no. 306-N-54-822)	127
6.1	A crowd of 20,000 South Koreans at a rally on 11 July 1951, listening to speeches calling for the rejection of the armistice on the grounds that it lacked provisions for unifying the two Koreas. (Source: National Archives photo no. 111-SC-372325)	209
7.1	Pastor Kang Ch'ungguk on his way to a T'aegŭkki rally carrying a cross with US and Korean national flags attached to it. (Source: © News&Joy)	230
7.2	A T'aegŭkki rally sporting three sets of national flags. (Source: © News&Joy)	231

Acknowledgements

Over the past two and a half decades, I have had the privilege of working in a caring community, the Department of English Language and Literature at Yonsei University. I would like to express my deep gratitude to my dear colleagues for their moral support throughout these years. In particular, I want to acknowledge Shin Kyung-sook, Yang Seok-won, Suh Hong-won and Rhee Seok-chae for their companionship, which has provided me with solace and reassurance. Theodore Jun Yoo from the Department of Korean Language and Literature deserves a special mention for his encouragement of my research. In addition, I would like to extend my appreciation to Terry Murphy and Peter Paik for serving as the first readers of my manuscript. In particular, Terry carefully reviewed each chapter as if it were his own.

Among all my cherished colleagues, I must give special recognition to Lee Kyung-Won whose presence in my life has been truly transformative. His insightful guidance and unwavering belief in my potential have played an indispensable role in shaping my life journey as both scholar and individual. Without him, I would not be where I am today. Over the years, his commitment to academic excellence and his passion for teaching have left an indelible mark on both the institution and on those who have been fortunate enough to have crossed paths with him. By his great sense of humour and genuine warmth, he has elevated our spirits. With both pride and a tinge of sadness, I offer this book to him upon his retirement, as a token of gratitude for the invaluable impact he has made on me personally as well as on the entire department.

During my tenure as the Managing Editor of *Situations: Cultural Studies in the Asian Context*, I have had the opportunity to learn from the mentorship of numerous distinguished scholars, including Chua Beng Huat, Chen Kuan-hsing, John Erni, Heonik Kwon, Lee Keehyeung, Larry Grossberg and Rey Chow. I would like to express my deepest gratitude to Joseph Jonghyun Jeon, Kyung Hyun Kim, Akira Lippit,

Sunyoung Park, Eli Park Sorensen, Winnie Yee and Fiona Law, who granted me the honour of co-teaching a number of graduate courses at Yonsei. Collaborating with these renowned scholars greatly expanded the intellectual scope of this book.

Engaging in discussions on the historical and political aspects of the Korean War Novel with my colleagues and students helped me to refine my arguments. I extend my heartfelt appreciation to Josephine Nock-Hee Park and Daniel Y. Kim for their special lectures for Yonsei students on the texts explored in this book. I want to thank the graduate students who participated in my course, 'The English War Novel and the Cold War'. Their vibrant discussions enriched my analysis of Korean War fiction. I also want to express my gratitude to those former students of mine whose insightful theses brought me great pleasure. The memories of working with Kim Eun-hae, Byun Jiyon, Mojca Penja, Choi Choa, Kim Hojung and Lee Seungyeon filled my heart with warmth and inspiration, and I am grateful for the incredible experiences we shared. I am deeply indebted to Choa, who went to great lengths to procure some valuable sources I urgently needed for my book. A special thanks goes to Kim Chang-Hee, Om Donghee, Shin Nami, Song Junggyung, Park Hyowon and Choi Seong-Woo for their steadfast friendships that supported me through some challenging times.

I would like to extend my thanks to the editors and staff members at Edinburgh University Press, Jackie Jones, Gill Plain, Kate McLoughlin, Elizabeth Fraser and Fiona Conn and my wonderful copyeditor Magda Wojcik as well as my anonymous reviewers, who meticulously read the manuscript and provided me with valuable suggestions. Lastly, I am grateful to my wife Kyung Nam and my two sons, Eugene and Euhyun, for their unwavering love and support. They are the foundation of my strength and happiness.

Series Editors' Preface

This series of monographs is designed to showcase innovative new scholarship in the literary and filmic representation of war. The series embraces Anglophone literature and film of all genres, with studies adopting a range of critical approaches including transhistorical and intercultural analysis. 'War' in this context is understood to mean armed conflict of the industrialised age (that is, from the late eighteenth century onwards), including not only conventional war between sovereign states but also revolution, insurrection, civil war, guerrilla warfare, cold war and genocide (including the Holocaust). The series is concerned with the multiple, often conflicting, significations that surround the act and event of armed combat, and volumes will also consider the causes, consequences and aftermath of wars; pro- and anti-war literature and film; memorialisation, trauma and testimony. The premise of the series is that new critical perspectives need to be developed in order to understand war representation better. Rather than simply analysing war texts, or even situating those texts in their contemporary cultural contexts, Edinburgh Critical Studies in War and Culture will identify the conceptual categories and forms by which war has been mediated in literature and film, and illuminate the cultural influences that produce them. Wars shape bodies, minds and literary forms; they mediate the possibilities of expression and create discourses of repression; they construct ambivalent subjectivities such as the enemy and the veteran; they invade and distort popular genres from crime fiction to fantasy; they leave tangible scars on the landscape and generate the production of memorials both concrete and imagined. This series explores the role of literature and film in mediating such events, and in articulating the contradictions of 'war' and 'culture'.

Kate McLoughlin and Gill Plain

Romanisation and Abbreviations

Korean and Chinese names and terms have been transliterated according to the McCune-Reischauer and the Pinyin system respectively, with the exception of Korean place names and personal names with commonly accepted alternative spellings such as Mao Tse-tung and Park Chung-hee. In instances where the Korean place names used in the novel differ from the South Korean government's official spellings, I have included both, with the novelist's chosen spellings placed within parentheses on first appearance. When referring to Korean and Chinese nationals, I have placed the surnames first.

CIES	Civil Information and Education Section
CPKI	Committee for Preparation of Korean Independence
DPRK	Democratic People's Republic of Korea (the Communist North Korea)
KPA	Korean People's Army
KPR	Korean People's Republic, a short-lived provisional government organised by South Korean nationalists in the wake of national liberation
MP	military police
POW	prisoner of war
ROK	Republic of Korea
ROKA	Republic of Korea Army
USIS	United States Information Service

To Lee Kyung-Won, My Esteemed Colleague

Introduction:
The War That Is Not One

Literature and history *qua* writing

This book seeks to uncover the ways in which six historical novels fashion or rewrite the history of the Korean War, seeking out the narrative strategies employed in each rewriting. As narrated in each of these novels, the Korean War ranges from an international war through a civil war to a war between the genders before culminating in what I will be calling the 'de-escalating of the Cold War'. Whichever shape it takes, however, this war cannot be considered apart from its international dimension – that is, the Cold War. In employing the term 'Cold War', this book aligns itself with the new perspectives advanced by scholars such as Heonik Kwon and Jodi Kim, who have suggested that the Cold War is an epistemology that not only informs and organises the social order but intervenes in meaning production. Seen in this way, the Cold War provides a new framework in which to consider both the Korean War and the historical or Korean War novel itself. This project is also indebted to the work of scholars such as Bruce Cumings and Kim Dong-Choon, whose revisionist expertise helped to recover a civil war dimension to what was known as a proxy war.

In this book, I have chosen to analyse three representative Korean-language novels – each of which is readily available in English translation – and three representative Asian American novels. The first group includes Choi In-hun's *The Square* (1960 in Korean; 2014 in English), Ahn Junghyo's *Silver Stallion* (written in 1964, published in 1986 in Korean; 1990 in English) and Hwang Sok-yong's *The Guest* (2001 in Korean; 2005 in English). The second group comprises Richard E. Kim's *The Martyred* (1964), Susan Choi's *The Foreign Student* (1998) and Ha Jin's *War Trash* (2004). If *The Square*, *The Martyred* and *Silver Stallion*,

2　The Korean War Novel

all written or published in the 1960s, constitute attempts to confront or manage in their own ways the still unhealed wounds of national division; the other three novels, all published after 1989, purport to revisit the Korean War from emergent post-Cold War perspectives that seek to re-evaluate critically the legacies of US military intervention.

In bringing together the works by Korean writers and Asian diasporic writers, this book aims at 'writing back' against the authoritative Cold War historiography. It does this by examining these differentiated rewritings of the Korean War and, at the same time, seeking to reckon with the dual role of Northeast Asians as both victims and agents of the Cold War, even if the scope of this reckoning is limited to those embroiled in the national conflict on the peninsula. In order to do this, the book subjects the texts to a process of rigorous scrutiny or 'dialogisation' so that each work, compared against both official and counter-historical discourses, may reveal the implicit ideological contours of its own historical perspective as well as those of the historical discourses themselves. The reason for proposing a re-examination of the texts is my strong sense that the ideological complexities of these narratives, both Korean and Asian American, have not yet received sufficient critical attention. In part, this ideological probing derives its justification from the everyday banalities of political discourse in the Republic of Korea (ROK) that suggest the Cold War was not simply an alien system imposed on innocent people but has shaped or penetrated our identities as well as our nation-state, consciously and unconsciously, even though we criticise it. The willing participation of Koreans in the ideological polarisation of the peninsula is recognised by Jongsoo James Lee when he asserts: 'the division effected in August 1945 by the two great powers led elements among the Koreans to ally themselves with either of the Powers, thereby themselves becoming forces that abetted and solidified this division' (2006: xviii). This project attends to the warning issued by Lim Jie-Hyun against what he calls a 'victimhood nationalism', which unquestioningly accords the status of righteousness to the members and their descendants of a nation persecuted at the hands of another (2010: 138–62). It also echoes Petra Rau's insight that while it refers to 'a foreign evil, an ideological otherness', fascism in the Western world is at the same time 'integral to the self precisely in those moments when culture casts [it] as other' (2013: 9, 10).

This study assesses the ways in which each of these novelists rewrites the Korean War and, where relevant, relates each novel to the dual dimension of the civil war and the Cold War. Whenever possible, the book brings to the fore the manner in which each work reinforces the Cold War framework or seeks to challenge or subvert it – in certain cases, the ways in which certain novels even attempt to articulate an alternative political vision. The investigation seeks out the potentially traumatising events associated with war – the slaughter of civilians, military sex crimes and prostitution, war crimes committed against prisoners of war (POWs) and major acts of civil strife – as particularly significant. Here, the absence of highly problematic events is viewed as potentially revealing as their presence in delineating the agenda of the novel, implicit or explicit. In maintaining this line of thinking, this book is inspired by Pierre Macherey, who, following Friedrich Nietzsche, suggested that it is 'useful and legitimate to ask of every [literary] production what it tacitly implies, what it does not say . . . for in order to say anything, there are things *which must not be said*' (1980: 85; emphasis in the original). In order to make the story speak of what it maintains silence about, the critic approaches it with a set of questions that Nietzsche formulated in the following manner: 'When we are confronted with any manifestation which someone has permitted us to see, we may ask – what is it meant to conceal? What is it meant to draw our attention from?' (Macherey 1980: 87). In those instances where certain events or certain aspects of the war receive extensive or even exclusive treatment, it is possible to ask what that treatment is meant to prevent us from seeing. This perspective allows for an extended rumination on the implications of what these war novels choose to be conspicuously silent about as well as on the more immediate significance of what they consciously bring to the fore.

Through this ideological investigation, I hope to be able to articulate the voice of a South Korean scholar's perspective on this trans-Pacific textual network, which may appear troubling to, rather than supportive of, the cause advocated by Sau-Ling Wong in her insightful work *Reading Asian American Literature: From Necessity to Extravagance*. It calls for the critics in Asian American Studies to make a concerted, but non-binding, commitment to the mission of building an Asian American literary tradition and, furthermore, making the voice of Asian Americans audible ([1993] 2001: 9). Although it welcomes and appreciates some sort of alliance among the literary and cultural works that challenge the self-legitimating legacies of the Cold War, this book takes a different route than the one recommended by the influential Asian American critic. Echoing Paul Ricoeur's hermeneutics of suspicion, of which 'willingness to suspect' helps to guard our preconceptions and moral certainties from masking the truth about the text (1970: 27), it prioritises the task of clinically examining the politics, implied or not, of the Korean war novels. Given the fact that criticism lacking self-reflection or self-criticism cannot hold very long, this project is my way

4   *The Korean War Novel*

of showing, if only by way of an extended detour, solidarity with the cause of promoting decolonisation for the people still struggling with the evolving legacies of the Cold War in the Asia-Pacific region.

The Cold War in a new light

The novels of the Korean War cannot be considered apart from the international dimension of the conflict – that is, from the overarching Cold War between the United States and the Union of Soviet Socialist Republics. The ways these works engage with the Cold War may be said to diverge. Sometimes, they end up working in collusion with the Cold War; they measure its realities against its propaganda or envision the war beyond its limits; in every case, however, these novels challenge Western-centric notions of the Cold War as a period of uneasy long-term peace centred in a conflict over the fate of Europe.

It would therefore seem useful to ask the question: When did the Cold War start? The trouble is that different scholars have offered different answers to this important question. The earliest historical date is the one suggested by Melvyn Leffler: the Cold War began in 1917 in the massive political and military upheaval signalled by the Russian Revolution (qtd in H. Kwon 2010: 3). Odd Arne Westad also takes note of the Russian Revolution as an important milestone in superpower rivalry by observing that 'over the years that followed Soviet Communism came to be seen as a deadly rival of Americanism, because it put itself forward as an alternative modernity' (2007: 17). A more conventional understanding of this global war would argue, however, that the Cold War really only begins in the aftermath of World War 2, with Winston Churchill's 'Iron Curtain' speech of 5 March 1946 at Westminster College, Fulton, Missouri.

For Westad, what is really interesting about the use of the term is this: while the US used it regularly when speaking of a 'war of containment' against the Soviet Union, until the advent of Mikhail Gorbachev, it was a term unknown to the Soviet leadership. The reason for the disinclination to use the term is that the Soviet leadership held to the narrative that their country was peace-loving: it was the US's aggressive policy of imperialism that threatened world peace (Westad 2007: 2). Whether this narrative has an element of truth or not, it is certainly true that the superpower distrust and fear was mutual. If we define the Cold War in a conventional sense – that is, as a competition between the United States and the Soviet Union for global hegemony – it is possible to argue that the Cold War began in the immediate aftermath of World War 2.

The Cold War was a fact of international politics some years before the outbreak of the Korean War.

Unlike the issue of its disputed beginning, the end of the Cold War does not appear to be a point of major academic contention. For most Cold War scholars, the Cold War ends with the fall of the Berlin Wall and the unification of Germany, shortly followed by the collapse of the Soviet Union itself in 1991. However, from an alternative perspective, the established views on the periodisation of the Cold War reflect only the viewpoint of the superpowers themselves. For the superpowers, the contest for global hegemony, which was paradoxically characterised by no declaration of war, was terminated in 1991 after a spell of about half a century.

As Walter LaFeber maintains, however, '[b]efore we conclude that the Cold War has ended, it might be as well to decide which Cold War is under discussion' (1992: 13). The reason for proposing this new perspective is that the experience of the Cold War is radically different, depending on the historian's location and involvement. That is, certain regional histories contradict the conventional understanding of the Cold War as the absence of a hot war. For instance, five most militarily expensive regional wars the US found itself engaged in in its entire history took place in Asia after World War 2 (Harrington and Suneson 2019). Andrew Hammond also states: '[t]he "Cold War" is an erroneous term for a global conflict which, spanning several continents and a multitude of coups, civil wars, insurgencies and interventions, was characterised by ongoing armed aggression' (2006: 1). In this light, Cumings maintains that the Western-centric notion of the Cold War is not appropriate to account for the experiences in the vast area beyond the Iron Curtain dividing Central Europe (1999: 51) – not least because to view the Cold War as an undeclared 'imaginary' war between the two superpowers elides the two major hot wars in Asia as non-existent or reduces them to proxy wars. In this way, the interested parties are stripped of agency. The reason why the traditional view of these wars has prevailed is partly due to the preponderance of the US-centric understanding of the wars in terms of anti-communist wars of geopolitical containment.

As Westad argues, however, the hegemonic contest between the superpowers on the one hand and the anti-colonial or postcolonial movements in Asia and Africa on the other have not evolved on parallel paths. Instead, these movements have affected the historical trajectory of each other by mutual interpenetration (2007: 3). For this reason, it is only when both the civil and the international aspects of the two major wars in East Asia are considered to be operating in tandem that a more balanced view can be reached. Such an act of reinterpretation must necessarily involve the comprehensive reconsideration of the narratives that then emerged to explain them.

As mentioned earlier, this research project is indebted to some recent studies on the history of the Cold War that help to expand our understanding of it. According to scholars like Heonik Kwon and Jodi Kim, the Cold War should be understood as a conflict between two dominant systems that produce, circulate and consume meanings unique to each of them. In other words, the contest between the two superpowers is a contest for politico-economic hegemony construed in terms of semantic and cultural issues. To quote Kwon's own words: '[t]he cold war was as much a "battle for the appropriation of meaning" between two competing teleological systems of historical progress as a battle for power between two competing social systems' (2010: 5). Here, the Cold War is seen as a competition between two incommensurable interpretations of the world. The interpretation that one group or nation chooses determines not only its relationship with the world but also offers to determine the telos of the global historical movement itself. In this light, the Cold War functions as a battle between two opposite sets of rival beliefs that organise what Louis Althusser calls one's lived, yet imaginary, relationship with the material world (1971: 162). In a similar way, Jodi Kim refers to the Cold War as an 'epistemology' (2010: 3). In the Korean American critic's words, '[t]he Korean War appears not simply as a congealed historical episode that is given narrative form after-the-event, but also as a Cold War epistemology in the making' (Kim 2010: 145).

The Cold War as a US-centred epistemology has encouraged certain knowledges while forbidding others, as a means of pursuing the US project of global hegemony. Although Kim limits the scope of the Cold War in the first place to the production of knowledge, this global war certainly had a material dimension. As an aspect of the US-led international political order, the Cold War required a significant investment in the set-up of the state apparatuses, both ideological and repressive, in the Western world – a project also repeated, even more visibly, in the non-Western nations under its influence. Since this system of rules that govern knowledge production operates both consciously and unconsciously, it may be called an 'episteme' in a Foucauldian sense. According to Foucault, an episteme is an underlying order of discursive practices that 'defines the conditions of possibility of all knowledge' ([1966] 1973: 168).

To define the Cold War as an epistemology or episteme instead of a time period or a military competition between the two superpowers has certain obvious merits. For example, it allows the researcher to consider, within a more appropriate framework, a more delimited geographical area like that of the Korean peninsula. Such a regional geography is affected – and continues to be affected – not only by the global dimensions of the Cold War but also by a more local or regional Cold War. This is a topic to which I will return in the conclusion. The notion of episteme also helps the literary critic to investigate the novelistic representations of the Korean War in a new light: the researcher may attend to the kind of thinking the Cold War episteme encourages or forbids, the historical facts to which it grants meaning or value, what historical facts it withholds and how it influences or helps organise cultural production and individual experience. This perspective enables the critic to appraise these Korean War novels in terms of the Cold War episteme: to ask the central question of the manner in which the novelistic engagements with the Korean War can be regarded as complying with or exceeding these preset limits.

The Cold War preceding the Korean War

Long before the outbreak of the Korean War, the Cold War had been waged on the Korean peninsula. The presence of this global 'imaginary' war had been felt in the division or rather in the interdiction of the possibility of reunification of the Korean people. Immediately following the achievement of independence from Japanese colonialism, the peninsula had been divided across the thirty-eighth parallel. At the February 1945 Yalta Conference, as William Stueck recounts, even before the cessation of hostilities ending World War 2, the US President Franklin D. Roosevelt had proposed to the Soviet Premier Joseph Stalin a twenty- or thirty-year multinational trusteeship for Korea (1995: 1–6). At this time, Roosevelt conceded to the Soviet leader, in return for the Soviet army's entering the war against Japan in East Asia, the Kurile Islands as well as special privileges in Manchuria. Although the United States and the Soviet Union did not work out concrete terms concerning the fate of Korea either at Yalta or later at the Potsdam Conference, both appeared to share an understanding that neither would attempt to occupy the entire peninsula. It was in early August 1945 that US President Harry S. Truman and Stalin consented to divide Korea along the thirty-eighth parallel and occupied the southern and northern portions of the peninsula, respectively (Stueck [1995] 1997: 19). That is to say, the seeds for the tragedy of the Korean War were sown when the superpowers took the decision to divide the peninsula. The division in turn brought into the much larger geopolitical division of the Cold War the people of a small peninsula who had lived as one nation for more than 1,000 years.

8 *The Korean War Novel*

Just as the Soviet occupying forces in northern Korea were responsible for the ideological fortification of the northern half of Korea, so the US occupying forces in southern Korea took control of a similar process that unfolded in its south. Perhaps unsurprisingly, then, as Cumings and other progressive scholars maintain, the US military government also took over responsibility and assumed accountability for the continuing legacies of Japanese imperialism in southern Korea.[1] Theodore Jun Yoo encapsulates the situation in the following concise terms: '[t]he mid-wives to the painful birth of the twin nations from a unified Korea were more concerned with their own Cold War agendas than the fate of the people' (2020: n. p.).

As Cumings, Lee Gyu-tae and Theodore Jun Yoo recount (Cumings 1981: Ch. 3; G.-T. Lee 2006; Yoo 2020), in the immediate run-up to the moment of national liberation, local Korean nationalists began to organise the Committee for Preparation of Korean Independence (CPKI). In southern Korea, the CPKI was established under the leadership of Yŏ Unhyŏng, a highly respected, moderate, leftist nationalist. It swiftly established a nationwide network of People's Committees, organised down to the township grass-roots level across the entire peninsula. On 6 September 1945, two days before the US Army moved in, the CPKI held a National People's Congress; this Congress was composed of 1,000 representatives and declared the birth of the Korean People's Republic (KPR). Nonetheless, when the US occupying forces assumed control over the South, Lieutenant General John Hodge, the US military governor, decided to work with the Korean Democratic Party rather than with the representatives of the left-leaning KPR. This was problematic since the Korean Democratic Party was led by conservative members of the propertied class who were known to have collaborated with, or were passive in resisting, the Japanese colonisers. According to Stueck's assessment, '[i]n discouraging the [Korean] People's Republic, Hodge broke the first and most promising effort at national cohesion in Korea's recent history' ([1995] 1997: 21).

As Cumings reports (1981: 139), General Hodge's alliance with the Korean Democratic Party was a violation of the direct orders from his superior commanders in both Washington and Tokyo to prohibit all Japanese or pro-Japanese Koreans from being retained in his bureaucracy. Bonnie B. C. Oh explains the reasons for this remarkable act of disobedience in the following manner:

> Apparently the majority of Koreans supported the KPR at that time. General Hodge, albeit an experienced soldier, was ignorant about Korea. He cared little that all Koreans wanted was rectification of past wrongs of the Japanese

Introduction 9

colonial era or that they had little knowledge of Soviet ideology. General Hodge was warned by the Japanese authorities still occupying administrative positions in Korea that the KPR leaned toward Soviet ideology. The Japanese also alleged that the KPR was inciting nationalistic and communistic agitation toward immediate independence. Hodge's main concern was that the KPR favored positions that appeared contrary to American ideals. Therefore, instead of the professed American aim of helping Koreans establish a government desired by the majority of the people, Hodge fell back upon America's own national aim of warding off a situation that might become too advantageous for the Russians. (2002: 3)

In this scenario, it was principally the fear of South Koreans leaning towards 'Soviet ideology' that led Hodge to side with the Korean Democratic Party, which conveniently took up the banner of anti-communism as a counter-ideology to the KPR's goal of decolonisation and popular self-determination.

In the same light, the US military governor labelled 'communist' each of the People's Committees, the local self-ruling government bodies organised by the CPKI. Hodge was unaware that these organisations took on different political complexions depending on the area in which they had been formed and that they mostly represented various forms of cross-class alliances uniting the main forces of left and right. Hodge also took the decision to re-employ the former bureaucrats of the Japanese colonial period in his government, thereby ensuring that the southern government was basically built on the old Japanese machinery (Cumings 1981: 429; Cumings 2010: 108). According to one study, for example, 78.6 per cent of the administrative positions and 71.2 per cent of the law enforcement personnel were recruited from the large group of pro-Japanese collaborators (M.-L. Park [1996] 2016: 133). According to Cumings, the continued presence of these particular elements in the officialdom of the First South Korean Republic was one of the causes of the Korean War. In his view, North Korea wanted to overthrow the military leadership of the South because it hated its record of pro-Japanese collaboration (2010: 44–5).

The Central People's Committee of the KPR, which replaced the CPKI soon after the provisional government of the KPR was organised, was clearly the only representative body that received nationwide support. In order to legitimise the new republic, the Committee intended to invite more right-wing leaders to join the KPR leadership and to stage a general election. Although right-wing nationalists like An Chaehong did participate in the CPKI and the KPR, neither Kim Koo nor Syngman Rhee, the two main right-wing leaders, freshly returned from exile, agreed to join. Meanwhile, the Korean Democratic Party began to

10   *The Korean War Novel*

'[attack] the nation-building activities of the CPKI and the KPR as a plotting of Communists' (G.-T. Lee 2006: 35). By actively antagonising the 'Communist' KPR, the conservative party aimed to position itself as the ideal political ally for the US military government. Under the terms of US military rule, then, the Korean Democratic Party began to work virtually as a ruling party, with Kim Sŏngsu, a central party leader, appointed as chairperson for the Advisory Board of the US military government.

If Hodge's decision to outlaw the KPR and disband the Central People's Committee is ascribable to his judgement that South Koreans, torn between a range of political groups, were not ready for self-rule yet, this is mostly attributable to his preconceived ideas about the KPR leadership. Anti-communism, in helping to lay the foundations for the alliance between the US military government and key groups of right-wing South Koreans, thus became the major factor in determining the course of history after liberation. For instance, the Jeju Uprising, which took place from 3 April 1948 to 21 September 1954, on an island fifty miles south of the Korean peninsula, resulted in the deaths of at least 30,000 and forced as many other Jeju Islanders to seek refuge in Japan due to the anti-communist terrorist actions carried out by the National Police and the Northwest Youth Corps. The latter organisation consisted of groups of ultra-right-wing men in their twenties and thirties with northern origins, who fought against the inhabitants of Jeju and who up to that time had been living peacefully under the leadership of the local People's Committee (Cumings 1990: 252–9; H. J. Kim 2014: 2; M. Kim 2019: 230–1; Yoo 2020).

The youth leagues deserve special mention because of the role they played in postliberation Korean politics. As Cumings recounts (1981: 74–6), a number of youth groups – shaped by both right- and left-wing ideologies – quickly emerged following national liberation from the Japanese. Among these groups were the CPKI's peace preservation corps (or *Kŏn'guk ch'ŏngnyŏn ch'iandae*), initially composed of students and other youths. These security forces organised as many as 162 branches and preserved peace throughout the country. After the demobbing of soldiers and officers from the Japanese colonial army, a number of military and quasi-military organisations also appeared in the south. The propertied elite who had collaborated with the Japanese colonisers used the formation of conservative youth groups as a means to contest the KPR's network and local jurisdiction. In this political evolution, the US military government became a major player by offering support to the largest rightist youth league called the Korean National Youth Association. As Monica Kim maintains, '[t]he youth of Korea – young men coming of age or demobilized from the Japanese imperial warfare apparatus – were the target population for the ambitions of both the US military government and the competing Korean political parties on the peninsula' (2019: 220).

During the US military rule and the early regime of President Syngman Rhee, the rightist youth groups acted as state-proxy organisations holding 'the monopoly of violence in post-1945 Korea, alongside the Korea Constabulary and the later establishment of the Republic of Korean Army' (M. Kim 2019: 215). It was one of these youth groups, the Northwest Youth Corps of northern refugees, that attempted with ruthless force to purge the left-leaning Jeju Island of communists. The organisation helped to turn the majority of the islanders against the government. These same anti-communist youth groups were also used by the US Counter Intelligence Corps. Because of the language barrier and physiognomic differences, US Counter Intelligence had to rely on Korean agents in conducting the espionage war against North Korea and its spies during the pre-war years. During the Korean War, these notorious youth groups were used by President Rhee as civilian vanguards in the recaptured territory of the North in order to terrorise political enemies and persecute perceived communist sympathisers. In short, the rightist youth groups were one of the major players, first created by General Hodge and then consolidated by President Rhee, in their project of anti-communist state-building. To quote Monica Kim again, 'the United States military and government used these youth groups, and the violence was not merely an inconvenience, but indeed integral to the US project of occupation and subsequent war' (2019: 217).

Nonetheless, these groups and their government-sponsored civilian brutalities are largely absent from the collective memories of South Koreans and the official discourse on the Korean War. In the chapter on Richard E. Kim, I summon these groups to bear witness to the enforced lapses in historical meaning that govern Kim's text and use this testimony as one means of recovering an obscured dimension of the war. In the chapter on Hwang Sok-yong, I analyse the postcolonial significance of the uprising instigated by these rightist youth groups. Finally, in my conclusion, I look at the emergence of their twenty-first-century variant, the national flag or *T'aegŭkki* protesters, in contemporary South Korean politics.

The South Korean historian Kim Kwangsik has analysed the options the US considered for the Korean peninsula after liberation in these terms: 'to establish a unified government or to secure its foothold through military occupation' (1987: 53; author's translation). Whichever option it pushed for, its unchanging ultimate goal was to 'set up a government

12   *The Korean War Novel*

amenable to the US's influence' (K. Kim 1987: 53). For the US, then, the fate of southern Korea was seen largely in terms of its potential role as a buffer against Soviet expansionism; and General Hodge was pursuing the Cold War in Korea well before this geopolitical reality erupted on the peninsula in the form of a regional hot war.

My emphasis on the Cold War as a determining factor in dividing Korea is not intended to suggest that the Korean War should be viewed merely through the lens of the international contest between the two major superpowers for global hegemony. After all, there is a dimension to the Korean War that cannot be entirely subsumed under a proxy war. Although the seeds for the Korean War were planted by the rivalry between the superpowers, it was the North Korean leadership that sought to cultivate it. In other words, the North Korean leader, Kim Il-sung, ought to be seen as the principal agent of the national tragedy. Since 10 September 1948, the day after declaring the establishment of the Democratic People's Republic of Korea (DPRK), Kim had been planning the war, calling it the project of *kukt'owanjŏng* (the completion of the national territory) (M.-L. Park [1996] 2017: 95–8), a euphemism for a war of unification against the South. In this context, it is worth noting that scholars who have entertained the theory of a civil war in the anti-communist South have typically been labelled as pro-communist – that is, to employ the Korean terms, as being *ch'ongbuk* (pro–North Korean) or *ppalgaengi* (Red). One major reason for this McCarthy-like reaction is that, in the eyes of many right-wing South Koreans, the act of drawing attention to the civil dimension of the war means denying the legitimacy or sovereignty of the First South Korean Republic.

In arguing in this way, however, right-wing South Korean intellectuals and politicians gloss over the fact that President Rhee, much like Kim Il-sung, also wished to advance his forces northward in order to reunify the land, justifying what would have been a northern-bound invasion as an intranational conflict – that is, as a civil war. For example, at a meeting with Kenneth Royall, the US Secretary of War, in February 1949, Rhee expressed a wish to arm his troops and march north as soon as possible (qtd in Y.-P. Hong 2000: 316). From the earliest days of the Rhee government, anti-communist rallies were staged. In this respect, the slogan of 'reunification by means of a military campaign' served as a rallying point for a government that quickly became unpopular. Figure 0.1 displays one such public rally for which the government mobilised many middle school students. The young students are holding a banner that reads: '[l]et us rescue our northern compatriots from their entrapment in hell'. This zeal for reunification would later re-emerge in the

Figure 0.1 An anti-communist rally on 23 September 1948 in a stadium in Seoul. (Source: National Archives photo no. 111-SC-308846)

form of opposition to the peace talks to end the Korean War, a point I will return to at the end of the sixth chapter.

Rhee's military staff were not very different in their bellicosity. Kim Sŏkwŏn, the Commander of the KOR First Infantry Division and hero among the Japanese in the colonial years for hunting out and executing Korean freedom fighters, once boasted that he intended to cross the line of division in order to have 'breakfast in Haeju, lunch in Pyŏngyang, and dinner in Wŏnsan' (Cumings 1990: 575). Such comments reflect the belligerent atmosphere of Rhee's government. What is more, in a letter to Robert T. Oliver on 30 September 1949, Rhee again expressed his desire to launch a war of unification: 'I am firmly convinced that right now is the psychologically most suitable moment to take aggressive steps and unite with our loyal Communist army in the North in order to eliminate the remaining part of it' ('Letter, Syngman' 1949). Over and over again, Rhee spoke of his determination to unify Korea in such a belligerent manner that the US tried to hamper his anti-communist initiatives by withholding military aid from the South (Oliver 1954: 299).

President Rhee's determination was not discouraged but rather strengthened during the Korean People's Army (KPA)'s sweeping,

14   *The Korean War Novel*

southbound advance. In a long telegram to President Truman, which was sent on 19 July 1950, about three weeks after the outbreak of the war, Rhee attempts to bring Truman's attention to the imperative of using the war for the purpose of national reunification:

> This war is not a conflict between north and south; it is a conflict between the few who are communists, and who by an accident got control of half of our country, and the overwhelming mass of the citizens of Korea . . . For anything less than reunification to come out of these great sacrifices of Koreans and their powerful allies would be unthinkable. (Oliver 1954: 306–7)

In this passage, Rhee justifies his desire to take advantage of the fact of communist aggression to wage a war of his own. He claims that the North Korean regime lacks legitimacy and has little support from the people. One grim irony of Rhee's position here is that this claim, if anything, speaks to his own situation after the general election of 30 May 1950, which involved him in a major political setback. With his supporters securing only 45 seats, as opposed to 128 out of the 210 seats won by the independents, Rhee appeared sure of missing out on a second term since the president was to be elected in the National Assembly (Stone [1952] 1971: 18). That is, he needed a national crisis in order to defuse his extreme unpopularity and thus stay in power. Indeed, Cumings even attributes the swift defeat of the Republic of Korea Army (ROKA) in the war to Rhee's loss of popular support (2010: 10–11). The main point, however, should be clear: given the Rhee government's professed and repeated desire to engage in a war for reunification, scholarly discussion of the nature of the Korean War needs to acknowledge the sad reality that the leaders of both the South and North appeared to require war.

A second way of testing the validity of the civil war theory is simply to try to answer how much the citizens of the South and the North before the outbreak of hostilities in June 1950 supported or identified with their governments (D.-C. Kim 2000: 32). Anything short of a completely positive answer would indicate the need for a reassessment of the nature of the war. Unfortunately, such honest and free discussions of the Korean War have rarely taken place in scholarly circles in the South in the past. One of the reasons for this situation is that questions about the role of the United States in the Korean War have been too readily subsumed under the larger umbrella of the traditional political divide between right wing and left wing (or, to be more precise, the liberal left). During the period of the military regimes in South Korea, which lasted from approximately 1961 until 1987, it was not truly possible to take a scholarly position that would argue anything other than the orthodox view that the Korean War involved the United States Armed Forces rescuing South Korea from the clutches of communist dictatorship. Any scholarly violation of this orthodox point of view would run the risk of swift legal prosecution on the grounds of anti-communism.

From the perspective of Kim Dong-Choon, the self-congratulatory view of the South that maintains that the Rhee government heroically defended the country from the communist invaders needs to be considered in the light of the rather chilly post-war reality. In Kim's own words, in the long run 'the ROK's "success" had created a control-oriented military society, an economic system under which more than 30 percent of the national budget (at present) is allocated for military expenditure, and a system of structural dependence under which U.S. armed forces are permanently stationed in South Korea' (2000: 32). Kim argues that 'the Korean War was actually an extension of a political conflict over what kind of nation-state to build, a struggle that went on after Korea's liberation' (2000: 19).

Given the unmistakably agonising path on which the North Korean people have had to walk under the patriarchal dictatorship of its family founder, Kim Il-sung, it was indeed fortunate that the South successfully defended itself against invasion. Yet, this fact should not be used to cloud over the separate issues concerning the nature of the successive dictatorial regimes subsequently established in the South. Nor should it be used to forbid asking pertinent questions about the Cold War itself or from offering scholarly speculations about possible hypothetical trajectories towards a reunified Korea. As for the repercussions of the Cold War in Asia and the Pacific, Christine Hong asserts these in unambiguous terms:

> In real terms the Pax Americana meant the suspension of decolonizing justice, the deaths of several million civilians, the displacement of many millions more, nuclear ruin [caused by more than 100 atomic bomb testings in the Marshall Islands] that eclipsed the magnitude of the atomic bombings of Hiroshima and Nagasaki, and the creation of a forward-deployed permanent garrison state anchored in hosting sites throughout the region. (2020: 3)

What serves to complicate this project is that the Korean War itself has existed as a heated issue of interpretive contention. It is, therefore, worth examining how this war has been understood and interpreted by historians and scholars of international politics since the conflict ended in deadlock and the signing of an Armistice Agreement in July 1953.

16   *The Korean War Novel*

The Korean War, proxy war or postcolonial conflict?

In the historical scholarship of the early 1960s, the Korean War is mostly understood as an international war, a war waged by the Soviet Union for a foothold on the Korean peninsula. In the terms of the so-called 'proxy war', North and South Korea fought against each other in the form of temporary substitutes or proxies for the wider conflict between the two most powerful global superpowers, the Soviet Union and the United States. Among the scholars who took up cudgels for this point of view are David Rees and David Dallin. According to Rees (1964: 19), Stalin was the major architect of a war primarily designed to expand communist influence in the East Asian region. To quote Dallin's famous formulation, the Korean War was 'planned, prepared, and initiated by Stalin . . . Moscow had to hold the reins in the Korean conflict; the war could not have been conducted in any other way' (1961: 60–1).

In 2005, Andrei Ledovskii, a Russian scholar, uncovered a letter in one of the three Russian State Archives, dated 27 August 1950, written by Joseph Stalin and sent to Klement Gottwald, who, at the time, was president of Czechoslovakia. In this letter, the Soviet premier spoke his mind: by tying US hands in East Asia, Stalin intended both to prevent the US from initiating a World War 3 and to strengthen Soviet hegemony in Eastern Europe ('Letter from Filipov' 1950). The belated discovery of this crucial evidence appeared to confirm the internationalist view of the Korean War as a Soviet war, while discrediting the civil war theory – a theory centred on the agency of North Korea in launching the war.

In the 1970s and 1980s, the internationalist or proxy view of the Korean War was challenged by scholars such as Robert R. Simmons and Cumings. Cumings questioned whether the Soviet Union was truly responsible for starting the Korean War and stressed the relative autonomy of communist-initiated action on the Korean peninsula. This newly emergent postcolonial perspective had the salutary effect of bringing to the fore the idea of the Korean War as an attempt to purge the peninsula of the legacy of Japanese imperialism and to unify a divided nation. In his celebrated two-volume Korean War history, Cumings argues that the origin of the war dated back to the liberation of Korea from Japanese control at the end of World War 2. According to this view, in the years of the immediate postliberation era, southern Korea witnessed an upsurge in demands for social justice voiced by unions of farmers and labourers. A failure to understand what was at stake in this unrest caused the US military government to aggravate, rather than alleviate, these social conflicts. The result was repeated farmers' riots

Introduction **17**

and labour strikes that drove southern Korea into severe turmoil. In his book, Cumings also takes note of the thousands of guerrilla fights that took place before the outbreak of the Korean War within the confines of southern Korea as well as skirmishes along the thirty-eighth parallel that eventually served to bisect the Korean peninsula. Based on these observations, the renowned historian maintains:

> The basic issues over which the war in 1950 was fought were apparent immediately after liberation, within a three-month period, and led to open fighting that eventually claimed more than one hundred thousand lives in peasant rebellion, labor strife, guerrilla warfare, and open fighting along the thirty-eighth parallel – all this before the ostensible Korean War began. In other words, the conflict was civil and revolutionary in character, beginning just after 1945 and proceeding through a dialectic of revolution and reaction. The opening of conventional battles in June 1950 only continued this war by other means. (1981: xxi)

Unlike the political situation in northern Korea, the purging of the Japanese imperialist legacy in the south was delayed; and even after it was launched, this purging was not successfully completed. For example, the advent of national liberation led the Korean people to envision a new nation that would be free of the old economic and political shackles, as voiced by the angry underclass members in Hwang Sok-yong's *The Guest*. For the vast majority of Koreans, most of whom were crop-sharing tenant farmers, postcolonial economic justice meant centrally the abrogation of the exploitative relations of farm tenancy. In the South, a process of gradual land reform was not implemented until May 1950; this reform, unfortunately, had only limited effects. Many large landowners had already disposed of their land before the reform process began; and individuals with pro-Japanese histories, a layer of southern Korean society that included large landlords, factory owners and other capitalists, were able to protect their interests by cooperating with the Korean Democratic Party. From the perspective of the oppressed classes, particularly that of the poor tenant farmers, decolonisation was indefinitely delayed. In this revisionist context, the Korean War may be seen as a revolutionary war aimed at liberating South Korea from the ancien régime that had managed to outlast the period of colonialism.

However, the revisionist claims of civil war over proxy war have themselves been challenged. Starting in the mid-1990s, following the collapse of the Soviet Union and the concomitant declassification of much of the old Soviet diplomatic records, the civil war theory of the Korean War has come under sustained criticism. Although defenders of this theory, like Cumings, never entirely ruled out the international

18   *The Korean War Novel*

dimension of the Korean conflict, a number of critics argued successfully that the revisionist scholars had placed too great an emphasis on the internal Korean factors in explaining the outbreak of the Korean War.

Basing her views on certain declassified Soviet documents that were presented to President Kim Young-sam, during his state visit to Russia in June 1994, Kathryn Weathersby was able to reconstruct a detailed account of the actual diplomatic dynamics between the Soviet and the North Korean leadership in the run-up to the Korean War. For example, when he visited Moscow for the first time in March 1949, Kim Il-sung came ready with a military campaign proposal; but Stalin disapproved of it, pointing out that both the internal and external circumstances were not ripe. It was only in January 1950, after Kim had presented suggestions for minor acts of military provocation and had been rebuffed twice more that the North Korean leader received Stalin's provisional permission. It would appear that certain major changes in the international balance of forces were key in altering Stalin's perspective. For example, in July 1949, the US Army withdrew from South Korea; in October 1949, the Chinese Communists under Mao Tse-tung successfully took power in Beijing; and on 12 January 1950, the US declared the existence of the Acheson Line, the US's defence line in the Pacific, which excluded South Korea from its zone of operation. In Stalin's mind, the emergence of Communist China under Chairman Mao would provide a guarantee of military and logistical assistance to North Korea, if that were needed. What is more, the exclusion of South Korea from the Acheson Line meant that the US would probably stand by if South Korea came under attack from the North (Weathersby 1995: 28–30). Weathersby also takes note of the role played by the North Korean leadership: '[t]hroughout 1949, [Kim's war] proposal was rejected by Moscow, but Kim Il Sung persisted in raising the issue until he finally secured Stalin's approval in January 1950' (1995: 31). The conclusion that the historian draws seems inescapable: as the revisionists had argued, Kim was not Stalin's puppet but 'a historical actor in his own right' who took the decisive initiative in planning the war. At the same time, however, contrary to the other major claim of the revisionist school, North Korea had been revealed in the diplomatic correspondence as absolutely dependent on Moscow; Kim's launching of the Korean War now appeared to have required both the approval and support of the Soviet Union (Weathersby 1995: 31).

Weathersby's thesis that balances both the international and the civil war aspect blazed the trail for the blossoming of a third view of the Korean War: the idea that the Korean conflict was the upshot of the intersection of emergent civil strife and a rapidly changing international

Introduction 19

balance of power. In other words, although the changed international situation was crucial in the North's unleashing of war in June 1950, it was Kim Il-sung who seized this opportunity, persuading first Stalin and then Mao to approve and support him. Among the scholars who have sketched out this third point of view on the origins of the Korean War are Stueck, Alexandre Y. Mansourov and Allan R. Millett. To quote Stueck, '[t]he Korean War can be understood only by integrating the internal and external components of its origin' (2002: 83). Although the issue of who initiated the war has now been resolved, the related issue of whether or not the South Korean leadership was also prepared for war still requires clarification. In the terms provided by Weathersby, 'the possibility remains that the South Korean leadership may have desired or intended to provoke the North to attack in order to gain American support for its own reunification plans' (1993: 428). From this perspective, the Korean War was already primed: it was merely a question of who was to pull the trigger first.

Another variant of the balanced perspective has been proposed by Kim Dong-Choon. Kim's thesis emerges from an acceptance of Simmons' hypothesis of the crucial role played by North Korea's preemptive strike and Isidore F. Stone's earlier argument that both the US and South Korea not only expected such an incident but were looking to benefit from the outbreak of hostilities themselves. According to Stone, the US needed war because elements within the Truman administration regarded political instability in East Asia as serving US geopolitical interests. From this vantage point, the US looked to war, rather than to peace, in order to extend its lease on its military and diplomatic hegemony in Western Europe. In addition, President Truman sought war in order to keep the US domestic economy ticking over by means of the expansion in government expenditures accompanying renewed military venture (Stone [1952] 1971: 106). Stone also quotes General Van Fleet's comments of January 1952 on the usefulness of the Korean War to the US: 'Korea has been a blessing. There had to be a Korea either here or some place in the world' ([1952] 1971: 348). In this light, the failure of the US and the Rhee government to act on the ample intelligence reports filed on the imminence of invasion was, to borrow Mark Caprio's words, 'a planned "failure" consistent with a calculated strategy' (2011). In other recent studies, including those by Jodi Kim and Hajimu Masuda, similar views are maintained, but with a new focus on the impact of the Cold War on US domestic politics. Taking the view that both Communism and Marxism form part of Western modernity, Jodi Kim argues that 'this Western inter-imperialist war helped prevent a civil war within the United States itself' (2010: 28, see also Masuda 2015: 2).

20   *The Korean War Novel*

The outbreak of the Korean War

By any criterion, the military power of the ROK was not comparable to that of the DPRK when the Korean War began. According to the *History of the Korean War* published by the Korea Institute of Military History, the total manpower of the ROKA consisted of 105,752 soldiers; in contrast, the DPRK's KPA could muster the significantly more formidable figure of 198,380 military combatants. At the time, the ROKA possessed not a single tank or self-propelled gun or combat plane; in contrast, the KPA was equipped with 242 T-34 Soviet tanks, 176 self-propelled guns and 211 fighter planes, including a number of training and reconnaissance vehicles. Whereas the North possessed 550 anti-tank guns, the South had only 140 anti-tank guns (KIMH 1997: 51, 89–90). In short, the South was thrown into the war almost completely unprepared. Given the North's superior war capabilities, the historian must find unconvincing any account other than the one that suggests the Korean War was an act of North Korean aggression. Perhaps most importantly of all, the classified documents that Boris Yeltsin handed over to President Kim Young-sam, during the latter's state visit of 1994 to Moscow, invalidate all claims in favour of South Korean aggression. Crucial among those 300 Soviet documents, including the diplomatic exchanges of 1949–53 between the Soviet Ministry of Foreign Affairs and its North Korean counterpart, are Stalin's initial January 1950 approval of Kim Il-sung's war proposal and the detailed accounts of the Chinese intervention in the Korean War. For this reason, the candid historian may safely conclude that North Korea invaded South Korea at 4:00 a.m. on 25 June 1950 – and started the Korean War.

Upon receiving reports about this momentous act of military aggression, President Truman convened an emergency meeting of the UN Security Council. On 25 June 1950, the UN passed a resolution calling for the 'immediate cessation of hostilities'; two days later, another resolution authorised UN forces to enter the Korean conflict. By 28 June 1950, a mere three days after crossing the thirty-eighth parallel, the KPA had occupied Seoul, the capital of South Korea (Stueck [1995] 1997: 12). Task Force Smith was immediately dispatched from Japan with the mission of deterring the KPA's southern advance. By 3 July 1950, forty-one out of the fifty-nine UN members had announced their approval of the Security Council's action. In Stueck's words, '[w]hat had begun as a conflict between Koreans aimed at eradicating the division of their country soon became a struggle of broad international proportions, one

Figure 0.2   North Korean attack, June to September 1950, and UN offensive, late September to November 1950. (Source: © Lee Wol-sun)

that threatened to escalate into a direct confrontation between the West and the Soviet bloc' ([1995] 1997: 12–13).

Arriving in Busan on 1 July, Task Force Smith engaged the KPA for the first time in Osan on 5 July; but there it suffered a huge defeat, as it was greatly outnumbered by the enemy. On 14 July, command of the ROKA was transferred to the commander of the UN forces. While the US Army 24th Infantry was attempting to delay the KPA's southward push, the ROK and the reinforced US Army were able to fortify the defence line along the Busan Perimeter (Figure 0.2). For six weeks, from 4 August to 18 September 1950, the UN forces resisted the North Korean army's major offensive at the Battle of Busan Perimeter.

With the US Marine Force's surprise landing at the strategic port of Inchon on 15 September 1950, the tide of the war began to turn. On 28 September, the US and the ROK forces recaptured Seoul. On 1 October, the ROKA crossed the thirty-eighth parallel, with the US Army following on 9 October. On 19 October, both the ROK and the US Army entered Pyongyang. In the meantime, however, undetected by

22 *The Korean War Novel*

the UN forces, Mao Tse-tung, as the Chairman of the Central People's Government, ordered the Chinese People's Volunteer Army to move across North Korea's northern border. On 25 October, the ROKA had its first engagement with the Communist Chinese Army north of Unsan. It nevertheless reached the Yalu River the next day (Figure 0.2). From 1–2 November, the US Army waged its first battle with the Communist Chinese Army near Unsan. On 29 November, the US Army started its general withdrawal to the defence line at Pyongyang. On 4 January 1951, Seoul fell for the second time, with UN troops recapturing Seoul on 14 and 15 March. By May 1951, the war had reached a form of stalemate, with only regional battles taking place for strategic points along the thirty-eighth parallel.

The first round of armistice negotiations was held on 10 July 1951. Tragically, these negotiations dragged on for two years due to difficulties in reaching a consensus on the military demarcation line – and then later over the issue of the repatriation of POWs. The Communist delegates called for a non-voluntary repatriation, demanding that all POWs be returned to their respective home countries immediately, following the terms of the Geneva Conventions. The US delegation, however, proposed a voluntary repatriation, insisting that the POWs should be allowed to choose to which country they wished to be returned. The compromise eventually reached was the agreement that the Five Neutral Nations' Repatriation Commission would handle the process of verifying the intentions of the POWs and then handing them over. On 27 July 1953, the armistice agreement was finally signed by General Mark Clark for the UN, Kim Il-sung for North Korea and General Peng Dehuai for China; the ceremony was boycotted by the South Korean delegates.

Writing the conflict

In their historical novels, writers have chosen to deal with the issues arising from the Korean War in a variety of ways. In some novels, for example, the ravages of war take the form of post-war trauma. Protagonists such as Frank in Tony Morrison's *Home* (2012) or Hector and June in Chang-rae Lee's *The Surrendered* (2010) need to come to terms with what they have gone through in order to affirm meaning in their otherwise distraught and empty post-war lives. It is noteworthy that Lee's portrayal of the Korean War in *The Surrendered* relies on a few iconic scenes that are reflective of his father's war experience while blanking out most of the war years: they forbid an easy historicising interpretation. *The Surrendered* uses scenes or tropes from the Korean

War that are easily recognisable. These include images of the south-bound journey of starving war refugees and the rape and slaughter of civilians suspected of sympathising with the enemy by US soldiers or Communists. Lee's protagonist, for instance, loses both her mother and elder sister to the US Air Force's bombing and later, two other siblings in a train accident. Later still, her brother, a conscripted KPA soldier, kills himself because of the excruciating torture he has endured as a POW at the hands of US soldiers. Although Lee dwells at some length on the gruesome details of these tragic scenes, the author does not contextualise them; what is more, he fails to engage with the significance of this ideological struggle to the Korean people. The omission of the political dimension of the Korean War is encapsulated by Josephine Nock-Hee Park in this manner: 'though Hector [the male protagonist] remarks that the war is "too hot and too cold," no understanding of either hot or cold war touches the story' (2016: 131).

The war's earlier fictionalisations included James Salter's *The Hunters* (1956) and James Michener's *The Bridges at Toko-ri* (1953), both of which are tales about the war experiences of US Navy pilots and both of which were later made into feature films. To some extent, these films served to form the orthodox US-centric view of the Korean War. Within an existential drama of life and death, both books parade the patriotism of the protagonist. Perhaps as a result, a critical, yet fragmentary, view of war pervades these novels. For instance, the absurdity of war becomes a target of criticism in one episode of Michener's novel in which Admiral Tarrant acknowledges the Soviet role in the war during a press conference. The interview is subsequently buried by the embarrassed UN Command because it wishes to maintain the narrative of the Korean War as a strictly limited war (Michener [1953] 1973: 50–1).

Similar criticism may be found in Pat Frank's *Hold Back the Night* (1951). In what is probably the earliest work of fiction in English on the Korean War, a critique of the war is interspersed within a narrative framework that remains faithful to the explanation of the Korean War as an attempt to defeat a major threat to the peace-loving West. The protagonist believes that the Korean War is a 'war between the free world and the slave world'; and, as such, it may prove decisive in determining the future of freedom-loving people. At the same time, Mackenzie, the central character, is entirely capable of becoming frustrated by the war's absurdity: 'a boy like Bishop got blown to shreds by a Russian shell out of a Russian barrel fired from a Russian tank, when Bishop had never had a chance to shoot back at Russians' (Frank ([1951] 1953: 132). What is characteristic of these early novels is that the Korean War has no significance in itself; both Korea and the Korean War exist only

24 The Korean War Novel

in relation to the global geopolitics of US–Soviet rivalry. As Frank's hero ruminates: '[t]his thing in Korea didn't look like much. It looked ridiculous. It was a skirmish over a piece of third-class real estate of no strategic importance' ([1951] 1953: 131).

In these early works of fiction, the depiction of the Korean War mostly exemplifies the US-centred Cold War framework. Alternately, the experience of the war on the part of American POWs is rescripted as a McCarthyist form of scare fiction about Soviet or Chinese Communist attempts to control the US administration. This type of fiction is best exemplified by Richard Cordon's *The Manchurian Candidate* (1959). As Steven Belletto suggests, this novel, which also later formed the basis of a cult feature film, narrativises 'Western fears about the dangers and mysteries of the Orient' (2015: 59) as these are represented by the American POWs' Chinese handlers.

My first chapter opens with the question of what Richard E. Kim's 1964 novel *The Martyred* chooses to expose and conceal. Pace those critics who base their revisionist interpretations on the author's exclusion of foreign armies from his narrative, this chapter maintains that such exclusion is selectively executed to leave intact the image of the UN forces as saviour figures. That is, while it takes the KPA's religious persecution as its centre of concern, this novel, by means of a process of enfiguring and substituting, displaces the war crimes of the US and ROK armies and the rightist youth corps. This does not mean that *The Martyred* is blind to the realities of war. The book is entirely self-conscious in the manner in which it expresses a central cynicism about the hypocrisy of international politics; yet this possibly elucidating moment does not develop into a sustained criticism of the Cold War nor is it rewarded with a deserving narrative trajectory. What the novel does instead is to focus on the issues of faith and the absurdity of the human condition. This existentialist turn serves to displace the dual aspect of the Korean War as both civil conflict and international war, enabling the author to rewrite the Korean War as a metaphysical struggle. This chapter recovers the anti-communist persecutions beneath the narrative's professed agenda of Communist anti-religious persecution by reading a religious mob action in the recaptured Pyongyang as analogous to the Red-hunting perpetrated widely in the North by the rightist Korean Youth Corps, the notorious paramilitary forces of the first South Korean government.

The second chapter examines the ways Ahn Junghyo in *Silver Stallion* (written in 1964, but only published in 1990) rewrites the Korean War as a gender war waged over the ownership of women. Initially, the author portrays the Korean War as a civil conflict: he describes the peace of a rural village unaffected by the KPA's arrival, while highlighting the civilian sufferings emerging from the development of what was at first a civil war into a major international war. Such a portrayal is intended to question the supposedly humanitarian cause of American intervention in the Korean War. Contradicting the US's self-image as a kind of global police force, the novel invites the reader to wonder whose interests the 'police action', to borrow President Truman's expression, was really aimed at protecting. The author's anti–Cold War project coincides with a sexual politics that rewrites the Korean War as a contest between South Korean patriarchs and American GIs (enlisted members of the US armed force) over the bodies of Korean women. In turn, this contest sets off a new war waged against the traditional system of Korean patriarchy by military prostitutes who wish to reclaim the rights to their bodies. While foregrounding the female protagonist's achievement of full subjecthood in this war, this chapter also restores anti-communist persecution to the novel by placing the protagonist and her family's ordeal within the context of an ideological branding or marking of certain individuals by the authoritarian South Korean government. Read in this way, the protagonist and her family's social ostracism, this chapter argues, alludes to the notorious anti-communist punishment of guilt-by-association persecution.

The third chapter discusses Susan Choi's much more recent novel, *The Foreign Student* (1998), in terms of the Cold War and American Orientalism. The novel has been noted by several critics for its condemnation of the South Korean political system and the US-led Cold War waged on the Korean peninsula in the wake of national liberation. Indeed, the author makes a number of metacritical comments on the inefficiencies of both the US military government and its local successor, the Rhee government, which creates a difference in knowledge between herself and her protagonist, who is initially portrayed as uncritical. In her depiction of the protagonist's life in the South as well as in the US, Choi also subjects both US notions of supremacy and ethnic paternalism to criticism. These episodes appear to confirm the anti–Cold War perspective of this novel, in the eyes of some critics, including Jodi Kim and Daniel Y. Kim. However, these critics have failed to discuss the way in which the author sometimes compromises her epistemological superiority in relation to her protagonist. There are moments when she significantly fails to sustain a critical acumen in diagnosing the political situation of southern Korea during the first few years of the postliberation era. This lapse causes Choi to gloss over a crucial, postcolonial dimension to the peasant riots and workers' strife of the time. By attributing the political instability of the period to communist agitation rather

26 *The Korean War Novel*

than to the decolonising aspirations of the Korean people, the author, this chapter maintains, ends up aligning herself with the anti-communist episteme of the Cold War. This chapter concludes with an analysis of the political implications of the author's portrayal of Japan Town in Chicago. Contrary to claims that Choi's depiction of the ethnic enclave upholds a new vision of inter-Asian solidarity, this chapter asserts that the novelistic rendering of Japan Town represents a displaced form of American Orientalism.

The fourth chapter measures the achievements and shortcomings of Ha Jin's *War Trash* (2004) against its professed anti–Cold War project. As Rosemary Foot maintains, both the US and the Communist forces began to make moral and political capital out of the issue of POWs repatriation as it became clear that neither side would be capable of winning the Korean War outright (1990: 200–1). Whereas the Communist delegates at the armistice talks called for non-voluntary repatriation and all-for-all exchanges, the US insisted on voluntary repatriation, a position that granted the POWs the ability to choose whether or not to return to their home countries. According to a preliminary screening of POWs, an overwhelming 70 per cent of the Chinese Communist POWs chose Taiwan over China. The US advertised this as a moral victory of the Western liberal world over the communist alternative. It is exactly this 'moral victory' that Jin chooses as his focus in his portrayal of the US-run POW camps in South Korea. If Jin criticises the US's Cold War propaganda about this victory by revealing its ugly realities, the author, at the same time, subjects both the leadership of the Communist POWs and the Chinese Communist Party to similar criticisms. This challenge to both the Western and the communist world seems to make *War Trash* an objective, anti–Cold War text. However, this chapter asserts that the significance of Jin's project is substantially compromised by the solipsistic form of liberal individualism and capitalist thinking that the protagonist-narrator embraces. In analysing Jin's political project, this chapter compares Jin's Korean War novel to one of its source texts, Zhang Zeshi's memoir, *Wo de Chaoxian zhanzheng* (My Korean War, read in Korean translation).

The fifth chapter analyses Choi In-hun's 1960 novel, *The Square*, in terms of a critique of both Korean regimes. The novel concerns a man who escapes from anti-communist persecution in the South in order to seek exile in North Korea, only to end up disappointed with the regime he finds there. In the journey of the protagonist, the novel puts forward a biting critique of the South Korean government for its oppressive politics and its echoing of US ideology as well as the North Korean government for betraying its people's revolutionary hopes. According to the protagonist, if the 'political square' in the South is deserted because of right-wing terrorism and the murderous exploitation of the people, its northern counterpart is nothing but a 'stadium' hosting a series of perfectly choreographed mass games. From this point of view, both the South and North Korean regimes are not only products of the Cold War but systems that work in collusion with it. The novel articulates its author's disapproval of the twin political orders begotten by the Cold War through the protagonist's choice of a third country during the POWs repatriation interview. This chapter considers the significance of this choice with regard to the neutralisation plan that attracted South Korean attention. In the immediate aftermath of the Korean War, the US suggested that the Korean peninsula be neutralised as a first step towards eventual reunification, only for this suggestion to receive a cold shoulder from the Rhee government. However, following an uprising led by college students that resulted in the downfall of Rhee's oppressive, anti-communist government in 1960, liberal intellectuals engaged in discussions about the possibility of a military neutralisation of the Korean peninsula. Choi's protagonist's choice in *The Square* echoes this shift in the intellectual climate of South Korea in the early 1960s.

The sixth chapter reads Hwang Sok-yong's *The Guest* (2001 in Korean; 2005 in English) in the historical context of the rightist uprising that took place during the Korean War in Shinch'ŏn (Sinch'ŏn), Hwanghae Province, North Korea, an uprising that was followed by civilian massacres and counter-massacres. In all, a quarter of the township's population – some 35,000 residents – was lost. These massacres have not received due attention either from scholars or the mass media under the military regimes of the South, something North Korea has exploited using a virulent form of anti-American propaganda. In the South, only the uprising, absent the subsequent massacres, has been commemorated as the '13 October Patriotic Anti-Communist Incident' by both the surviving participants and South Korea's Ministry of Patriots and Veteran Affairs. Hwang rewrites the deadly clashes between right-wing and left-wing forces as a crusade against Communism, with a hidden postcolonial dimension that dates back to the conflicts during Japanese rule. The novel centres on the insistence of the large landlords on their semi-feudal rights and the demands of the tenant farmers for economic justice. This rewriting of the heroised, anti-communist uprising as a reverse postcolonial conflict constitutes a counter-discourse to the official memory of the South Korean government. Hwang's anti–Cold War project, this chapter argues, emerges most clearly in his targeting of right-wing Christians among a variety of nationalist insurgent groups that participated in the uprising. Contextualised within the post-war system of Korean division, the novel summons to trial the anti-communist, right-wing Christians for helping to solidify this division, all the while suggesting a form of communal responsibility based on the ethics of mea culpa as a prerequisite for inter-Korean reconciliation. This dual gesture, a gesture that encourages the South to rise from its old, vengeful victimhood and to take a more constructive initiative in inter-Korean relations, constitutes the author's proposed first step towards a reunification of the two Koreas.

The conclusion begins by pointing to a certain imbalance and self-contradiction structuring these war portraits. It also analyses a group of Korean partisan fictions and memoirs featuring communist protagonists that were hugely popular among South Korean readership despite or perhaps because of the repressive, anti-communist ambience of the times. The controversies over these partisan novels and memoirs between conservative and progressive critics, along with the persecution of several of their authors at the hands of South Korean authorities, indicate that many decades after the armistice was signed, South Korea is still waging its own Cold War. Although the military rule which served as the great pillar of anti-communism in South Korea for three decades ended in 1988, this did not lead to the cessation of the regional Cold War in South Korea. On the contrary, the conflict has engulfed even more people over time. In today's South Korea, the old ideological conflicts that once divided the Korean peninsula militarily have taken on new, often highly volatile, forms that separate the forces of the right and the liberal-left. This has been particularly true since the beginning of the reign of President Roh Moo-hyun, who led the country from 2003 to 2008. If, in the old days, the ideological clashes that took place between the military regime and democratic activists, including left-wing intellectuals and college students, primarily involved conflicts over the issues of the National Security Law, workers' rights and political reform, the frontline of this ideological war has more recently been redrawn in such a way as to polarise the masses themselves into two very large, hostile groups. As a result, conservative citizens who call themselves *T'aegŭkki* protesters and ultra-right-wing Christians have positioned themselves at the one end of the ideological spectrum, with liberal and liberal-left citizens positioned at the other. The book concludes with some reflections on the implications of the appearance of this new form of mass politics in terms of the local Cold War.

Three concentric frameworks

The Korean War Novel foregrounds the representation of this complex and under-examined war across a range of influential Korean and Asian American novels. Its conceptualisation is greatly indebted to both Josephine Nock-Hee Park's *Cold War Friendships: Korea, Vietnam, and Asian American Literature* (2016) and Daniel Y. Kim's *The Intimacies of Conflict: Cultural Memory and the Korean War* (2020). While both Park and Kim focus on the dynamics between certain Asian American narratives and US imperialism, my purpose here is to examine Korean War novels within three concentric frameworks: the domestic politics of South Korea, the context of the national Korean civil war and the context of the international Cold War. Considered within these concentric horizons, some of the novels that have received critical acclaim either for their criticism of the role of the US Armed Forces in the Korean War or their radical conceptualisation of the Korean War as a civil war reveal themselves as subtly influenced by the persistent and pervasive, US-centred Cold War episteme. What is more, other novels that reputedly indict the Cold War or the overseas ventures of US militarism, this book maintains, are found recounting a gender or a class war, holding the Korean people ultimately responsible for the internecine savagery, a position that aligns itself with the notion of the Korean War as a civil conflict.

The study brings into discussion a range of diverse views, published in both Korean and English, on such compelling historical issues as the conflict between left-leaning nationalist forces and the anti-communist, pro-Japanese collaborator class during the US military occupation and the Rhee regime, civilian massacres during the Korean War, anti-communist persecutions during the military regimes and the early twenty-first-century mass politics of South Korea. In particular, the book's reflections on the conjunction between the Korean War and the Cold War offer a continuation, within the exclusive field of the Korean War novel, of the anti–Cold War discussions advanced by postcolonial Asian Studies scholars, such as Christine Hong, Jini Kim Watson, Joo Ok Kim, Sunny Xiang and Crystal Mun-hye Baik. If Hong in *A Violent Peace* (2020) investigates the US war machine's necropolitical functions targeting racialised people in the Asia-Pacific through the lens of the military tactics of counter-intelligence, Watson in *Cold War Reckonings* (2021) examines the trajectories of Cold War decolonisation in the Global South – that is, its genesis and contestations – by exploring the resistant, literary and visual productions of the region from the 1960s through to the early twenty-first century. The racialised US Cold War

30   *The Korean War Novel*

historiography, what Joo Ok Kim calls the Orientalist 'origin story' of Korea, in particular, is also contested in the critic's *Warring Genealogies* (2022). These issues strongly resonate with the conclusion of my book.

This, then, is a book about the ideological complications of the Korean War novel. Above all, it distinguishes itself by its refusal to see the representations of the conflict-afflicted through either the commiserating lens of victimhood or the morale-boosting one of decolonising resistance. To be more specific, this book's engagement with the six war novels has a dual focus: it seeks to bring to light the experiences of Northeast Asians as both victims and agents of the Cold War – that is, their sufferings and their agencies. My re-examination of the impact of the suspension of decolonisation on the Korean peninsula, for example, which still informs the polarised politics of the Korean peninsula today, contributes to East Asian and Korean Studies by denaturalising the authoritative Cold War historiography through the recovery of counter-hegemonic memories and voices. A second crucial contribution of this project lies in its analysis of the ways Koreans under authoritarian regimes have viewed themselves in relation to the outbreak of the war and its concomitant establishment of the militarised division system. In this view, the Cold War was not simply their war – that is, a conflict between the two superpowers that conscripted us – but our war. That is to say, Koreans waged it as their own. This refusal to see the Cold War from the usual victim perspective will help elucidate the complexity of the Cold War and its legacies in South Korea and provide a new window to look at other decolonised regions as well.

In truth, the Cold War is far from over in Asia. There are still nations in the region that are struggling with the consequences of US military engagement. If South Korea or Taiwan is still faced with the threat of annihilation from the divisive system installed in the wake of World War 2, other nations struggle to come to terms with the consequences of what Hong in *A Violent Peace* calls 'an anti-communist necropolitical order in which unfreedom would be presented as freedom, democratisation as democracy, and militarism as the basis for life itself' (2020: 3). For the people of the 'decolonised' countries in Asia and beyond, the Cold War, and not just its legacy, is still a felt reality. In other words, to quote from Don Mee Choi's *Hardly War*, the Cold War is only 'partly history' here.

Note

1. Most of the Korean officials and organisations chosen by the administration of the American occupation as political allies had connections to the

Japanese era. As Cumings maintains, 'The southern administration [of the American occupation] took on the reactive and negative cast that marked its birth and offered little to the Koreans that was better than the previous colonial regime, save that it was, for the most part, Korean' (1990: 429). Similar views have been advanced by Korean scholars (G.-T. Lee 2006: 7–48; K. Kim 1987: 49–72).

Chapter 1

The Metaphysical War

When it was first published in the US, *The Martyred* (1964) received the highest acclaim from both critics and the general reading public. This debut novel of Richard E. Kim (1932–2009), the first volume of a trilogy, remained *The New York Times*'s bestseller for twenty weeks and was nominated for the National Book Award. Translated into more than ten foreign languages, *The Martyred* enjoyed global popularity, eventually leading to the author's nomination for the 1971 Nobel Prize in Literature.

At first blush, such an instantly warm reception is certainly not something one would anticipate from a debut novel by an immigrant writer whose mother tongue was not English, someone who immigrated to the US at the age of twenty-three. In 'Another War Raged Within', a review published in *The New York Times Book Review*, Chad Walsh offered a eulogy, along with a caution against possible disappointment for those who might have expected either exoticism or scenes of military combat from this 'Korean War' novel:

> Though Richard E. Kim, now teaching at Long Beach State College in California, was himself an officer in the Republic of Korea (ROK) Army, his purpose here is not to tell the deeds of war but to probe the involutions and ambiguities of conscience, the meaning of suffering and of evil and holiness, the uncertain boundaries between illusion and truth. This he has done with a skill so great it is almost invisible. (1964: 1)

In the above passage, the reviewer sketches out the main agenda of Kim's novel in non-political, moral terms, signalled by the use of such terms as 'conscience', 'the meaning of suffering and of evil' and 'illusion and truth'. Walsh's review was soon followed by a second one entitled 'A Moral Tale'. This review also took note of the moral and religious issues of the novel with the observation that the author had chosen to emphasise 'the spiritual trouble generated in his characters' instead of 'all the important kinds of conflict and suffering' of the war (Elliott 1964).

It seems only natural that the overall message of *The Martyred* centres on what appeared to be an advocacy of humanism: there is an emphasis on both the redeeming value of self-sacrifice and the moral imperative of affirming life against nihilism. Foremost among Kim's critics, it is David Galloway who has most insisted on the novel's affirmation of life. According to Galloway, 'absurd heroes', such as the protagonists of novels by Richard E. Kim and Saul Bellow, 'began their quests with a vision of the apparent lack of meaning in the world, of the mendacity and failure of ideals which they saw about them, but concluded with gestures of affirmation' (1964: 171). This line of criticism, which is one subscribed to by later critics of the novel, including Mario J. Valdés, Lee Kihan and Jooyeon Rhee, tends to be reinforced by the epigraphs that Kim himself employs, such as the one in which he dedicates the novel to Albert Camus for the latter's 'insight into "a strange form of love"' that helped him overcome 'the nihilism of the trenches and bunkers of Korea' (R. Kim 1964).

Later criticism of *The Martyred* distinguishes itself from this moralistic, universalising perspective by shifting its focus from the theme of humanism to the politics of the Cold War. Josephine Nock-Hee Park, for example, uncovers within the text 'two different orders of conflict layered together: the war against communism and the war to reunite a divided nation' (2016: 52). Both Christine Hong and William Nessly note the conspicuous absence of the US armed forces from Kim's portrayal of the war. Hong, for instance, sees a homology between Kim's portrayal of the Korean War and the military operation of counter-intelligence, based on the fact that both employ the tactics of elision, fictionalisation and popular manipulation (2012: 156), while Nessly puts forward a compelling argument that the author, by muting the presence of the US Army, imagines Korea as 'a more fully sovereign modern nation, [one that is] capable of decisive military warfare' (2018: 56). In the book, the Korean War is represented as a civil war.

This chapter is premised on the idea that in *The Martyred*, Kim consciously pursues moral and religious issues. By bringing into focus the spiritual dimension to Communist religious persecution, the author eventually refashions the Korean War as a metaphysical war. In this process of rewriting, the barbarism of the UN rollback campaign – that is to say, the war crimes committed by the UN army and the rightist Korean Youth Corps, who have been sent out as security forces to the recaptured North – are figuratively displaced and further substituted

34   *The Korean War Novel*

for by moral and religious concerns. The war becomes of significance because of the manner in which it sheds light on the existential and religious dilemmas of the main characters.

This chapter maintains that one needs a different hermeneutics in order to read back the effaced realities of the recaptured Pyongyang. To quote Pierre Macherey's hermeneutics of narrative silence, 'what the work cannot say is important, because there the elaboration of the utterance is acted out, in a sort of journey to silence. The basic issue, then, is to know whether we can examine that absence of speech' (1980: 87). As a means of elucidating the dynamics underpinning what the novel chooses to say and chooses not to say, this chapter examines the ways in which the novel employs such rhetorical devices as omission, substitution and displacement. It takes note of the conflicting testimonies made about the anti-religious massacre by both its perpetrator, Major Jung, the captured Communist officer, and one of its survivors, Reverend Shin. The latter's initial silence and his subsequent, selfless act of lying about the massacre repeatedly precipitate him into religious persecution at the hands of his fellow Christians, a moment that this chapter metaphorically interprets in the context of the anti-communist persecutions in the recaptured North. The chapter concludes by arguing that, although such spiritual issues as religious persecutions and apostasy occupy centre stage, it is the very same set of religious issues, which take the form of the upsurge in the repressed religious fervour of the citizens of Pyongyang, that conjures up for the reader those otherwise eclipsed anti-communist brutalities perpetrated by the Rhee regime's security forces in the recaptured North.

An anti–Cold War text?

The Martyred begins with the occupation by the US Military of Pyongyang, the capital of North Korea, in mid-October 1950. Colonel Chang, the ROKA Chief of Political Intelligence, orders Captain Lee, the protagonist, to probe a case of religious persecution by the KPA. The North Korean Communists, who had previously arrested fourteen Christian ministers a few days before the outbreak of the Korean War, have executed twelve of them, a few hours before the invasion. In this way, the story revolves around Captain Lee's investigation into the mysteries of the civilian slaughter, including how the twelve ministers were murdered and why two of the ministers were spared execution. One of the two survivors, Reverend Shin, however, refuses to talk about the execution, while the only other survivor Reverend Hann is experiencing a mental health crisis due to his ordeal at the hands of the Communists.

The Metaphysical War   **35**

Only after Major Jung, the captured North Korean military officer in charge of the execution, reveals what he saw and did does Shin open his mouth to deny what Major Jung says. Later still, Shin reveals to Captain Lee that what he has said in contradiction to Jung's testimony was in fact a lie: the truth is that he wanted to play the role of a latter-day Judas so that his fellow Christians, who have lost everything in the war, might have twelve martyrs to look up to for faith and guidance. The novel ends with a report about how many of the novel's characters, following the example of Shin, have also sacrificed their lives for the cause they believe in.

In a recent essay, Nessly takes notice of the possibility that the author may have deliberately de-emphasised the role of the US forces in *The Martyred* as part of an anti–Cold War project. Kim's novel, in other words, recasts the relationship between South Korea and the US as 'a partnership of equal sovereign states' (Nessly 2018: 55). From this standpoint, Kim's historical imagination resists the US-centred Cold War framework that reduces the significance of Korea and the Korean War to the role of an accessory or as simply part of a wager in the global political game of the two superpowers. Steven Belletto, who divides Korean War novels into two groups – the first written by US combatant veterans, the second by first- or second-generation Korean Americans – maintains that if the war literature of the first group makes 'claims about the Korean War as a noble Cold War venture', that of the second questions and dismantles a framework that creates novelistic meaning only in relation to the US's geopolitical imperatives (2015: 62–3). In his opinion, *The Martyred* initiates the literature of the second group, a tradition that now includes such titles as Theresa Hak Kyung Cha's *Dictee*, Ty Pak's *Guilt Payment*, Susan Choi's *The Foreign Student* and Chang-rae Lee's *Native Speaker* (Belletto 2015: 65–71).

As both Nessly and Hong note, it is next to impossible to find foreign soldiers in Kim's novel. The only moment when American soldiers are seen in the work is when the ROKA blows up a bridge on their retreat from Pyongyang, with the purpose of deterring the southern advance of the Chinese People's Volunteer Army. Even then, the US troops are assigned almost negligible, supporting roles. A member of the American Military Police is seen controlling traffic on the bridge, and a few American soldiers in one of the southbound army trucks are heard to express surprise at the sudden explosive demolition of the bridge they have just crossed. Other than these two brief incidents, members of the US military do not appear in person in the novel. Captain Lee mentions a high-ranking American military officer attending a joint memorial service for the executed Christian ministers; but this official

36   *The Korean War Novel*

is never seen – by the time the protagonist shows up, the official has already finished his speech. His presence is only registered by Lee's brief mental report of the incident. The Chinese Communist Army is also absent, despite the fact that its entry into the conflict served to turn the historical tide dramatically; its presence is only registered in an ROKA intelligence report. In this regard, one might agree with Nessly's view that the muted presence of the two major foreign armies in the novel ensures that the international dimension of the Korean War is largely obscured.

And yet, this novelistic practice of heavily editing historical facts does not alone justify the claim that Kim reimagines the Korean War as a civil war. De-emphasising the international dimension of a war is not the same thing as representing it as a civil war. What distinguishes a civil war from a proxy war is the possession and exercise of full agency by the two warring parties. The unfolding of *The Martyred*, however, does not support but rather confuses the claim that the ROKA exercises such complete agency. On the one hand, this claim is buttressed only a single time by Colonel Chang's expression of his resolute determination not to allow anyone to 'defile the cause of *our war*' and 'give the Reds an upper hand' (R. Kim 1964: 91; emphasis added). His emphasis on the war being 'our war', along with his belief in its cause, appears briefly to confirm what Nessly calls the South's 'autonomy from US control' (2018: 57–8). However, this emphasis is later contradicted by the military intelligence officer himself. When Captain Lee asks him why he passed a fabricated report on to local newspapers about the twelve Christian ministers being heroic martyrs, Colonel Chang replies by asking him if he has ever considered the consequences of telling the truth to a war-afflicted people:

> [W]ould you rather tell them this war is just like any other bloody war in the stinking history of idiotic mankind, that it is nothing but the sickening result of a blind struggle for power among the beastly states, among the rotten politicians and so on, that thousands of people have died and more will die in this stupid war, for nothing, for absolutely nothing, because they are just innocent victims, helpless pawns in the arena of cold-blooded, calculating international power politics? (R. Kim 1964: 107)

Colonel Chang's words serve to disabuse the reader of both the heroic view of the US as a benign global police force and any belief in independent South Korean military agency. Seen from this perspective, the Korean War has never been 'our war' but has always been their war – namely, 'the sickening result of a blind struggle for power among beastly states'. The US's intervention, stripped of its grandiose Cold War

The Metaphysical War   37

rhetoric, is seen as a self-serving move to exploit Koreans as 'helpless pawns' in a global power game.

At the same time, the Korean War in *The Martyred*, in spite of the claim to be 'our war', remains distinct from, or falls short of, the kind of civil war imagined by revisionist historians such as Bruce Cumings. From the revisionist historical perspective, the Korean War is understood in a fundamental way as a 'postcolonial civil war', the origins of which date back to Japanese colonial times. The war is seen as primarily an inter-Korean conflict prompted by the popular desire both to liquidate the Japanese colonial legacy and to unify a divided country (Cumings 1981: xxi). In contrast, the war in *The Martyred* may be termed 'civil' only in the sense that it is depicted as a fraternal conflict.

When read in the light of his remarks about the victims of Communist religious persecution, Colonel Chang's critique of the US-centred Cold War is compromised still more. After Reverend Shin contradicts Major Jung's shocking revelation, the colonel decides that the army will glorify both victims and survivors of the persecution as 'good and saintly'. When Captain Lee wonders about the obvious absurdity of this decision, the colonel's impatient explanation is offered in the terms of Manichean logic:

> What you don't understand is that there should be no doubt about the glory of the martyrs. They were good and saintly. Why? Because they *are* martyrs. Because they were murdered by the Reds. It is as simple as that. Now, what about the survivors? Well, they are good and saintly, too. Why? Because they too have been imprisoned by the Reds. Because they too have been tortured by the Reds, and above all, because they are Christian ministers. Don't you see? That is how everything ought to be. They all deserve to be praised. They must all be good and saintly, do you understand? ... Every minister in this case is and must be as immune to any charges of impurity as fresh snow. And that's that! (R. Kim 1964: 76–7; emphasis in the original)

The passage elucidates the ideological cast of the colonel's mind as much as the political necessity of his decision. If the military intelligence officer's simplistic logic that those who suffered at the hands of the Reds 'must all be good and saintly' reverberates with the black-and-white logic of Cold War propaganda, such a blanket granting of immunity to the victim group also echoes the claims of 'victimhood nationalism' (Lim 2010). In the work of scholars of post-war memory, ethical dichotomies are managed by schematically dividing victims from aggressors: while the claims of the former group are sanctified, the claims of the latter are demonised. Colonel Chang's blind commitment to Cold War propaganda cancels out the accuracy of his criticism that accuses

38   *The Korean War Novel*

the superpowers of a 'blind struggle for power'. It also undermines the critical view that sees the potential for an anti–Cold War project in this novel.

The ideological befuddlement embodied by a high-ranking officer like Chang may be seen as an indicator that, in contrast to the claims made by Kim's critics, the intent of this Korean War novel is neither to interrogate the Cold War framework nor to offer a 'resistant reimagining of the Korean War' as a civil war. Nor does it represent in an allegorical manner 'the political task of building a Korean nation' as 'an existential crisis' (J. K.-J. Lee 2021: 340). Instead, Kim's intent lies elsewhere, that is to say, not in what he chooses to say but, perhaps, in what he does not want to say. As Nessly once admitted, '[t]he text is dominated as much by what is not depicted and determinate as what is actually shown and known' (2018: 57). This line of thought leads one to wonder what realities of the Korean War the novelist would rather sidestep than confront when fictionalising it for his conservative American readership.

What gets narrated, what is withheld

In the novel's opening scene, Captain Lee describes a grim, desolate scene of war-related mass destruction. From his new office in Pyongyang, Lee is able to see people down below digging into the heaps of street rubble:

> The people were back at their labor, working as silently and stubbornly as they had day after day. Ever since I arrived in the city, I had been watching these people. Occasionally, I saw them drag out of the debris some shapeless remains of their household goods or, sometimes, a dead body, which they would quietly carry away on a hand-pushed cart. Then they would continue digging in the crumbled mess of brick, boards, and chunks of concrete. (R. Kim 1964: 3)

The street the protagonist sees is in 'ruins'. The 'debris' strewn everywhere appears to be all that remains of an entire neighbourhood. Intent on salvaging anything of value from the wreckage, some of Lee's neighbours uncover their broken 'household goods'; at other times, it is the grislier discovery of a 'dead body'. In this ghastly scene of devastation, the tragedy of human loss is downplayed. It is particularly noteworthy that the discovery of a dead body is treated only as a kind of a by-product of a salvage operation designed to uncover forsaken household goods. No description of the dead is offered; no cries of sorrow are uttered nor tears shed by those who must lift it up, from amid the debris. People 'quietly carry away' the body and 'continue digging' 'silently

The Metaphysical War   39

and stubbornly'. It is as if nothing truly important has happened. With their emotionless, almost automaton-like behaviour, these war survivors appear almost as lifeless as those whom they drag out from under the rubble. It is as if the novel wants to compensate for the relative absence of physical death from the story it shares by presenting another kind of death, a malaise of emotional and spiritual desperation, in abundance.

Kim relays the aftermath of a mass-scale destruction in a completely neutral tone, unconcerned about the agent of this massive destruction. In his account, for instance, dead human bodies are lumped together with broken furniture. Although the author is silent about locating accountability for the horrors of this devastation, a reader familiar with the history of the Korean War can soon work out the identity of the perpetrator. One historical record provides a detailed report about it:

> From June to late October [of 1950], B-29s unloaded 866,914 gallons of napalm. Air Force sources took delight in the virtues of this relatively new weapon, introduced at the end of the previous war, joking about communist protests and misleading the press about their 'precision bombing'. They also liked to point out that civilians were warned of the approaching bombers by leaflet, when all pilots knew these were ineffective . . . When American forces came back to Seoul, Major Gen. Frank E. Lowe was outraged that retreating KPA forces had torched the capital building (yielding but partial damage): for this act of 'wanton pillage', he urged 'immediate retaliation in the form of complete destruction of Pyong-yang [sic] by aerial bombing'. (Cumings 1990: 707)

According to this report, the US Air Force bombed enemy cities and towns heavily and indiscriminately from the very start of the Korean War. The capital city of North Korea was not exempted. The US Air Force, for instance, targeted the army arsenal, marshalling yards and storage houses in Pyongyang early on.

Figure 1.1 illustrates the wreckage of one of these facilities after the attack of US B-29s was carried out in the first few months of the war. The same photo is also significant in indicating the extensive damage that the surrounding areas suffered. Although these bombardments were intensive enough to wipe these strategic targets off the map, they did not stop the US Command from stepping up its devastating air campaign, after it adopted what was called a 'scorched earth policy' towards the North. Before the war, the capital city had been mostly filled with houses. Thus, it was the civilians who absorbed the heaviest blows from the US Air Force. A classified report of March 1954 from the Soviet Embassy in Pyongyang to Moscow estimates that the US air-bombing alone during the war had decreased the total population of North Korea by 282,000 persons (qtd in S.-C. Lee 2004: 143).

Figure 1.1 Pyongyang Central Marshalling Yards on 25 October 1950 after a raid by US B-29 bombers. (Source: National Archives photo no. 342-FH-4A38936-B87162ac)

Richard E. Kim's protagonist, while stationed in Pyongyang, offers neither a real-time report of the massive air strikes and their resultant human losses nor makes any direct reference to the agents responsible for this massacre. Only once does he give a real-time report of an air raid, yet only much later in the novel – in the last, single-sentence paragraph of the twenty-eighth chapter. On one particular day, Captain Lee drives his friend First Lieutenant Park to the airbase to see him off to Busan (Pusan); and, coming back to the headquarters, he finds Reverend Shin waiting for him. After the meeting with Shin is over, Lee feels both despondent and embittered when he realises that he has hurt the noble-minded minister's feelings. The protagonist finally concludes his reminiscences about the events of this particular day by mentioning an air raid, in an extremely perfunctory manner: '[t]hat evening we had the first air raid in Pyongyang' (R. Kim 1964: 144). Again, no report of the devastating consequences of the air war follows, and, perhaps unsurprisingly, there is no mention of the agent responsible for what has happened. Here, if anything, an 'air raid' serves as a temporal marker, a mere chalk mark on his mental calendar, the sole significance of which lies in differentiating one particular evening from the run of others.

The Metaphysical War   **41**

In spite of that, it is not very difficult to infer that the wrecked streets of Pyongyang are the result of a bombing campaign attributable to the US Air Force. Somewhat conveniently, what Kim instead offers is a murderous civilian outrage committed by the Communists, a diversion that takes the form of a compelling series of mysteries, including why the twelve Christian ministers were killed and why Reverends Hann and Shin inexplicably survived the mass execution. With the carpet bombing elided and its civilian slaughter replaced by a focus on the religious persecution carried out by the army of the Communist enemy, the US Air Force finds no place in Kim's emplotment of the Korean War. Nonetheless, the repressed details of these sustained air campaigns are not completely lost. Curiously, they reappear in the form of a strangely hostile natural landscape that seems to be at war with the city of Pyongyang. In the same opening scene in which he describes the salvage work of the survivors following the unreported attack, the protagonist remarks, almost in passing, the state of the weather:

> From the white-blue November sky of North Korea, *a cold gust swept down the debris-ridden slope, whipping up here and there dazzling snow flurries, smashing against the ugly, bullet-riddled buildings* of Pyongyang. People who had been digging in the ruins of their homes stopped working. They straightened up and looked toward the top of the slope, at the remains of the nearly demolished Central Church, and then at *the gray carcass* of a cross-topped bell tower where the bell was clanging. They gazed at one another as though they understood the esoteric message of the bell. *Some old women knelt down on the ground, and the old men removed their dogskin hats and bowed their bare heads.* (R. Kim 1964: 3; emphasis added)

The freezing high winds that have 'swept down' on the city perform what appears to be a strikingly similar action to the US mustangs and bombers that had, in actual fact, swept down earlier on Pyongyang. The swift, unchecked actions of the winds, their 'whipping up' of the 'dazzling snow flurries' that pour down on the people with a blinding brightness, the way in which they are observed 'smashing against' the buildings, evoke the memory of the actual aerial bombings carried out by the US Air Force in the North. If the US air strikes are figured in this scene as a period of remarkably inclement weather, their extensive damage to both the human population and their dwellings become metonymically condensed in the gigantic, ruined edifice of a church belltower, which the narrator aptly calls a 'gray carcass'.

With the US Air Force's notorious bombings encrypted into the actions of the natural elements and the victims figuratively displaced onto an inanimate religious edifice, one may question whether the focus

42 The Korean War Novel

of this novel is truly concerned with the course of a calamitous tragic war that took the lives of about two to three million civilians and almost as many soldiers.[1] As if answering this inquiry in a somewhat pre-emptive manner, the author initially offers the reader the 'proper' story material of a mass murder. This mass murder, casting North Korean Christians as victims, unambiguously points an accusing finger at the Communists and 'exhibit[s] to the entire world the Korean chapter in the history of Christian martyrdom' (R. Kim 1964: 6). The major conflict in the novel thus takes the form of a proxy struggle between the forces of Korean Christianity and those of Korean Communism. This motif of Korean Christianity opposed to Communism repeats itself in Hwang Sok-yong's *The Guest*. The only difference is that the tables are turned around in Hwang's novel, with Christians taking revenge on Communists in the form of a counter–mass murder.

Not unrelated to the narrative manoeuvre of figuring US attacks as weather is Captain Lee's depiction of the odd behaviour of the people on the street. As mentioned earlier, like thoughtless or emotionless automatons, these people show no emotional responses to the discovery of dead bodies, who are most probably members of their family or known neighbours. In contrast, the same automaton-like people respond quickly to the ringing of the church bell. The women immediately kneel on the ground and the men, taking off their hats, bow their heads and pray. In their almost automatic performance of the religious ritual following the signal from the church bell, they evoke none other than their worst enemies, that is, the dogmatic Communists who obey the orders of their political party with the same alertness and unquestioning punctuality – or perhaps their alleged champions of freedom, the ultra-right-wing youth groups sent north by President Rhee that followed the latter's orders with a very similar zeal. Tangential as it may appear at first in a fiction about the Korean War, this uncanny resemblance is crucial in understanding a later narrated episode that concerns an event of intra-communal violence among the Pyongyang Christians. If his encrypting of the US Air Force's indiscriminate bombardment in the form of inclement weather leaves traces of excessive violence that threatens the success of such enfigurement, Kim's portrayal of the citizens of Pyongyang as highly devoted Christians ends up imbuing them with the bizarre quality of blind zealousness or else turns them into grotesque automatons.

Almost, but not quite, erased

Despite the fact that most of the actions in *The Martyred* take place in Pyongyang, the reader is only barely informed of what the city looks like, with the partial exception of the immediate neighbourhood around Captain Lee's office. The protagonist drives out in a military jeep to go back and forth to Reverend Shin's house several times, but there is no mention of pedestrians or buildings or even traffic on the streets. It is the presence of snow that assists this selective blindness, providing the protagonist with a convenient excuse not to dwell on what is really happening in Pyongyang. Each time he looks out of his office window, Lee finds himself fixated on the blindingly bright snow, which covers the surroundings like a gigantic blanket. When he goes out to visit Reverend Shin's church, even trivial details like the different layers of the old and new snow and their different textures are what serve to occupy his mind: '[b]eneath the soft new snow under our feet lurked the old snow as hard and slippery as ice' (R. Kim 1964: 33). When he drives out to a meeting with some other Christian ministers to discuss the fate of the twelve ministers who have been executed, Lee once again directs his attention to the way in which the snow from the previous night serves to conceal everything from view: '[t]he blizzard of the night before had quietly left the city, leaving behind it a thick layer of fresh snow over the battle-scarred earth' (R. Kim 1964: 80). When he leaves the joint memorial service later, he again observes, '[i]t had begun snowing again; the soft, thick snow fluffed down over the gray city' (R. Kim 1964: 140). And even after shutting himself inside his office, Captain Lee's attention is drawn to the window where he looks out in order to watch seemingly every movement of the wind and the snow, from 'a whistling gust whipp[ing] past the box, spraying a silvery mist of pulverized snow' to the 'snow . . . turning into a blizzard' (R. Kim 1964: 9, 69).

Rather surprisingly, then, apart from the description of the general retreat, there is only a single scene in the entire novel in which the protagonist describes a procession of US armoury through the Pyongyang streets:

> The snow was getting heavier, the sky darker. Through the window I saw columns of medium tanks, their guns prostrate, crawl past the ruins, trailed by another column of howitzers, northbound. The snow soon covered the tracks left by the heavy treads. Silence returned to the streets, and with it the brooding afternoon of a dreary northern city. (R. Kim 1964: 63)

44 *The Korean War Novel*

Even in this scene that registers the US Force's northbound heavy armoury for the first time in the novel, it is the natural element of the snow that soon prevails. The snow obliterates the proof of the passage of the armoured vehicles and weapons by covering their tracks immediately after they have been made. What is more, once the rumbling heavy machines pass through, the streets once more become silent. During his entire stay of about two months in Pyongyang, the protagonist finds these city streets quiet and deserted except for two solitary occasions, the significance of which I will return to. Apart from these brief incidents, nothing about the cityscape of Pyongyang is registered in the consciousness of the protagonist; Captain Lee therefore has nothing to say about it.

In its portrayal of the recaptured Pyongyang, Kim's novel makes a striking contrast with certain Chinese Korean War novels such as *Dongfan* (The East, 1978) by Wei Wei and *Yongbingtuan gushi* (A Tale about the Mercenaries, 1968) by Huang Lu. According to one Chinese critic, the author Huang in *Yongbingtuan gushi*

> focuses on portraying both Pyongyang occupied by the ROK and US armies and pro-communist struggles by North Korean workers at a printing factory. American soldiers are described in many negative ways in this novel. It tells us about the Pyongyang streets that were turned into red-light streets because of the American soldiers and also about the local pedestrians who were worried about their safety because of the American soldiers' reckless driving. (Xu 2018: 78; author's translation)

In the eyes of this review, Huang depicts the struggles of the North Korean workers against the 'liberating' forces of the UN and the ROKA. The novel includes scenes about the US troops becoming a source of public concern because of their disorderly and even criminal acts, such as reckless driving and seeking out the services of prostitutes on the streets of Pyongyang. Naturally, in considering these charges, the possibility must be considered that certain passages in these novels form the stuff of communist propaganda designed to emphasise the lawlessness of the US troops as a means of legitimating the Chinese intervention in the Korean War. However, accusations about the US Army's criminal acts and moral licence in Pyongyang are not entirely groundless, if viewed in juxtaposition with the reports from war correspondents such as Reginald Thompson and Mark Gayn. In his aptly named article, 'So Terrible a Liberation – The UN Occupation of North Korea', Callum MacDonald summarises the eyewitness accounts of these journalists. According to MacDonald, reckless acts of drink-driving were a popular form of harassment among many of the occupying US soldiers:

The Metaphysical War   **45**

When Pyongyang fell, whole companies became drunk, throwing grenades and firing at random. A participant compared the scene with Dodge City. A common form of harassment was to drive vehicles at Koreans for the sake of seeing them jump off the road, a practice witnessed by Gayn as early as 1946 . . . As late as July 1951, the U.S. Eighth Army had to issue an order against the practice: The increasing number of daily accidents in which Koreans are injured by army trucks is becoming a matter of great concern . . . Some, who feel they have developed great skill, have been observed trying to see how close they can come to pedestrians without hitting them. This recklessness is not worthy of the U.S. soldier and draws condemnation from Koreans and right-thinking soldiers alike. (1991: 18)

According to the same report, more serious crimes like rape and murder were also perpetrated by US soldiers against both POWs and North Korean civilians with impunity. During the occupation of the North, official North Korean sources estimate that about 170,000 civilians were murdered by the US military (MacDonald 1991: 3). The war crimes by the US troops were so rampant that in April 1951, two US chaplains filed a complaint with the new Eighth Army commander, General Matthew Ridgway. The chaplains protested that poor discipline and the refusal of the appropriate authorities to investigate serious crimes 'made murder, rape and pillage easy for the criminally inclined' (MacDonald 1991: 18). As one journalist reports, sex crime was used as 'a weapon of war' by both the US and South Korean soldiers: 'One North Korean eyewitness described how 300 politically suspect Korean women were held in a warehouse and used at will by U.S. soldiers after the recapture of Seoul in 1950' (Kindig 2021). If the US Army was capable of perpetrating these crimes against civilians in the recaptured South, which was supposed to be under the control of the National Police, it is not difficult to imagine the possibility of still worse crimes in the recaptured enemy territory. The sexually charged atmosphere of pillage and piracy informally fostered among the US servicemen in the Korean War is summarised in the popular US GI slang of the period: 'R&R leave, in Korean War–era GI slang, could also mean "Rape & Restitution" or "Rape & Ruin"' (Kindig 2021).

By excluding the US troops from his narrative, Kim saves himself the trouble of dealing with their war crimes. At the same time, the author occasionally shows an acknowledgement of the significance of the US Army as the protector of North Koreans. Towards the end of the novel, for instance, as the conflicts between the UN and the Chinese Communist Army escalate to full-scale war, the ROK Counter Intelligence Corps begin a series of psychological campaigns aimed at the citizenry of Pyongyang. To calm down the panicking residents, the

46 *The Korean War Novel*

military counter-intelligence unit appeals to the might of the UN troops: 'jeeps with loudspeakers prowled through the streets, grinding out martial music ... appeal[ing] to the populace to be calm and steadfast in their trust in the United Nations Forces; it was only a matter of a few days before the Chinese invaders would be beaten back across the Yalu River' (R. Kim 1964: 145). When anti-communist citizens in Pyongyang march on the street in protest of the intervention by the Chinese, they also call on the UN forces to take immediate reprisals against the Chinese Communist Army (R. Kim 1964: 176). That the ROKA has to invoke the authority of the UN forces in order to placate an anxious local population and that the anti-communist North Koreans had to plead specifically with the UN military, rather than with the ROKA, to protect them from the Chinese invaders, indicate that the presence of the UN army is not something negligible, despite its 'muted' status. It is an irony that, although the UN forces are muted almost to non-existence in the novel, that presence is perceived by the Pyongyang citizens to be more powerful and important than the Korean forces whose presence in the novel is highlighted.

If he turns a blind eye to the US military's war crimes against the citizens of Pyongyang, Kim also eliminates the atrocities committed by both the ROKA and paramilitary forces, such as the Commando of the National Police and the rightist youth corps. Instead, the author chooses to emphasise the honourable efforts of the ROKA to preserve Christian places of worship from the raging destruction of the war. As Colonel Chang explains to Captain Lee – after he remarks on the fact that Reverend Shin's church has remained standing, despite all the destruction around – it has not been a matter of luck but the efforts of the ROKA that have saved the building. According to Chang, however, the South Korean army had to go through 'one of the bloodiest battles' (R. Kim 1964: 34) while capturing this strategic point without destroying it. Well aware that their enemy would not be permitted to shell it with artillery fire, the Reds utilised this church as their observation post, effectively deterring the advance of their enemy forces (R. Kim 1964: 34). In this way, the ROKA is portrayed in an entirely noble-minded way, whereas the KPA comes across, comparative speaking, as despicable.

In contrast with the ROKA, whose commitment to the monumental challenge of both conquering and preserving the enemy territory is highlighted, both the Commando of the National Police and the posse of youth groups, whose terrorist acts earned notoriety in the recaptured North, are practically eclipsed in *The Martyred*. These groups were sent north by the South Korean regime in order to maintain 'order and security'. They zealously conducted manhunts and committed sex crimes against both Communists and their sympathisers in the recaptured North, just as they did in the recaptured South. The murders perpetrated by these special forces were so extensive that even Dean Rusk, Assistant Secretary of State for Far Eastern Affairs, regretfully pointed out that the ROKA's brutalities were too numerous. Although local governments were set up in the recaptured major northern cities for an interim period, in reality they were run by the National Police and the rightist youth corps. This reality was confirmed by the US embassy itself, when two officials visited Pyongyang on 25 October 1950. In the recaptured city, they found

> [g]roups of young men with rifles were roaming the streets wearing armbands that proclaimed them as belonging to the Security Party or the Northwest Youth Corps. In theory they were there to protect property and to maintain public order, but they had more the appearance of vigilantes than police officers, and their probable conduct was 'open to speculation.' (MacDonald 1991: 12)

Cumings also reports that in Pyongyang, '[a] state of anarchy existed, with no effective administration, police reprisals against suspected collaborators (including many assassinations), and rightist youths roaming the streets looting what little property was left' (1990: 718).

In *The Martyred*, the author represents the notorious youth corps in Pyongyang as an entirely innocuous outfit. One of these groups is referenced a single time in the novel when members of the 'Anti-Communist Youth Association' briefly appear as part of a protest march of Pyongyang citizens against the Chinese intervention. The chairman of the group momentarily appears at the joint memorial service in order to give an anti-communist speech to the congregation, a service at which the city's mayor is also introduced. Kim's overall portrayal of Pyongyang gives the false appearance that law and order are maintained within a peaceful city under the control of a legitimate provisional civil government. Even when the general retreat is imminent, the streets of Pyongyang appear free from disorder:

> Armored cars patrolled the hushed streets; a man pushed a cart across the empty, wide avenue; a Military Police jeep, blinking red lights, its radio antenna swinging, screeched around a corner. A cold wind whipped about, fluttering torn pieces of war posters on the shop windows. (R. Kim 1964: 156)

The only thing that threatens to upset public order and security is the harmless 'cold wind' that threatens to make a mess of some patriotic war posters on the shop windows.

48   *The Korean War Novel*

Christianity as a surrogate agent of the Cold War

With the narrative focus initially fixed on the religious persecution carried out by the Communists, the storyline of *The Martyred* unfolds along the line of a proxy conflict between Korean Christianity and Korean Communism in the North. The development of this other war between Communism and Christianity is first insinuated at a symbolic level in the opening scene. Here, the destruction suffered by the Christian church is brought to the fore, along with the automaton-like features of the faithful Pyongyang Christians. In a surprising turn, however, after Major Jung of the KPA makes a defamatory statement against the murdered ministers, Reverend Shin comes forward to offer a counter-statement. Refuting Jung's claim that the twelve ministers 'died like dogs', denying both God and one another (R. Kim 1964: 86), Shin makes a confession first to a group of fellow ministers and, later, to the public. Shin suggests that it was he who denied God and that he was in return spared from execution while the twelve Christian ministers died as true martyrs. In this account, the twelve ministers were tortured and eventually killed because of their refusal to support the Communist regime and to sign a petition for admission to the Communist Party (R. Kim 1964: 122). Of course, as Shin later admits to Captain Lee, this is a lie. What is intriguing about this episode is that it suggests that showing support for Communism is considered to be an act of defiance in the face of God. And yet, all that the Communists had requested from the arrested ministers was to sign up for political affiliation, not to give up their religious beliefs. The Communists even offered to release some other arrested Christians and to allow the churches to keep their property in return for the ministers' cooperation. Yet, this request was not considered an option for the Christian ministers. Why not? How does a political issue predetermine a religious matter? The answer to this question may be sought in the politics of North Korea, not in Christian theology or practice per se, nor in the notorious atheistic tenets of Communism.

As mentioned in the introduction, immediately after national liberation on 15 August 1945, Korean nationalists established the CPKI and set up People's Committees. As Cumings reports, 'In 1945 and 1946 the entire Korean peninsula was covered with "people's committees" (*inmin wiwŏnhoe*), existing at province, city, county, and village levels' (1981: 267). It was Protestant ministers and other nationalist leaders who played a key role in establishing the CPKI in the North; it was in this way that the political vacuum in northern Korea was filled during the interim period. By creating political parties, the religious leaders tried to protect their social influences. For example, the Reverends Han Kyŏngchik and Yun Hayŏng created the Christian Socialist Democratic Party in Shinŭiju, North P'yŏngan Province as early as 18 September 1945, while Presbyter Cho Mansik established the Chosŏn Democratic Party in Pyongyang, South P'yŏngan Province on 3 November 1945. While serving the economic interests of the bourgeois class as a bulwark against the Communists, these political parties tried to protect religious freedom. The bourgeois base of the Chosŏn Democratic Party is emphasised by Kim Jae Woong: '[a] considerable number of the bourgeois classes who were discontent with land reform enrolled in the Chosŏn Democratic Party. Their acquisition of Party membership was a realistic means of rallying against the Communist Party of the have-nots that implemented land reform' (2020: 268; author's translation).

As reported in many historical studies (Cumings 1990: 316–20; Ko 2016: 878–83), the Communists initially cooperated with the local Christian leaders, inviting them to the Provisional People's Committees. The main reason was that when they crossed the northern border of Korea with the occupying Soviet army, Kim Il-sung and his followers had no substantial political infrastructure in northern Korea. For this reason, they decided to form a united front with the Christian nationalists, who also professed to be socialist, partly as a way of keeping themselves on the right side of the Soviet occupation and partly because they also felt the 'need for socialist policies' (S. Kim 2020: 114). However, once they had power in their hands, the Communists began to oust the Christian leaders from positions of influence. The turning point in their relationship was represented by the Christian leaders' break with the Communists over the issue of international trusteeship. For his refusal to support the trusteeship, Presbyter Cho, the most respected Christian nationalist in the North, was detained by the Communists. The rest of the right-wing Christian leaders of the Chosŏn Democratic Party were then gradually ousted from their own political party, with many of whom then deciding to defect to the South. After this, Christians and Communists in the North continued to clash on a number of issues, including land reform, the scheduling of representative elections to the People's Committees and the hosting of the Commemoration Ceremony of the 1 March 1919 Independence Movement (Ko 2016: 880). The remaining landed-class Christian leaders received the greatest blow from the Land Reform legislation of 5 March 1946, which was initiated by the People's Committee and whose seats by then were mostly filled by Communists. Given the confrontation in terms of political and economic interests, along with the issue of religious freedom, it appears

50   *The Korean War Novel*

unsurprising that public support for Communism is not an option for the arrested Christian ministers in *The Martyred*. As a matter of fact, the North Korean Christians in the novel are on the frontlines in the anti-communist war: they have taken upon themselves the mission of antagonising the Communist power structure, as witnessed in the novel's depiction of a Christian-led rally in Pyongyang.

One might say that Christianity in Kim's novel plays the part of a surrogate agent for the missing armed forces of the right, including both the UN military and, most importantly of all, the South Korean paramilitary youth groups. For example, the status of Christianity as a militant player in the inter-Korean politics can be ascertained in the scene in the novel where some Christians break into Reverend Shin's house, looking for him:

> The mob was there, even if Mr Shin wasn't, or the young minister, only the old woman. They demanded to see Mr Shin and when they were told he wasn't there they broke into the house. Those good Christians searched the whole house. Then they got mad and began to smash the furniture, windows, everything they could lay hands on. I found the old woman outside in the snow, hysterical, while they were literally tearing down the house inside. I tried to talk them out of it, but nobody listened to me. Meanwhile more people, mostly women, were coming up the hill. They milled about the house chanting hymns and screaming, 'Judas! Judas!' It was uncanny. (R. Kim 1964: 72)

These people have clearly stormed Shin's house with the intention of punishing him for selling himself out to Communism. At the same time, a group of laywomen circle the house, beating their breasts and calling the Christian minister 'Judas'. What deserves special mention is that this 'uncanny' incident happens even before Shin has made his false confession: the suggestion is that these people are acting on their preconceptions about the minister's integrity. As this chapter argues, the punishment prompted by this suspicion of betrayal has a parallel in the tragic history of the Korean War: the terrorism perpetrated during the war by both the Korean Youth Corps and the National Police against civilians suspected of pro-Communist sympathies.

The violent nature of the behaviour of the Christians at Shin's house appears to go well beyond what might be a likely Christian reaction to the apostasy of a fellow Christian. The excess appears to be due to the pent-up resentment of the North Korean Christians against the Communist regime for harassing the churches and confiscating the property of both the Church and its more affluent members. It is in this context that both the Church congregation's rage against apostates

The history of the Korean War bears witness to the fact that the North

and their eager participation in the protests against Chinese intervention in the war can be understood. At this point, the city dwellers and the peasants of the North part ways. Unlike those of the urban bourgeoisie, peasant grievances against the Communist regime were not particularly significant. Whereas the former had everything to lose under Communist rule, the latter were the beneficiaries of the land reform implemented in the Communist North. According to Cumings' estimation, '[l]and reform had made 70 percent of the peasants "ardent supporters" of the regime' (1990: 718). The anti-communist fervour of the Northwest Youth Corps and its sequel, the Korean Youth Corps, can also be understood within the same context: all of the members of these rightist organisations were of northern origins, having defected to the South as a sign of their hatred of the Communist regime.[2] Many of the northern refugees were either pro-Japanese collaborators, who knew that they would number among the first group to be executed by the Communist regime, or were Christians or members of the landed class who also expected harassment and confiscation of their property and thus chose to flee south.

The history of the Korean War bears witness to the fact that the North Korean regime executed the right-wing nationalists they were holding in custody right before their retreat; the prisoners in both Pyongyang and Wŏnsan Penitentiary were slaughtered (S.-C. Lee 2004: 160). In Pyongyang, the KPA 'threw civilians [prisoners] down the prison well or dragged them to a nearby air raid shelter and shot them to death' (D.-C. Kim 2000: 167). When the ROKA and the Korean Youth Corps moved into the same areas, they in turn executed a great number of suspected Communists and their sympathisers. The UN Command in theory had both the ROKA and the South Korean National Police under its control, the latter of which moved north as an attachment to the UN formations. In reality, however, they were out of the UN Command's control. President Rhee considered the National Police and the Korean Youth Corps operating in the recaptured northern territory as vanguards of the advancing military forces. To quote MacDonald again: '[t]he police and youth leagues were acting as Rhee's political agents in the North, intimidating the masses by a policy of terror and political assassination under the guise of pacification' (1991: 11). The most serious problem of these groups is that the criteria they used in judging a person's possible pro-Communist tendencies were too arbitrary. The reign of terror which these paramilitary forces brought to the recaptured northern territory is strikingly described in the following account: '[t]he greatest percentage of victims of the civilian slaughter in the [recaptured] North include Communists, officials of popular

52   *The Korean War Novel*

associations and political institutions, their families, and the People's Army's families, that is, people suspected of leftist leanings' (S.-C. Lee 2004: 148; author's translation). According to this testimony, the rightist youth corps and the National Police indiscriminately slaughtered civilians. In their view, kinship, by birth or marriage, to a Communist was good enough to warrant the death penalty. During their forty-day occupation, North Korea claims that US troops killed hundreds of thousands of civilians, 15,000 civilians in Pyongyang and 120,000 in Hwanghae Province alone (D.-C. Kim 2000: 167).

The arbitrary practice of incriminating and executing civilians on the basis of suspicion alone was also common in the recaptured Seoul. A dispatch for 31 December 1950 from the US Embassy to the US Department of Defence states that 142,760 out of an arrested 305,523 civilians had been released and that those remaining in custody were either being tried, in a civil or military court, with a small number under further investigation (I.-H. Lee 2010: 123). The number of people arrested on the suspicion of Communist collaboration is shocking, given that, as Kim Dong-Choon maintains, about one million Seoul citizens remained under Communist occupation (2000: 66). And yet the mere fact that over half of the arrested had subsequently been released is even more outrageous: it testifies to how indiscriminately the arrests had been made in the first place. In the recaptured territory of the South, Communist suspects were considered 'guilty until proven innocent'. This McCarthyist policy, which President Rhee employed before and after the war in order to eliminate his political enemies,[3] was inherited by South Korea's later military regimes when incriminating democracy activists.

But in Kim's novel, there are no references to civilian carnage committed in the recaptured North by either the Commando of the National Police or the rightist youth corps. By transposing the war between the Communist North and the democratic South into a conflict between a group of militant Christians and some alleged apostates, the issue of anti-communist war crimes is foreclosed. Nevertheless, this absence speaks of itself through its very displacement onto the religious dimension of the narrative. The bizarre self-betrayal of the novel is caused by an accidental homology between what the text represses and what it foregrounds – that is, the resemblance between the Korean Youth Corps' manhunt for political renegades and the young Christians' zealous persecution of religious renegades. Having heard twelve ministers lose their lives to a Communist atrocity, a number of the young Christians try to seek justice by persecuting the two survivors, viewing them as betrayers who have sold out their colleagues. The dictum 'guilty until proven

The Metaphysical War   53

innocent' here also applies to Reverends Shin and Hann. Suspicion of their apostasy is based on the flimsy grounds that they simply survived the mass execution. Founded on suspicions, the episode of religious persecution strongly resonates with the mass civilian harassments and executions in both the recaptured northern and southern territories by the National Police and the rightist Korean Youth Corps. Just like the two Christian ministers, the mere survival of the Communist occupation was later used by those who fled to Busan as evidence of disloyalty against those who did not or could not flee from the North Koreans. As MacDonald reports, '[m]any in Seoul claimed that they were mistreated by the "Pusan patriots" in the police and youth leagues simply because they had remained in the city during the communist occupation' (1991: 10).

After Reverend Shin makes his false self-condemning confession, admitting that he betrayed both his fellow ministers and God, the mob once again gathers around his house, chanting and screaming. Captain Lee, hurrying to Shin's house, greatly concerned about the safety of the two ministers, finds the place besieged by angry Christians:

> Young voices kept on screeching, 'Judas! Judas! Judas! Judas!' A roaring voice boomed, 'Come out, Judas! Repent, Judas!' I could not tell how many of them were there in the dark – perhaps forty or fifty. Suddenly I heard Park's voice commanding, 'Who is your leader! Who is responsible for this mob!' I saw him snatch a submachine gun from a guard and fire into the black sky. The crowd grew silent briefly, but Park lost his chance to speak as several voices screamed out, 'There he goes! Catch him!' 'Kill him! Kill him!' (R. Kim 1964: 115)

Before Lee arrives at the scene with First Lieutenant Park, the Military Police are already in place to maintain public order, but their armed presence fails to curb the frenzy of these furious Christians. The grim irony is that these Christians, who profess to want to defend their religion, end up betraying it by turning into the harassers and murderers of innocent people. Reverend Hann, whose life was spared because he was judged insane, is murdered by the mob, who mistake him for Reverend Shin. In their madness, their craving for blood and their hatred of those who prove disloyal, these militant Church members resemble nothing so much as the rightist youth corps members who also hunt down and kill the faithless. The two seemingly discrete groups converge in their tendency to condemn their own side, based only on suspicion. In this regard, the crazed Christians' cries for blood, their yells of 'Catch him!' 'Kill him! Kill him!', might just as well be those of the revenge-thirsty Korean Youth Corps in the recaptured territory of the North.

54 *The Korean War Novel*

A metaphysical turn from anti-communism

Moved by his courageous confession of his sins, many members of the congregation come to accept Reverend Shin. Once more at the front of the Pyongyang rallies, Shin is reinstated as their leader, a champion of Christianity against Communism. His self-sacrificial act of unjustly condemning himself while glorifying the real apostates as martyrs inspires others to rise up from despondence and fight with faith and hope. But curiously enough, at the time when the faith of the congregation in their leader reaches its zenith, Shin confesses to Captain Lee that he ceased to believe in God many years ago. When Lee criticises him for deceiving the public with his feigned faith, the minister replies:

> Despair is the disease of those weary of life, life here and now full of meaningless sufferings. We must fight despair, we must destroy it and not let the sickness of despair corrupt the life of man and reduce him to a mere scarecrow ... I saw how men can come to be beasts without hope, how men can come to be like savages without the promise, yes, the illusion of the eternal hope. Men cannot endure their sufferings without hope, without the promise of justice. (R. Kim 1964: 160, 171)

Here, the Christian minister reveals that he has had to lie because it was imperative to keep up people's hope for salvation at any cost. Having seen the loss of hope degrading many people to the status of 'savages' and 'beasts', Shin has decided to help them, although this means he must bear the guilt of deceit alone until he dies. Shin thus becomes a martyr for a religious cause in which he himself no longer believes.

In a way, it would be more precise to say that Shin becomes a martyr for his personal belief, a belief in hoping against hopelessness. Shin inspires Lieutenant Park to follow him, helping out the Christians at his late father's church, although he himself does not believe in God. In explaining to Captain Lee how important it is to have hope, Park makes an interesting comparison between a fairy tale and a worthwhile belief:

> Do you understand that a fairy tale can be an integral part of our lives? Then it ceases to be a fairy tale. It becomes real. It becomes something that is meant to be. What those Christians wanted and needed was not merely a nice little story that would give them comfort and confidence but something that would make their lives meaningful, something that would make their sufferings worthwhile. Do you recall this, I forget from where? 'Deeper truth lies in the fact that the world is not meaningless and absurd but is in a meaningless state.' ... Yes, those Christians have something that sustains their lives in a world that is in a meaningless state. But we don't. Why should we call what they have a fairy tale? (R. Kim 1964: 142–3)

In this passage, Park speaks of the value of a 'fairy tale' or other illusion in helping to overcome despair. According to him, an illusion well lived is no longer illusory since it has become an 'integral part' of one's life. In highlighting the life-constituting power of an illusion or its capacity to become 'something that is meant to be', Park's argument smacks of existentialist thinkers. As Camus argues, a true existential rebel is one who affirms 'the part of man that must always be defended' ([1951] 1984: 25) and acts in identification with others. By saying both 'yes' and 'no', that is to say, by refusing to accept the human condition as it is and by affirming the value of being human, one can create meaning in this meaningless world. Camus called this the rebellion against absurdity (Camus [1951] 1984: 22–3).

In *The Martyred*, all of the main characters, inspired by the example of Reverend Shin, fight for their belief in man and sacrifice themselves in the end. Lieutenant Park, the atheist, accepts Shin's advice that if he cannot have faith, he should at least pretend to have it. As a consequence, he decides to help the church served by his late father, one of the executed ministers whom he formerly hated so much. In the end, he dies with his men in a heroic defence on the eastern front. Chaplain Koh resigns from his post in order to run a church for refugees on a small island off Busan. Even Colonel Chang, the cynic, dies as a hero, holding the enemy back so that his men can make safe passage. Each of them has become a martyr, sacrificing himself for others.

The last moment of each of these characters evokes Kim's understanding of what he calls 'small history versus grand history'. In his Korean-language essay, *Irŏbŏrin shiganŭl ch'ajasŏ* (In Search of Lost Time), the author explains his views on humanity and the meaning of his work in the following terms:

> Conflicts and struggles necessarily take place when a man confronts the grand history with his small history. Tensions from such conflicts and struggles, I believe, become the core content of my work. Although the characters with a small history become commandeered, swallowed, and destroyed in the end by the ruthless, heartless grand history, it is in the critical moments of such conflicts and struggles that we get to see a dazzling slice of a human life like an epiphany that reveals what men are and, furthermore, what men should be. It will be a true liberation of man, and at that time one will say, I cry no more. (1985: 47–8; author's translation)

The crux of the author's message is that a rebellious individual will inevitably be destroyed by grand history, but in the very act of being destroyed, he can prove his greatness. This is the essence of humanity. Paradoxically, the individual's destruction is proof of their greatness

56   The Korean War Novel

or proof of their freedom from the servile yoke of the given. Naturally enough, the heroic individual Kim has in mind here resembles Reverend Shin and his followers.

In *The Martyred*, most of the characters fall in the end, rebelling against the dire human condition of simply being outnumbered. Colonel Chang and Lieutenant Park die heroic deaths. Major Minn, the Hospital Commander, whose personality Josephine Nock-Hee Park traces back to the model of Dr Rieux in Camus's *The Plague* (J. N.-H. Park 2016: 69), also sacrifices himself: he decides to stay in the otherwise forsaken Pyongyang in order to take care of those patients who are too critically wounded for evacuation. Reverend Shin's fate is uncertain. Although his tuberculosis has progressed to a critical state, he decides to remain in the North to help those in need of his guidance. If there are rumours that people have seen him in one place or another, there are also other rumours, perhaps just as convincing, that he has been executed by the Communists. If the reader adopts a rational point of view, it seems unlikely that a character with Shin's health issues would last very long. Worth noting here is that Shin, alive or dead, along with his disciples, is placed on a high pedestal as an existential hero in this novel. To borrow the author's words, each act in which a character gives up his life partakes of those 'small histories' that create meanings and values in an absurd world. The glorification of these heroes' common virtue – that is, self-negation – is befitting as the ending of the novel that suggests a metaphysical rebellion as an alternative to a political one.

Nonetheless, the attempt of Richard E. Kim to heroise those individuals who fight against grand history finds itself in collusion with a certain brand of that grand history – namely, the US-generated teleological history of the world. *The Martyred*, for instance, starts by lending its support to the US-led Cold War by centring itself on the theme of Communist religious persecution and displacing the war crimes of the massive US air-bombing campaign. The author's rescripting of the Korean War as a conflict between Communism and Christianity also results in the effective displacement of the civilian mass murders and other anti-communist brutalities perpetrated in the recaptured North by the UN/ROK forces and the Rhee regime's security forces. Above all, the spiritual dilemmas and spiritual victories celebrated in the small histories of Kim's novel deflect the reader's attention from the realities of the war that may incriminate the Good Forces of Freedom. The moral victory of the martyrs in the end substitutes for the victory these forces could not achieve in the real war.

However, this victory is a precarious one. The eclipsed realities of the Korean War, in the form of their narrative repression and the unpredictable evocativeness of literary language, directs the reader's attention toward the novel's ideological bias. On the wayward nature of literary language, Macherey has asserted: '[t]he writer, as the producer of a text, does not manufacture the materials with which he works. Neither does he stumble across them as spontaneously available' (1980: 42–3). The materials or discourses which a novelist chooses for their work are not transparent; instead, they come already inscribed with particular values or associations or allusions, depending on the history of their prior inscriptions in aesthetic and cultural forms. It is due to the intractable, associative function of the language that Kim's rewriting of the Korean War as a metaphysical war ends up bringing to the reader's mind those very things it was written to displace.

Notes

1. According to Rosemary Foot's statistics, the number of civilian casualties was about two or three million individuals, while military deaths ranged from 1.5 to 2.5 million. These figures included an estimated 33,629 US battle deaths, plus 20,617 from other causes; there were 400,000 South Korean military fatalities as opposed to one or two million Communist deaths (1990: 208).
2. The author himself worked for the Northwest Youth Corps as one of its student leaders when he settled in Mokpo in 1947 after crossing the border. His relationship with this anti-communist organisation lasted throughout his high school and college years (W. D. Kim, 2007: 44, 51–7).
3. In July 1959, Rhee had the key members of the oppositional Progressive Party imprisoned and the latter's leadership executed after a show trial on charges of espionage and violations of the National Security Law. The leader of the Party was Cho Pongam, Rhee's strongest rival who served as the nation's first Minister of Agriculture and first Vice Speaker of the National Assembly. In 2007, the Korean Truth and Reconciliation Commission decided that Cho's case was a judicial murder. The Supreme Court, when it retried the case in 2010, cleared him of the espionage charge ('Cho Bong-am' 2011).

Chapter 2

The UN Ladies' War

Ahn Junghyo (1941–2023) published two novels based on his war experiences. The first is *White Badge*, a novel about the Vietnam War, which was published first in Korean in 1983 under the title *Of War and the Metropolis* and then in English, in 1989. While *White Badge* relates the author's participation in the Vietnam War as a South Korean soldier, while he was in his mid-twenties, *Silver Stallion* contains the author's experience of the Korean War, which broke out during Ahn's second year of elementary school. Ahn first started writing *Silver Stallion* – the first draft was written in English – during his stay at his college friend's grandfather's house in the summer of 1964. The grandfather, Master Hwang, on whom the author modelled one of his main characters, was the chief of Kumsan village in the mountainous Kangwon Province. In *Silver Stallion*, it is Kumsan village that is used as the background of the story. Although he finished writing the English manuscript in November 1964, Ahn had difficulty in finding a suitable publisher. In the end, Ahn published the Korean translation of *Silver Stallion* under the title *Galssam* (The Autumn War) in 1986; the English version, with the title *Silver Stallion*, came out in 1990 (Ahn 2012: 11–16).

In one of the earliest reviews of *Silver Stallion*, the literary critic Herbert Mitgang offers his compliments for the novel's authentic portrayal of the war from the perspective of the Kumsan villagers. Mitgang suggests that the author 'succeeds in writing an anti-war novel that might have been, but is not, an anti-American novel' (1990: 17). One of the reasons for Mitgang's verdict is perhaps the fact that the novel mostly focuses on the conflicts among the villagers rather than on the much larger conflict involving the US Army and the Koreans. A second early review gives credit to the novel for its 'true to life' characters and its depicting of 'the profound effects of sudden, unsolicited contact between two cultures' (Fulton 1992: 224, 226). The early encounter of South Korea with modernity during the war is noted by a third critic who directs attention to the financial rise in the novel of a miller, a nouveau riche proto-industrialist, and to the female protagonist's exposure to 'the ways of the foreigners' (Gowman 2008). By way of contrast, *Silver Stallion* has produced a number of controversies among its Korean critics. One of the earlier Korean critics, for instance, accused the novel of 'vilif[ying] the lives and experiences of the raped mother and women engaged in sexual labor' (H. Kim 1998: 181). Other critics, including Park Joohyun and Suh Jungkyu, have read in the novel a deconstruction of the stereo-typical images American GIs often have of Korean military prostitutes (Park and Suh 2009: 271). In his comparison of the novel in its Korean and English versions, Pak Inchan has suggested that the English version caters to Western Orientalism with its sensational, sexual descriptions of the South Korean female prostitutes. Curiously, these descriptions are not found in the Korean version. From this perspective, the critic argues that Ahn's cultural translation exemplifies 'self-orientalization' and thereby provides 'another source for Orientalism' (I. Pak 2009: 218).

Silver Stallion begins with the UN military forces' rollback campaign in full swing and the UN army arriving in Kumsan, a secluded village which lies across the Soyang River and the North Han River from the city of Chunchon, Kangwon Province. When the battle between the UN forces and the KPA enters a temporary lull, a couple of foreign soldiers are seen prowling Kumsan and a neighbouring village, seeking out some likely female victims to grab hold of for rape. In the event, Ollye, a widowed mother, becomes the victim of these predators in Kumsan. Not long afterwards, a detachment of the UN army arrives in order to construct Camp Omaha on Cucumber Island, a small islet which lies a short distance from the village. The presence of the UN forces on this island soon attracts a group of South Korean military prostitutes, locally known as the 'UN ladies' who follow the military routes of the foreign armies. On the island, these prostitutes soon build a shanty town of brothels called 'Texas Town'. Yonghi and Sundok, two UN ladies, decide to move to Kumsan where the housing is cheaper and then try to purchase or rent a snake hunter's shack to open a bar. The move quickly attracts unwelcome attention from the village elders and creates a source of conflict within the neighbouring environs. In the meantime, Ollye, who has been cast out of the village by her neighbours follow-ing her rape, finds it impossible to feed Mansik and Nanhi, her two children. She eventually decides to join Yonghi and Sundok in working in the brothel in order to make some money, and it is Ollye's tumultu-ous life trajectory that the novel follows. The narrative also centres on the little world of Mansik, Ollye's elder son, who suffers from the

60   *The Korean War Novel*

repercussions of his mother's rape, in the form of being alienated from his playmates. By fighting bravely in the frontline of an annual autumn battle with the boys of a neighbouring town, Mansik tries to win his friends back. However, this attempt fails when he discovers that his two friends, Chandol and Kijun, have been spying on the prostitutes, including his own mother, when they have sex with the foreign soldiers. An apparently small but serious dispute among some children quickly escalates to a larger struggle between Ollye and the other villagers. The novel concludes with almost the entire population fleeing Kumsan when the rumoured general retreat of the UN army appears set to become a reality.

This chapter begins by analysing some of the ways in which *Silver Stallion* engages with the major US-led Cold War propaganda about the Korean War. It suggests that Ahn is making a pointed revelation about the true dimensions of the Korean War in its initial stages as a civil conflict, through his comparison of the situation before and after the UN forces enter the war. Ahn's novel successfully deconstructs much of the Cold War propaganda about the Korean War by foregrounding what the majority of other Korean War novels gloss over: both the war crimes of the supposedly friendly military forces, including sexual violations and massive air-bombings against civilians, and the complicity of pro-American South Korea in concealing these atrocities. In this regard, Ahn's novel undermines the dominant tropes of what Olivier Courteaux would call mythologising 'postwar narratives' that serve to glorify patriotism and nationalism at the expense of historical facts. In his analysis of General Charles de Gaulle's post–World War 2 discourse, Courteaux brings to the fore the ways in which a hegemonic French post-war narrative distorted or ignored certain historical facts with the purpose of heroising the French Resistance's movement while minimising the importance of the Allied military intervention in Normandy. In this way, the French authorities were able to construct an alternative memory of the war including the myth of 'Paris . . . liberated by its people' (2015: 13).

Stated in Macherey's terms, *Silver Stallion* speaks of the 'silence' that grounds much of the South Korean post-war nationalist narrative that valorises the intervention of the US Army (1980:85). However, to speak of this silence, this chapter maintains, begets another kind of silence. In other words, as a means of questioning the legitimacy of the US military intervention, Ahn highlights the peacefulness of the village before the US Army's arrival, sidestepping the brutality of the class struggle that erupted after the advent of Communist rule in the occupied South. By focusing intimately on the details and social repercussions of a friendly force's sex crime as a central upshot of US military intervention, the author in effect rewrites the Korean War as one involving a major gender conflict over women's rights. Refashioned in this way, the Korean War becomes an object of potential appropriation by the different groups within the village, ranging from the Kumsan patriarchs, to the military camp prostitutes, to Ollye, the victim of rape herself. While charting the war waged by Ollye against her community, this chapter reads the protagonist and her family's social ostracism in the wake of her rape within the larger historical context of the anti-communist practices in the South. Viewed through this approach, the challenges faced by Ollye and her children, following the revelation of her 'tainted' status, parallel the guilt-by-association persecution perpetuated by the Rhee administration and the subsequent military regimes' anti-communist policies.

The occlusion of class issues

In *Silver Stallion*, Ahn narrates the impacts of the Korean War on a traditional village of Kumsan from a series of different and even conflicting perspectives. Kumsan village is described as a place almost outside history, tucked out of sight of the seismic political shifts of the past that have caused the nation to suffer such dizzying turmoil. Initially, the Korean War was no exception:

> The farmers of Kumsan village had never considered that the war had anything to do with them. Until as recently as yesterday morning, in fact, they had hardly believed that a war was actually going on. Some of the villagers had seen Communists guarding buildings draped with red flags when they went to town to sell radishes or straw ropes . . . But the presence of those soldiers in town was the only visible evidence of war for the villagers, although it had been three months since this war had broken out. Some townspeople said the Communist Army had come to liberate the South and unify the divided nation; others that the Reds were nothing but bloody murderers who were determined to wipe out the southern half of the nation. Confused by these conflicting rumors, the villagers listened and nodded or shook their heads half-heartedly: 'Whatever you say, whatever you say.' (Ahn 1990: 4)

The passage testifies that for the Kumsan villagers, or the people of the larger West County, life went on much the same, even after the outbreak of the war. Naturally, the villagers know all about – some have even seen – the Communist soldiers armed with 'strange Russian rifles' stationed in the town. However, despite the KPA occupation of Chunchon, the people feel they have nothing to do with the war, an attitude that can be attributed to the remoteness of their village from the main military

62   *The Korean War Novel*

action, the upshot of the fact that the village of Kumsan is segregated from Chunchon by the course of two large rivers, the Soyang River and the North Han River. More importantly, the reason for this lack of concern may also be attributed to the class structure of this small village. Kumsan possesses no large landlords, something that helps to explain why there has not been 'a single incident of confrontation between the rich and the poor, the land owners and the peasants' here (Ahn 1990: 6). The choice of such a quiet secluded hamlet, of course, enables Ahn to highlight the peacefulness its residents have enjoyed before the arrival of the UN forces.

This way, the impact of Communist occupation upon civilians exists only in the contradictory rumours that the people of Kumsan village hear from the townspeople. According to these rumours, the KPA soldiers are both 'liberators' and 'bloody murderers'. This contradiction, however, does not merely signify the absurdity of the rumours. Placed within the wider historical context of agricultural South Korea, it reveals the different ways the rule of the advancing KPA affected their newly acquired southern territories. According to historical reports,

> the most important projects pursued by the Communist regime in the recaptured South were land reform and electing People's Committees. On 4 July [1950], the Supreme People's Committee issued the standing committee's decree that it would impose land reform in 'the southern territory of the Communist republic'. Ten days later, on July 14th, the standing committee of the Supreme People's Committee declared that in the liberated South, elections would be held to fill the seats on county-, township-, and village-level People's Committees. (Jung 2012: 41; author's translation)

From this point of view, the otherwise puzzling dual nature of the Communist Army depends upon which class the particular villager belongs to. Stated differently, those who had substantial property to lose perceived the KPA as armed robbers, whereas those who felt they had something to gain saw them as liberators. As Kim Dong-Choon maintains, '[t]he KPA occupation during the Korean War is remembered as heaven by some and hell by others, a disparity very rare in similar situations' (2000: 93). In this regard, the contradictory rumours that the Kumsan villagers hear about the KPA are true. The arrival of the KPA also meant a complete upheaval within the political hierarchy in the South. The seismic changes the southerners experienced under Communist rule can easily be guessed from the fact that in Kangwon Province, as well as in the other provinces under Communist control, peasants and labourers constituted an overwhelming 90 per cent of the members of the People's Committees (Kee 2012: 50). What is more, those classified as pro-Japanese or pro-American became targets for execution.

However, Ahn leaves to one side the severe repercussions of Communist popular power. In truth, a family like the Hwang's, one described as the wealthiest and the most learned family in the West County, would undoubtedly not have survived the anti-landlord, anti-elitist and anti-pro-Japanese policies of the occupying Communists. Under Communist rule, members of the lowest class, including the snake hunter and Yom, the ferryman, the vast majority of the villagers look down on, would most likely have filled the ranks of the People's Committee. It is these formerly despised lowest-caste citizens, the so-called 'base Reds' (D.-C. Kim 2000: 135–6), who suddenly find themselves in power under Communist rule, following the mass execution of their old masters during the war. In turn, these lower-caste people found themselves the victims of the subsequent Red manhunt when the Korean National Army reoccupied the village. The tragic dimensions of this class struggle are absent from the novel. In this regard, one might argue that the Korean War as a revolutionary civil conflict is merely symptomatically present in Ahn's novel, registered only in the self-delegitimising form of sensational but contradictory rumours. Eliminating the visceral class struggle from his portrayal of the occupied South, the author focuses on challenging the imperative need for the US military intervention, not to mention its humanitarian rhetoric, while foregrounding the war crimes of the US soldiers.

Debunking the liberationist rhetoric of the UN forces

In an out-of-the-way village like Kumsan, even the jubilant incident of national liberation celebrated among a majority of Koreans, according to the narrator, appears not to affect the lives of the villagers at all: '[t]hey were supposed to have been officially liberated from the Japanese Imperialists, but nothing actually happened' (Ahn 1990: 6). Since, for these villagers, the economic realities of the colonial class structure do not change with liberation, the postliberation era appears to be no different from the Japanese colonial period itself. In a similar way, 'liberation' by the UN military forces from Communist rule is viewed in much the same disinterested manner:

> These out-of-the-way farmers were not much impressed by the news that an American general with the queer name of Megado [MacArthur], commanding thousands and thousands of the United Nations Forces, had landed at

64   *The Korean War Novel*

Inchon to liberate the South Korean people. *The villagers thought nothing would be changed if they were liberated once more by the famous American general. Old Hwang did not believe it mattered too much even if his county remained unliberated.* There were many things the old man could not understand about the war. (Ahn 1990: 6; emphasis added)

Master Hwang's attitude toward both the first liberation by the Communists a few months previously and a second that is supposed to happen soon is marked by complete indifference. As a matter of fact, Hwang and the villagers do not believe it matters 'even if [their] county remained unliberated.'

Questioning the very meaning of 'liberation' is not unique to Ahn's fictional residents of Kumsan village. It is a view shared by Kim Sŏngch'il, a professor who taught history at Seoul National University during these years and was thirty-seven years old when the war began. His diary entry for 28 June 1960, three days after the outbreak of the Korean War, records his and other citizens' responses to the arrival of the KPA in this manner:

Although they have a strong north-western accent, they are our kind, sharing the same language, customs and blood. At first sight, it would seem that they, somehow, are not our enemy. They look more like brothers, who have come back home after living somewhere far away. I do not feel hostility when I see them speaking amiably with smiles. (S.-C. Kim 1993: 68–9; author's translation)

Although Kim Sŏngch'il did not welcome the arrival of the KPA, he did not feel threatened, either, despite his initial fear, when he first saw them marching in. For a short time at least, his family's life went on the same way as before. The only difference Kim noticed was on the evening of 28 June, when he saw among young people wearing red armbands, 'a young man who, until only yesterday, was seen riding a bicycle, wearing the armband of a chief inspector of the rightist Korean Youth Corps' (S.-C. Kim 1993: 69). The sudden change in allegiance noted by Kim serves to indicate that the line of demarcation between the Red forces and the right-wing forces was not always vigorously guarded: some people chose one side over the other or even flipped back and forth for personal reasons or out of expediency rather than for noble political reasons.

The lack of enthusiasm or excitement about the intervention of the UN army was shared both by the farmers of Kumsan and the members of a smaller community – an informal club comprising five small boys: Chandol, Kijun, Kangho, Mansik and Bong. Driven by the desire to see a real battle first-hand, four of the boys, with the exception of Bong who is too young to make the attempt, swim naked across the North Han River to Cucumber Island. Hiding themselves in the bush, the boys see the UN troops for the first time, with their military trucks and tanks. The wonderful, and yet strangely grotesque, sight of the faces of these foreigners attracts the boys' attention. The four boys animatedly discuss the differences between their physical features and the features of these UN soldiers, which soon leads to the topic of why all these foreigners have come to Korea:

> 'They must be the World Army,' Chandol murmured . . . 'They don't look like Koreans. Too tall and too big. And some of them have a strange dark color on their faces.'
> 'You mean they are the foreign soldiers who came to liberate us from the People's Army?' Mansik said.
> 'Yes.'
> 'Are we liberated?' Kijun said.
> 'That's right.'
> Kijun said, 'While we've been sitting here, naked? That's funny.'
> Chandol explained, 'We just watch the war. It's grownups who decide whether we are liberated or not.'
> 'That's confusing,' Kijun said. 'It's so different from our Autumn War.'
> 'It's really a very simple matter, Toad,' said Chandol. 'Whether we're liberated or not is decided by which side wins the war. If the World Army wins, we're liberated from the People's Army. If the People's Army wins, we are liberated from the World Army.' (Ahn 1990: 41)

Kijun's response – 'While we've been sitting here, naked? That's funny.' – to the explanation that the UN troops are there to deliver them from the Communist Army is the upshot of his ignorance of immediate realities. What is more, Chandol's clarification of the essential mystery of the war – that is, the question of who has been liberated by whom and who is the liberator and who the oppressor – is, at one level, too simple to merit serious attention and yet it is strikingly effective in exploding the hypocrisy and absurdity of liberationist rhetoric. This childish debate nonetheless raises some key issues when the reader considers that the explanations offered by these four awestruck young men function in the novel as a miniature version of the adult world surrounding them. The resemblance between the two worlds is unmistakable in several ways. For instance, the war raging outside Kumsan village is metonymically represented in the form of the fist-fighting and rock-throwing between the five boys from Kumsan and seven other boys from the neighbouring Castle village. Synecdochically, the modern weaponry deployed by the rival militaries is represented in the young gang's assembly of a sizeable

66 The Korean War Novel

armoury, including a bayonet, a DDT powder can, a full box of live ammunition and a rifle with its stock missing. This year, the war among the village boys is expected to be more intense than before since the two rival groups are now fighting over the right to raid the local US military camp's precious dumping ground. In this way, the internecine nature of the war between the two states is revealed in the unambiguous terms of a second war between the young combatants of the two neighbouring villages, with the material motive of one war exposed in the naked competition over the right to salvage refuse from Camp Omaha.

Considered in its relation to the military homology of the rival regimes, the conversation between Kijun and Chandol now begins to take on more important political significance. For example, what had seemed at first blush to be a historically uninformed and rather silly, if still funny, comment by Kijun, one which curtly trivialised the much-glorified UN military's attempt to liberate the nation, drives home Cumings' revisionist argument that the Korean War is after all a civil strife – a point which highlights the absurdity of the intervention by foreign armies.[1] By implication, much the same line of criticism is also applicable to the second foreign intervention, the entry of the Chinese Communist Army heralded at the end of the novel. For those who consider the war as a mostly civil conflict, the intervention of foreign forces, whether under the auspices of the United Nations or of the Chinese Communists, makes no sense. And even less sense can be made of their 'funny' claims of coming to save Korea from its own people. There can therefore be little wonder that the village farmers do not care which side liberates them or conquers the other side. The 'liberationist' rhetoric employed by both the UN army and the KPA and its Chinese ally is also undermined by Chandol's reply, even if he does not realise it. According to the leader of the gang of boys, the question of who liberates whom is simply a matter of who will win the war. In an all-out war, the winning side defines justice – retrospectively. Once their pretensions are removed, the weighty issues of the adult world turn out to be nothing more than a childish dispute where might always plays the deciding factor.

The rather carefree attitude towards the war on the part of 'the people' under Communist occupation is expressed by Kim Dong-Choon in the following manner:

> The majority of farmers who had not actively supported either regime, South or North, did not evacuate when the South was invaded or follow the retreating North Korean troops. They did not consider life under the KPA a hell, nor did they consider the return of South Korean forces a liberation. Most of them just settled down in one place and carried on with their lives. (2000: 136)

The UN Ladies' War **67**

Read alongside this historically grounded point of view, Ahn's account of the boys' conversation alludes to two largely unacknowledged truths about the Korean War. The first is that it is military strength that determines righteousness. The second is that the conflict in Korea had a hidden civil dimension. In this regard, Ahn's novel subverts Cold War propaganda by stripping it of its grandiose, liberationist rhetoric.

If he critiques the foreign military intervention in the Korean War by emphasising its civil dimension, Ahn takes direct issue with the US Air Force's problematic practices of bombardment. The author makes it clear that it is the US air strikes that have changed the attitude of the Kumsan farmers towards the Korean War from indifference through anxiety to fear. The farmers first experience anxiety regarding the excessive nature of the US bombing when they find the city of Chunchon still ablaze the morning after, following the two hours of bombing that took place on the previous afternoon. Master Hwang, for one, feels 'vaguely apprehensive', thinking that '[w]hat was happening might eventually affect his village, too' (Ahn 1990: 4). This initial response escalates as they watch the US air strikes continue and begin to hear first-hand testimony of the havoc the bombing has wreaked on Chunchon. Kijun's uncle, for example, graphically conveys what he has just seen in the town:

> 'It kept coming and coming, explosions, in all directions. Wham! Wham! WHAM!' he went on . . . 'Many houses were engulfed by smoke and clouds of dust, and people were running away, helter-skelter, stumbling and screaming. They were running, running, running with their children in their arms, shrieking and whimpering and calling, their hair all in tangles and their clothes torn to flying shreds. They did not know where they were going, where they should go, or what they were supposed to do. They ran back and forth going nowhere. And I saw a woman whose arm had been just blown off . . . Blood was gushing out of the ragged stump of what was left of her arm. She was digging in a pile of dirt on the curb, sobbing, "Where's my arm? Where's my arm?"' (Ahn 1990: 17)

Despite the speaker's well-known flair for exaggeration, this vividly rendered description of the aerial bombing makes the villagers 'nervous'. The subsequent fear caused by the seemingly indiscriminate nature of the air raid takes such a strong grip on the minds of the local residents that 'even a faint purr of the bombers' is enough to send everyone running in panic for their lives (Ahn 1990: 33). What is worth noting about the portrayals of the US Air Force's air strikes on the 'enemy territory' is that not a single Communist soldier is mentioned. By bringing to the fore the sufferings of the civilians, Ahn makes an emphatic statement about the indiscriminateness of the warfare waged by the US Air

68   *The Korean War Novel*

Force, a point that is starkly absent from the account offered in Richard E. Kim's *The Martyred*.

A patriarchs' war

However, with the arrival of the 'liberating army' of the UN, the Kumsan farmers find that a life of relative seclusion is no longer possible. If the US Air Force had been jeopardising the lives of innocent people with excessive air strikes, the US soldiers that arrive soon after now threaten the safety of the traditional village's womenfolk.

As night descends and the battle between the UN forces and the KPA comes to a temporary halt, two UN soldiers decide to go prowling in the village for women. They end up at the widowed Ollye's Chestnut House and rape her. What turns out to be truly devastating for Ollye, however, is not so much the horrendous sex crime itself but its social repercussions. After the incident, the neighbours completely cut off all contact with Ollye and her family. Master Hwang's comments sum up the attitude of the entire village concerning what has happened:

> [V]ictim or not, she was a dirty woman. Loss of feminine virtue, under any circumstance, was the most profound shame for a woman – so profound a shame, in fact, that in the old days, a disgraced woman did not hesitate to drink a bowl of lye to terminate her life. The act of taking her own life symbolically restored the chastity of the defiled woman. (Ahn 1990: 67–8)

Still ruled by ancient Confucian precepts, the community can find no place for the victims of sex crimes such as Ollye. The only option for a 'defiled woman' to restore her status as a full member of the community is to take her own life. Initially, the incident traumatises Ollye and her older son, Mansik, who are filled with an overwhelming sense of shame and then with the paralysing fear of meeting their neighbours. However, Ollye eventually decides to defy the Confucian demand that she restore her honour by dying by suicide.

Instead, *Silver Stallion* is primarily occupied with exploring the dynamic conflict between the human rights of Ollye and the social rigidity of the village patriarchy. For the Kumsan patriarchs, the nature of the Korean War changes, depending on how its twists and turns affect their traditional privilege. In this respect, the Communist occupation of the South means nothing to them as long as the village is left alone. Only when they feel the impact of the UN rollback campaign do they start to recognise danger and begin to mobilise against it. At this point, each of the Kumsan farmers digs an air raid shelter for his house and a ban is placed on all trips to Chunchon, the site of the frequent US air strikes. When the UN forces arrive, the village patriarchs find the chastity of their womenfolk endangered, and as a result, take action in order to protect their women against these foreign sexual predators, and assert their authority within the sphere of gender relations. When Camp Omaha is set up on Cucumber Island, the village leaders sense a grave threat to the moral health of their community and, obviously, are doubly concerned about their ability to enforce the edicts of female chastity. A moral crusade is waged against Texas Town, the name for the brothels set up on the islet for American GIs. According to Ahn, this crusade is even more important to the farmers than the outcome of the Korean War itself, as is evident from Master Hwang's response to the report that the Communist guerrillas have opened an upstream floodgate as a means of attacking the ROKA stationed downstream. When the river starts being flooded, Hwang secretly sides with the Communists: he declares his wish that 'the *bengko* ['the big-nosed', a reference to the Western soldiers] camp and the whore town had been wiped out by the river' (Ahn 1990: 172). When he learns that the surprise flooding has failed in its objective, the county chief is sorely disappointed.

Toward the end of the novel, when the tide of war begins to turn against the UN military forces and the news of their general retreat reaches Kumsan, the villagers become highly anxious. This frightened response contrasts with their earlier reaction when they were informed that the North Korean Communists had arrived to 'liberate' them. Master Hwang's son, Sokku, explains the two distinct reactions in these terms:

> When the *Migook* [American] Army first arrived, they brought battle to West County and raped women. Now another horde of foreign soldiers from China was surging south like a human sea. The war was growing bigger and bigger, and its irresistible wave would crash over this village soon. The villagers, who were only too well aware of what the friendly forces of the Liberators had done to them, shuddered in anticipation of what the enemy forces of China would do. (Ahn 1990: 204)

What differentiates this second visit from the earlier visit of the Communists is the presence of a second pack of foreign soldiers arriving alongside the North Korean army. First and foremost, the painful memory of what the 'friendly' foreign army has done to their women causes the villagers to fear for their future.

As discussed above, what is most at stake for the Kumsan patriarchs in the war is not so much the sovereignty of their country as their male privilege, the control over their women in particular. According to Yang Hyunah, from a patriarchal point of view, the issue of chastity is

70   *The Korean War Novel*

fundamentally about the male desire for monopoly over female sexuality. This male possessiveness is explained in the following manner:

> Chastity involves not virginity as such, but rather that there is always a proper place where female sexuality belongs. A married woman's sexuality belongs to her husband, whether he is alive or dead; an unmarried woman's sexuality belongs to her future husband; and in general, Korean women's sexuality belongs to Korean men. (Yang 1998: 131)

In Kumsan, the gender hierarchy is pointedly revealed when Mr Han, the mill owner, discovers that, disobeying his instructions, his wife has visited Chunchon in order to pilfer rice from the granary of the retreating People's Army. As retribution, he gives his wife a severe beating with a conveyor belt 'until she foams at the mouth' (Ahn 1990: 30).

Within this rural community, the patriarchs' entitlement to privilege is warranted by their possession of a certain set of inherent qualities. According to the narrator, although most village women took trips to the city to obtain the free rice, few men did. The narrator attributes this to the separate code of values held by the men and women of Kumsan: 'Women did not care about pride or dignity, because only men were supposed to possess these qualities' (Ahn 1990: 32). It is these hierarchical gender relations that serve to justify the Kumsan patriarchs' view of women as private property. In their eyes, the Korean War takes on significance only when foreign armies, whether Communist or not, threaten to deprive them of their proprietorship over the bodies of their women. If it helped the patriarch to secure this birthright, switching sides would be easy, as illustrated in Master Hwang's wish for the hostile flooding of the river to succeed.

The unacknowledged, yet crucial, dimension behind the Kumsan patriarchs' fear for their women is xenophobia. The reason Master Hwang and the other villagers offer for their denunciation of the violated Ollye is her loss of chastity. This hidden dimension, however, emerges briefly in an unguarded conversation among the five boys of Kumsan. After Ollye and her two children are ostracised from the village, Kangho tries to invite Mansik to join a treasure hunt on the dumping ground of Camp Omaha. When Mansik shows up, however, the gang leader, Chandol, chases him away. This small incident is significant in what it reveals about what lies beneath the ostensible reason given for the villagers' ostracism of Ollye as a 'defiled' woman.

> 'I guess you came here to play with us, but we can't play with you,' Chandol said. 'We all know that your mother fucked a nigger. And you still expect us to play with you?'

'Yeah,' Kijun added. 'My mother told me your mother will have *a black baby* because she fucked a black man.' (Ahn 1990: 144; emphasis added)

From Chandol's and Kijun's mouths, we learn what was left unsaid in the villagers' stigmatisation of Ollye. Unlike the case in which Korean men sexually assault Korean women, the identity of the rapist in Ollye's case adds another dimension to the social repercussions of the crime. To recall Yang's argument, 'Chastity involves not virginity as such, but rather that there is always a proper place where female sexuality belongs' (1998: 131). Here, Ollye is not simply a victim: she is also figured as a transgressor, one who, in the opinion of the villagers, not only '[chose] to be raped' but also 'enjoyed it . . . so much' (Ahn 1990: 181, 68). If her victimisation at the hands of American GIs has compromised Korean male proprietorship over Korean female sexuality, it has also broken the racial taboo of the traditional community. Chandol's remarks, which are probably a paraphrase of something his parents have said, make it clear that the villagers' ostracism of the rape survivor is not just about her loss of chastity but also about the violation of the racial divide.

Ollye's 'crime' is aggravated by the fact that one of the two rapists is an African American. The way the villagers see the aspect of the inter-racial sex crime is expressed quite bluntly by Chandol, who sees Mansik as contaminated by association with blackness. In this sense, Ollye has violated the racial taboo attached to Korean female sexuality twice: she has been taken not just by a foreigner, but by a black foreigner. As Chungmoo Choi maintains, '[a]ll Korean women, as the discourse of homogeneous single-nation (*tanil minjok*) mandates, are expected to be chaste and vigilant against foreign males' (1998: 14). Kijun's relaying of his mother's words is revelatory of a second hidden dimension to the villagers' condemnation of the rape survivor. As Kijun's mother says, the villagers believe that Ollye may give birth to 'a black baby'. Kijun's mother's words divulge the unspoken fear of possible interethnic relationships as an outcome of the crime; they also, at a single stroke, expose the villagers' anti-black racism. For the conservative Kumsan community, with its strong attachment to the myth of ethnic purity, the mere thought that one of its women might bear a biracial baby, a half-black baby at that, is a nightmare. Significantly here, a biracial baby is subsumed under the category of black subjectivity. At this point, we can begin to grasp the depths of the communal anxiety underlying the villagers' condemnation of and its hostility to all foreign armies, ostensibly friendly or hostile, as the case may be.

72 *The Korean War Novel*

A women's war

If the Korean War is significant to the Kumsan patriarchs only in terms of their ownership of female sexuality, how is the war of significance for Ollye? After her violation by the US soldiers, no one will visit her any more. None of his friends will come to play with her son, Mansik. Suddenly, it appears that they have become invisible to their neighbours. The ostracism of her family from village life makes both Ollye and Mansik afraid to go out. During the course of a single night, Mansik has lost the comforting, familiar world he has known all his life. That world now simply refuses to recognise his family. In thanatological terms, Ollye expresses the same sense of non-existence:

> She had the frightening sense that she might be dead even now, sitting there under the tree in the dark, watching the bright artificial lights of another world across the river. Breathing, but dead with her eyes wide open. She had been confined in her home, dead, while the world, ignoring her existence, was busy living. (Ahn 1990: 124–5)

Ollye's horrifying sense that she might be '[b]reathing, but dead' is rooted in the experience of her social death within her community. It is this social death that leads the village boys to conceive their daring plan to spy on her while she is servicing American GIs in the brothel. It is obvious even to the youngsters that an abject subject like Ollye has no human rights. Tabooed by her community, Ollye has become what Giorgio Agamben refers to as a '*homo sacer*'. According to the Italian philosopher, a criminal ostracised from the society of ancient Rome was reduced to the bare state of existence known as *zoe*, in which they are deprived of all legal and political rights (1998: 9). This outlawed person was left to their own devices and exposed to the unconditional threat of death. In Ollye's case, exposure, humiliation and fear characterise her status as a social outcast.

In *Silver Stallion*, the major ideological issues associated with the Korean War, including those of class struggle and of anti-communist persecution, are doubly occluded. That is, if these issues are first back-grounded by Ahn's decision to debunk the liberationist rhetoric of the US military intervention, they are then de-emphasised by the author's decision to focus on gender issues. Nonetheless, this is not to say that these historical realities are entirely absent – nor indeed that gender issues cannot themselves mobilise the wider politics of the conflict. Inserted within the Cold War context of ideological struggle, certain episodes that seem at first to be exclusively rooted in gender conflict offer allusions

The UN Ladies' War **73**

to the forms of ideological persecution practised by both the South and the North. For example, anti-communist persecution may be discovered when the Kumsan villagers punish Ollye, stigmatising her and depriving her of membership in the community. This method of ostracising the 'transgressor' as a means of punishment recalls the way Communist subversives and Communist sympathisers were treated in South Korea.

As Kim Dong-Choon reports, '[b]randing someone as a Red was practically a form of violence that could socially ostracize someone for life. As Cho Pongam pointed out, those accused of collaborating with the North were completely deprived of their status as citizens' (2000: 123). In her autobiographical novel, *Who Ate Up All the Shinga?*, Park Wansuh, the South Korean novelist, recounts in similar terms the ordeal she had to go through: '[t]hey called me a Red bitch. Red bastard, Red bitch, it didn't matter – anyone stained by red was no longer human. And since our humanity had been forfeited, we couldn't demand our human rights' ([1992] 2009: 234). The metaphorical reading of Ollye's ostracism as a form of anti-communist persecution is bolstered by the fact that the villagers' communal penalisation is extended to the children of the original victim. In this way, the village children also treat Mansik, Ollye's son, as a *'homo sacer'*. Because she is too young to have a social life, Nanhi is the only member of Ollye's family who is spared from this ordeal. This system of punishment using guilt by association recalls the example of the vicious ideological politics of South Korea.

During the period of the Rhee government as well as the South Korean military regimes, from the taking of power by Park Chung-hee in 1961 until the end of the reign of Chun Doo-hwan in 1988, if a member of a certain family was known to be a Communist or a defector to the North, the rest of the family became subject to various forms of persecution. Not only were they forbidden to hold public office but they were also treated in general as second-class citizens. Many of them found themselves placed under constant police surveillance as possible spies and traitors. Heonik Kwon describes the social discrimination suffered by these people because of their blood ties to a known Communist:

> For people whose genealogical backgrounds include ancestors once classified as Communist subversives, sympathizers of communism, or defectors to the Communist North, red blood line has been a terrifying idea associated with the memory of summary killings and mass murder, surviving family members' experience of social stigma, and the restriction of their civil rights. (2010: 41)

In the McCarthy-like atmosphere under the Rhee and the South Korean military regimes, ideological markers were treated as genetically

74 *The Korean War Novel*

inherited. When read metaphorically, the punitive ostracism suffered by Mansik testifies to the anti-communist practice of conflating the ideological and the biological. This conflation is something that the Cold War brought into being in South Korea. Hence, Kwon's observation about South Korea and Vietnam, two nations in which this policy was practised: '[i]f racial colors were ideological constructs, not biological conditions, political ideologies, in turn, took on biological and racial imagery in the history of the twentieth century' (2010: 42).

Alienated from the outer world, the protagonist Ollye misses the life where she could safely rely on help from the people she once knew; at first she fears meeting anyone because she sees herself as a rightfully disgraced person. However, as time passes, Ollye begins to cease fearing renewed encounters with the villagers, including even Master Hwang, the village patriarch himself. Just as she has stopped existing for the villagers, so the village has stopped existing for her (Ahn 1990: 125). By accepting her status as an outcast, Ollye has freed herself from her apparently lifelong sense of bondage to her community and its traditional ways. Before, she thought that it was she who had disgraced and aggrieved the villagers because of her 'fallen' state. From her new critical perspective, however, it is the village that is now responsible for her current predicament. Instead of consoling one of their own at the time of her greatest need, not to mention failing to protect her as a widow from the dangers of sexual violence in the first place, the villagers not only ignored her suffering but then shamelessly and irresponsibly cast her and her family out. In this way, the village punished the victim for the actual crime. This train of thought leads Ollye to declare her intention to cut off ties with her community. In her own words, '[i]t was time for her to do her own casting off – of her past life' (Ahn 1990: 175). Ollye's 'casting off' of her past life coincides with her attempt to '*lead* her life' as a UN lady.

It is important to note that Ollye does not become a liberated individual on her own. Born and raised in a traditional village, Ollye has no obvious mental or cultural assets for achieving independence. Indeed, from the villagers' act of ostracism, she is all too aware of the extreme difficulty and even unbearable nature of trying to stand alone. Speaking of the difficulties female subjects face when trying to break with traditional patterns of dependence, Almudena Hernando asserts:

> Individuality comprises anxiety, searching, instability, and unstoppable and inevitable transformation. That is a load too heavy to be carried on one's own. It cannot be done. It is too cold inside individuality, for it leaves human beings naked before the universe. (2017: 112)

From Hernando's perspective, 'individuated identity' cannot be developed without maintaining some sort of 'relational identity'. As a consequence, perhaps, Ollye chooses to bond with Yonghi and Sundok, two Texas Town prostitutes, and comes to see them as role models. As a matter of fact, it is her early exposure to the perspective of these women that leads Ollye to question the righteousness of her community in dealing with her crisis. Even before she understands all the details concerning Ollye's predicament, Yonghi pities the widow for having to put up with such a backward community: 'you must get a lot of grief from these characters all around you' (Ahn 1990: 113). In Yonghi's case, her sympathy stems from her knowledge of the details of the village elders' conspiracy to sabotage her plan to open a bar in Kumsan. On a separate occasion, Yonghi passes negative judgement on the general ethics of the village, based on a comparison between Kumsan and her past experiences of other communities: 'I've never seen people like them, really . . . Bad neighbors are worse than wasps'. At this point, Sundok chimes in, inviting Ollye to wake up and reconsider her reality: '[y]ou should know who your real enemies are. And who your true friends are' (Ahn 1990: 122). Of course, this advice is primarily designed to invite the widow to join them as an ally in their struggle against the morally uncompromising villagers. Nevertheless, Ollye benefits from consorting with these despised women. It is her exposure to this extra-communal perspective that encourages Ollye to disengage psychologically from the village.

With her new profession, Ollye faces many changes in her life. She learns to use new Western products, which, in time, leads to a transformation in her perspective on life. Since she now has some money, she is able to buy for the first time expensive foreign goods such as cosmetics, clothes and even a camera. With this camera, she 'took pictures of Mansik and Nanhi standing before the chestnut tree, standing before the house, standing by the kitchen door, standing on both sides of the rabbit cage, standing side by side on the footpath, standing everywhere' (Ahn 1990: 115). In this passage, Ollye is doing more than just taking snapshots of her children. She is becoming familiar with Western technology, basking in her new affiliation, however tenuous that might be, with the modern world. At the same time, playing with this new camera allows her to express herself creatively. It is Ollye who must choose the exact location for the snapshots; and it is Ollye who must ask her children to pose in a certain way for the camera. Familiarising herself with other modern products enables her to develop new sensoria for enjoyment: she not only comes to feel comfortable wearing skimpy Western dresses, including short skirts and sleeveless blouses, but she also 'like[s] the soft touch of her stockings' (Ahn 1990: 175) that cover her legs to the thighs.

76   *The Korean War Novel*

Her new experience with cosmetics even changes her traditional view on aesthetics and femininity: '[m]aking up one's face was vulgar, Ollye had been raised to think. But she came to believe that it was something highly elegant and truly feminine' (Ahn 1990: 174).

A second remarkable transformation that comes with her work in the brothel is the way in which she learns not just new manners in order to entertain her customers but, more fundamentally, begins to transform into a wholly new person with much better control of her life. This change is signalled when Ollye undertakes a series of daring initiatives, ones she would not have even dreamed of in the past, in the brothel business:

> Her manners toward the soldier customers also underwent a change. Once, when she was very drunk, Ollye attempted a clumsy imitation of the striptease. She even learned to express her displeasure the Yankee way. If somebody tried to tie her down with a rope or tried to force her to do unmentionable things such as sticking a bottle in her crotch and sucking the beer in, she did not hesitate to shriek, 'Goddamn fucking sonabech gerrary,' and in case her feelings had not been fully communicated by those *Migook* words, she went on screaming and cursing in Korean. If Korean swearing did not work either, she knew how to call the MPs and get the 'sonabech' dragged away for punishment . . . [N]o body doubted that she was now a regular U.N. lady. (Ahn 1990: 175)

What happens as Ollye learns the tricks of the brothel trade is her simultaneous acquisition of self-confidence, adventurousness and boldness. She is self-confident enough to act toward men in ways that her old community would condemn as 'unfeminine' and 'immoral', including 'screaming and cursing' at men when they displease her. She has also learned to exercise her legal rights as a co-proprietor of the brothel business when her patrons cross the line: she has the military policemen (MPs) drag them away. In this regard, the narrator's summary of the transformation in Ollye's situation – 'she was now a regular U.N. lady' – appears as something of an understatement. For the first time in her life, she has become *a full human subject*. She is now someone who is entirely aware of – and knows how to protect – her rights. Naturally, it is grimly ironic that it is only when Ollye has fallen to the level of the military prostitute that she earns the right to a full human dignity. At the same time, it is her insertion as a brothel owner into the web of capitalist relations that enables Ollye to achieve genuine subjecthood. The fact that this reluctant entry into a local market economy dependent on the US military forces offers not only economic survival but also potential prosperity to the social outcast constitutes another point of irony in the much wider context of US military intervention in Asia. As

The UN Ladies' War   **77**

Christine Hong asserts, since World War 2, US militarism has aimed at establishing 'a system of dependent capitalism' in order to consolidate its interests in Asia (2020: 15).

If her former life is compared with her new life as a military prostitute, Ollye will be seen to have become her own mistress. 'She wanted to *lead* her life' (Ahn 1990: 175; emphasis in the original), and now she does. Perhaps the greatest change of all those she has experienced concerns her views on prostitution itself. This awakening has been facilitated by Yonghi, who is also known as 'Sister Serpent'. Although 'Yonghi' originally means 'Dragon Girl', her friends at a certain point started to refer to her as 'Sister Serpent' in jest due to her obvious failure to become as illustrious as the celestial creature. In view of the fact that it is Sister Serpent who opens Ollye's eyes to the kinds of futures possible for UN ladies, however, the nickname, with its Biblical associations with the sharer of forbidden knowledge, appears aptly given. According to Yonghi, some of the UN ladies, having married US soldiers, have gone off to live in the United States, the country known as the earthly 'paradise' (Ahn 1990: 123). Using a highly consumerist vocabulary, she expresses her limited notion of this Brave New World: '[l]ots of canned food. Nice warm blankets. And . . . almost every family has its own car in that big country' (Ahn 1990: 123–4). In consequence, her advice to Ollye can be summarised in the language of opportunism: '[p]lay it smart and you will come to thank heaven for this war for bringing the *bengkos* to this country' (Ahn 1990: 124). For this group of wily women, who have lost everything except their marketable bodies, this is what the Korean War means. Even if the war has deprived them of almost every resource needed for survival, including money, human dignity and a system of social and emotional support networks, they are still able to find a way to turn it to their advantage, by attempting to utilise it as the source of a new life in the diaspora that holds out the promise of a hitherto absent material comfort.

Nonetheless, a plane ticket to a wealthy life in the US is not their only option. According to Yonghi, these young women can also start a new life with the capital they have accumulated servicing foreign soldiers:

> Work like a dog for just one year until you make enough money to open a small shop somewhere . . . Then you can go and settle down at a remote town in Chungchong or Kangwon Province, open a cotton shop or a noodle house and live as happily ever after as you want with your children. (Ahn 1990: 164)

From this point of view, military prostitution can guarantee a middle-class life as a shop owner as long as they are willing to work hard,

78   *The Korean War Novel*

relocate and never mention to anyone their previous line of work. When the reader stops to consider that the best life that Master Hwang can now hope for with the money he has raised by selling both his big house and his harvest of rice is to open 'a small shop' (Ahn 1990: 243) somewhere further in the South, Yonghi's prospect of owning 'a cotton shop or a noodle house' does not look so bad.

Ollye also learns to take an active role in the emerging modern Korean commercial economy. She disposes of the goods Yonghi smuggles out of Camp Omaha in the town's black market, making as much money for herself and Yonghi as they both earn from entertaining American soldiers. In the sense that these women's new subjectivity as *homo economicus* is achieved through demeaning brothel work, the reader may wonder whether their life trajectories illustrate a case of female empowerment or just another form of female victimisation. In this regard, one may be reminded of the criticism that this text confirms the 'pejorative views that render [Ollye] more a commodified object of play than a self-determined subject' (H. Kim 1998: 184). Yet, this kind of critique takes account of only one side of the story. The author's insight is that for women of the underclass, a second chance does not come in the form of a sudden Cinderella-like fairy-tale transformation. For those who lack privilege, the ladder to the stars starts with one's feet planted firmly in the dirt.

Ollye shows her defiant, independent spirit when Master Hwang visits her with his plan to stop the operation of the Lady Dragon Club, the brothel set up by Ollye and her co-workers, Yonghi and Sundok, at the snake hunter's shack across from the protagonist's Chestnut House. The shack was the only property these women could purchase in Kumsan village for their bar business. The owner sold it to them, disobeying Master Hwang's direct order against it. The village patriarch has sold some of his latest harvest, finally procuring enough money to pay back Yonghi for the snake hunter's shack. He asks Ollye to pass the money on to Yonghi, relaying at the same time his order for her to leave the village immediately. Although it is not explicitly mentioned, this order implies that Ollye must leave the village too. Ollye flatly refuses. Shaken up by this unexpected, daring response, the village patriarch tries to reason with her, pointing out the harmful effects of the existence of the brothel on the villagers. He tries to make her agree that 'this is best for both of us' (Ahn 1990: 179). Ollye's rebuttal smacks of the ways of the modern businessperson: 'What benefit is there in that for me?' (Ahn 1990: 179). The brutal candidness of her response causes Master Hwang to lose his head completely: 'I don't want to hear any argument from you!' (Ahn 1990: 179). Refusing to be cowered by her old master's

The UN Ladies' War   **79**

display of anger, Ollye declares war against the village in a language of cold, naked hostility, reversing her earlier resignation to the living death:

> [The villagers] thought I ceased to belong to this village, to exist. That is fine with me, too. I won't blame you. In return, you must not blame me for what I am doing – for what I had to do – because you cast me out of your world. Just don't tell me to leave. I will stay here as long as I live, hating every single one of you . . . Even if all the villagers get killed in this war or by an earth quake, we will stay here and go on living, forever! (Ahn 1990: 181)

The protagonist justifies her 'immoral' activities by the fact that Kumsan's traditional code of behaviour no longer applies to her because she has already been ostracised; the order from the village patriarch cannot be binding on her for the same reason. Not only does she openly express her hatred for all the inhabitants of the village but she also expresses her adamant will to fight for her right to stay. She even declares that she and the other prostitutes will take over the village when the villagers leave in fear of the returning Communists.

Later, Ollye stands up against the entire village when she tries to hold Chandol responsible for the hand injury her son suffers when trying to stop his former playmates from spying on his mother's sexual activities in the brothel. Chandol verbally abuses Ollye, calling her a 'whore' and a 'dirty slut', in order to discredit her. With Chandol's mother defending her son, this conflict naturally develops into a fight between the parents. Ollye calls all the villagers out to bear witness to Chandol's foul act only to find that they are all on the side of the lying boy. She violently accuses the villagers who dispute her words only because of her disreputable profession:

> Everybody in Kumsan village knows that I am a whore . . . Everybody despised me because I am a dirty woman and I found many scribblings on the walls describing me as a Yankee whore. I was too ashamed even to use the same boat with other decent West County people. I've become a shameless woman. And now I will behave like one. I've undergone all sorts of insults and humiliations, but were *you* all really so estimable that you could treat me that way? (Ahn 1990: 257; emphasis in the original)

In this passage, Ollye summons the entire village to her court of justice and accuses them of narrow-mindedness and self-centredness by raising the rhetorical question, 'were *you* all really so estimable that you could treat me that way?' Implicit in this question is her verdict that the villagers have no right to judge her. According to this line of thought, it is her community, not Ollye, that should be ashamed of itself since it abandoned its collective duty to look after one of their own, a

80 *The Korean War Novel*

defenceless, violated woman in distress. Ollye's war against this shameless community is soon joined by Yonghi when Chandol and his mother denounce the protagonist as a liar and the villagers side with Chandol's false accusation. After a brief series of expletive exchanges, Yonghi attacks Chandol's mother using her sharp fingernails to take revenge for the latter's insulting remarks. This small brawl immediately escalates, with a great number of people becoming entangled with one another, some joining the fight and others trying to pull the warring parties apart (Ahn 1990: 261). The pandemonium-like fighting brings to the fore the warrior spirit of Ollye and Yonghi, both of whom show themselves willing to antagonise the whole village for the sake of the social justice and human rights each believes in so strongly.

Biopolitics and the twin Texas Towns

It is worth mentioning here that the ways in which the Kumsan villagers react to Ollye's victimhood create a curious, ambivalent psychological pattern of denial and identification, of distance and empathy. Completely cut off from any aid from the village after the rape, Ollye's family is faced with the possibility of actual starvation. Too young to understand at the time what has really happened to his mother, Mansik wonders why the villagers all of a sudden have started to shun them. He asks his mother if it is because they hate his family, but she responds to the question only indirectly. Indeed, why did the village, which, according to Master Hwang, had lived for generations like 'one single huge family' (Ahn 1990: 67), not rush to her house to offer words of consolation and assist her family in every possible way they could? One possible answer may be found in the following critique of the biopolitics of colonialism:

> In order to articulate the sovereign nation-state and its body politics, and in order to consolidate the modern subject into the fulcrum of the modern nation state . . . it was necessary to construct the body of the incurable, the Other of the healthy body itself. Once the incurable is established as the limit concept of the healthy, the idea and instrumentalisation of the normative national body becomes tenable. It is possible to grasp what the healthy body means only through its antinomy, the incurable body. (H. J. Yoo 2012: 171)

From this point of view, a modern nation needs a diseased colonial Other against which to define itself as a healthy body politic. That is to say, a nation can be sure of its healthiness only through a comparison with that nation's antithesis – an unhealthy alternative self.

The notion of 'the incurable' as a 'limit concept' of a healthy body politics is not only applicable to the colonial context; it also assumes importance in the manner in which a community interprets its relationship with itself and its various limit figures, including slaves, untouchables and outlaws. The action taken by the villagers of Kumsan immediately after the rape makes Ollye and her children feel that they are quarantined. Mansik, for instance, muses agonisingly as he dwells on the thought that an invisible fence or sanitary cordon has been set up around his house: '[h]e felt the world beyond had been suddenly forbidden him by some unknown force and he was confined to his house by invisible walls' (Ahn 1990: 65). By setting the 'diseased' victim and her family apart, the Kumsan villagers can imagine themselves once more as a normal cleansed community. What is more, the womenfolk of Kumsan, by comparing their own states with that of the fallen woman, can bask in a happy, narcissistic self-reflection. For example, Kijun's mother declares to her husband:

> 'I heard Mansik's mother enjoyed it with the *bengkos* so much that she yowled like a crazy bitch, but I am different. I don't want to be raped.' This woman, whose eyes bulged forward like a goldfish's as far as her nose, shook her head emphatically. 'If that ever happens to me, I'll bite my tongue off and drop dead right there even before they put their dirty thing in me.' (Ahn 1990: 68)

In this polarising comparison, Ollye becomes a sexual pervert who enjoys being raped, whereas the speaker, Kijun's mother, elevates herself to the paragon of female virtue, one who is unafraid even of killing herself to protect her chastity. And yet Kijun's mother's moral self-promotion is here undermined by the narrator's description of her in disturbingly unappetising terms, including noting that she has the bulging eyes of a goldfish.

In her confrontation with Master Hwang, Ollye reveals that there is also a certain psychology of denial behind the villagers' act of ostracism:

> I never wanted the soldiers to rape me. It was an accident. They happened to pick my house and violated me. If I had not been there, they must have done the same thing to some other woman. But people preferred to believe that I was *a filthy slut who had chosen to be raped*. (Ahn 1990: 181; emphasis added)

According to Ollye, the villagers now consider her as someone who was somehow already diseased before the crime took place, a view corroborated by Kijun's mother's denigration of her as a pervert. By defining Ollye in this way, as a kind of rape-inviting nymphomaniac, the

82   The Korean War Novel

villagers can deny both the criminality and sheer happenstance of what has transpired. The twisted interpretation makes the crime a function of the victim's free will in the eyes of the village women. In this way, the women can relieve themselves of the otherwise lingering anxiety that one of them could just as easily fall prey to such crimes.

What is still more intriguing, however, is the fact that over time the villagers' attitude towards the victim gradually changes from one of fear and revulsion to a new stance of curiosity and even identification. The villagers' burning curiosity about the 'defiled' woman is illustrated when Ollye runs across the wives of Sokku and the miller, who are on their way home after delivering lunch to the villagers. Since she knows that these women will turn at the crossroads, Ollye slows her pace in order that they may arrive ahead of her and go off in a different direction. Surprisingly, however, the two women also begin to slow down, as they see Ollye doing the same, an action that implies that they are fully intent on meeting with her at the intersection. As a consequence, the two parties come face to face at the turnoff. Out of a sense of sheer embarrassment, Ollye waits for the two other women to speak first. But her hope for some kind words from her old friends turns out to be a heartbreaking mistake: the two women instead '[observe] her from head to toe curiously' without saying a word (Ahn 1990: 100). It is only when Ollye finally turns away from their uncomfortable, persistent gazes that they turn and run off giggling. For the Kumsan womenfolk, Ollye has become a kind of ambivalent spectacle, an abject being whose moral depravity repulses even while it continues to titillate.

If Ollye serves Kumsan village as its diseased Other, her otherness also provides them with the occasion for a secret form of identification. In this strange form of libidinal investment, the villager utilises Ollye's abject body as a dark surrogate self, with each villager operating as an active, affective exploiter of Ollye's misfortune rather than as a passive beneficiary. Unabashedly, the crime victim's tragic story not only circulates in its retelling but it also becomes a tale that is co-authored, transformed and dramatised to suit their own needs.

> By noon many farmers at other villages in West County had learned of the Chestnut House incident, and almost everybody at Kumsan had heard it at least twice . . . They relished it anew, from the very beginning to the last word, as enthusiastically as the first time, and nobody minded that some of the details had changed . . . In the late afternoon, the stories evolved faster and faster, and some said that Ollye had bitten the black rubber stick off the Negro *bengko* when she could no longer resist the rapist, . . . and some said that the *bengkos* had such huge tools that the Chestnut woman had bled a whole chamber pot of blood 'down there.' The village women washing

clothes at the stream giggled and exchanged delicately bawdy anecdotes and some farmers insisted that Mansik's mother actually enjoyed it a lot, for she had had no man at all for two full years. (Ahn 1990: 63–4; emphasis in the original)

Here, dictated by their own sexual appetites and desires, the residents of Kumsan and some of the surrounding villages contribute to the endless rewriting of the heart-wrenching calamity into a form of sadomasochistic pornography. In this revision, the rape survivor is cast as a prurient subject who enjoys sexual violence.

The continual rewriting of Ollye's tragic narrative allows the villagers to indulge themselves in a general vicarious pleasure, with the males in particular able to exorcise their inferiority complexes. By means of an imaginative identification with these '*bengkos*' with 'such huge tools', the village farmers can hope to overcome their collective emasculation, their impotent inability to deal with the impact of the war on their nation and the violent entry of the foreign army into the life of their village. The females also earn their shares in this libidinal investment in a victim's suffering. By projecting their forbidden desires on the 'unclean' woman, the females can safely indulge their repressed sexual fantasies. In other words, seizing this rare opportunity, the Kumsan women vicariously identify with 'Mansik's mother [who, they suggest,] actually enjoyed it a lot'.

A set of uncanny parallels exist in the novel between the adult world of Kumsan and the club that the boys in the village form among themselves. Just as the village is ruled by the patriarch Master Hwang, so the boys' club is headed by Chandol, its captain. Chandol's power over the others is such that none of the boys dare to challenge his authority, even when he is acting in an obviously foolhardy manner. Even in terms of the kinds of taboos each enforces, the two worlds mirror each other. For example, when the villagers ostracise Ollye, the boys' club, following the logic of the adult world it imitates, ostracises one of its own as well – Mansik. If the parents tell each other pornographic stories, their children tell each other less coherent narratives of lust and violence. Having heard the adults gossiping about a rape, for example, the children are gradually awakened to the facts of life. Not content with the obscure lessons they can derive from the overheard snippets of their parents' conversations, the children decide on a plan to satisfy their own curiosity more directly. In carrying out their plan, though, they turn out to exercise greater daring, cunning and violence than their parents. All the boys, apart from Mansik, secretly visit Texas Town in order to peep in on one of the sexual acts taking place inside there. When Yonghi and

84 *The Korean War Novel*

Sundok, with the assistance of Ollye, open the Lady Dragon Club, both Chandol and Kijun, emboldened by their earlier success in Texas Town, pursue further vicarious pleasure on home ground.

When Mansik catches Chandol and Kijun spying at the brothel, Chandol forces him into a deal by threatening to ostracise him again from the boys' club, which he has been only just allowed to rejoin. Afraid of losing his playmates again, Mansik agrees to look the other way on condition that Chandol peeps only into Sister Serpent's room – not into the room occupied by Mansik's mother. Learning about this later from Chandol, Kijun demands the same deal, threatening to tell about the earlier agreement with Chandol to all the adults, including Mansik's mother. Infuriated at both Chandol's treacherousness and Kijun's impudence, Mansik tries to keep both away from the brothel, only to end up getting severely beaten by Chandol. When he next catches the two boys spying on the Lady Dragon Club, Mansik tries to chase away Chandol by threatening him with a makeshift pistol – but accidentally ends up blowing off two of his own fingers.

What is interesting here is that neither Chandol nor Kijun appears to worry about possible punishment at the hands of their parents for their daring immorality. When Mansik will not comply with their demands, they threaten to publicise the earlier deal with Chandol. Their belief that they can threaten Mansik without fear of consequences while he is powerless to threaten them back is ultimately a function of Ollye's abject status in Kumsan. Overhearing the adult gossip about Mansik's mother, Chandol and Kijun have become aware that she not only no longer belongs to the community but occupies the status of an outlaw. It is this knowledge that induces the two boys to pursue their fantasies about the naked body of their friend's mother.

If the casting and recasting of Ollye as a sexually deviant subject in the fantasies of the local community is made possible by the lowly status of their victim, it illuminates at the same time the psychosexual world of the dreamers. As Master Hwang fears, it appears that the ultimate source of depravity that is capable of contaminating the public morals of West County is neither the sex-hungry US soldiers nor their immediate victim. Instead, a renewable fund of lascivious desire has existed inside the mind of each of the villagers, and the rape of Ollye has merely served as a means of exposing it. In this respect, the villagers, at least in their imaginations, have been running their own private Texas Town where they have been free to pursue whatever perverted sexual fantasies they desire – all at the expense of the 'defiled' body of Ollye. This alternate Texas Town has been in existence long before the series of brothels were set up on Cucumber Island. On Cucumber Island, there is a form

The UN Ladies' War   85

of mutual self-interest established by the cash nexus between service provider and fee-paying clientele. In the Texas Town of the imagination, a violent kind of sexual intercourse is performed unbeknownst to its victim. What is more, while no more incidents of rape succeed the two notable instances in the novel, the everyday violations of Ollye's body in the speech and thought of the villagers of West County would appear to know no end.

The traditional patriarchy in disintegration

According to the narrator, the village of Kumsan has been without social conflict for generations and generations. And yet, this does not mean that the village subsists as an ideal or idyllic community, as it will have become obvious to the sceptical reader by now. Kumsan is, in fact, a backward or premodern community built on a strong foundation of gender and class hierarchy in spite of the liberation of the servant class many decades before. In this social hierarchy, the farmers constitute the layer of lower-middle-class citizens, while the snake hunters and similar marginal professions occupy the lowest rung. Indong, Ollye's husband, whose parents and grandparents served in the Hwang household, belonged to a semi-servant class, whose social status is somewhere between farmers and the very lowest occupations. At the top of the social pyramid sits Master Hwang, the county chief and the only man of learning in the neighbourhood. His words are law both in Kumsan and in the neighbouring villages. According to the narrator, '[n]obody questioned the authority of the Hwangs, the wealthiest and most educated family in the West County for the last eight generations' (Ahn 1990: 5). Master Hwang is the local adjudicator whose counsel is sought by those who find themselves involved in everyday disputes. The patriarch's unquestioned authority over the village reveals itself when several Korean military prostitutes try to buy houses in order to open an entertainment business for the UN soldiers. The old man orders each of the villagers not to sell their house to these women. When he finds out that the snake hunter has already sold his hut to Yonghi, he rebukes the man severely, even ordering him to try to cancel the sale. The snake hunter, 'one of the lowest men in the community' (Ahn 1990: 103), cannot dispute this order.

According to Ahn, the premodern, domestically violent Kumsan patriarchy sometimes shows a benevolent face to the needy. Master Hwang, for instance, gives Ollye domestic chores so that she can buy some extra food to feed her two children after Indong drowns in a flooded

86 *The Korean War Novel*

river. The paternalistic village patriarch, however, proves to be without meaningful resources when the peace of the community is threatened by external forces. When the villagers, worried about their safety due to the US Air Force bombing, turn to him for advice, the learned man finds himself unable to offer any. As further contacts with the outer world continue, the traditional structures of the community are undermined. Despite his initial success in warding off infiltration by the UN ladies, Master Hwang experiences extreme humiliation at the hands of the brothel workers. When he turns some of the prostitutes, who are looking to purchase houses, out of the village, the women verbally abuse him and his son:

> What the hell do you think you are? Do you own this village or something? No son of a bitch ever drove us out of any town. You bastards won't be able to keep us out of this damned place for long either . . . Fuck you, old man! You will pay for this. We'll come back and fuck everybody in front of your gate! I'll fuck your son and piss in your face! (Ahn 1990: 107)

These women more than effectively challenge the authority of the county chief by their willingness to resort to the language of the body. The damage wreaked on the old village patriarch's authority by what one may call a discourse of the 'carnival-grotesque' (Bakhtin 1984: 34) is massive. It is almost certain that this is the first time in his life that Hwang has been the target of women he believes the entire village regards as low, coarse and despicable.

Despite his initial successes, Master Hwang's plan to protect his community from the intrusion of military prostitution is permanently damaged when the snake hunter runs away at night with the huge windfall he has received as payment for his shack. The county chief then attempts to counter the unwelcome development by ordering Yom, the ferryman, not to provide boat passage to any of the brothel workers. This ruse forces Yonghi and Sundok to give up their idea of opening a brothel in Kumsan – but only for a time. The women soon renew their verbal conflict with the aging patriarch when Master Hwang and his son ask them to move their immoral business somewhere else for the sake of the villagers. Ridiculing Hwang's suggestion, Yonghi challenges the old patriarch using highly abusive language:

> 'What the hell does this old cock think he is anyway?' said Sister Serpent, not a bit intimidated. 'An MP or something? What right do you have to tell us to stay away from this place? I bought this house with my own money, and nobody is going to drive me out of my own house. You think you can treat me like a dirt because I'm a whore, but, you fucking bastard, you'll see that you have it all wrong.' (Ahn 1990: 111)

The UN Ladies' War   87

In this passage, there is a clash between fundamentally divergent ethical codes. The first is the Confucian ideal that prioritises communal interests over the rights of the individual; the second is the modern ideal of individualism in which the rights of the buyer are inviolable. It is the latter ideal that undergirds Yonghi's claim that since she has legally purchased the business property, nobody has the right to interfere with what she does. For this UN lady, the only legitimate agency having jurisdiction over this issue is, oddly enough, an 'MP'. This recognition of the authority of foreign military law may sound peculiar, given that what is at stake is the rights and communal duties of South Korean citizens. Yonghi's belief that the highest form of authority, exercising jurisdiction even over civil matters, is the US MP raises questions about how the US Army must have appeared to the Korean people during the war. South Korean subjection to US military power certainly did not start with the US intervention in the Korean War but instead dates back to the first day of national liberation. As Monica Kim reports, during the time when the southern part of Korea was under the military control of the US, the military relied on threatening death as a punishment for disobedience, rather than respecting the wishes and authority of the local populace (2019: 50–1). The US occupational forces' authoritarian attitude is plainly indicated by General Hodge's proclamation at a press conference that 'In effect, I am the Korean government' (qtd in M. Kim 2019: 48).

Utilising a modern discourse that blends the inviolability of individual rights with a torrent of coarse, abusive language, Yonghi decisively wins the verbal battle with the village's only learned man, Master Hwang. Master Hwang's valorisation of communal ways and collective good turns out to represent an anachronistic form of judgement when juxtaposed against the modern discourse of individual property rights. The old man eventually acknowledges this defeat when he thinks to himself that 'the Serpent woman had every right to stay at the shack' (Ahn 1990: 170). In this regard, Yonghi and Ollye, the female characters in Ahn's novel, emerge as winners in the women's war against the traditional patriarchy. At the novel's end, the reader witnesses the total disintegration of Kumsan, when virtually the entire village chooses to flee.

And yet the author does not neglect to emphasise that the impact of the Korean War should not be held solely responsible for the breakdown of such traditional Korean communities as Kumsan. As a matter of fact, this premodern community had been silently crumbling even before the UN soldiers and the UN ladies helped to turn it upside down. No more central a person than Master Hwang himself, the staunch champion of Confucian values, has already begun to experience his own personal emasculation. According to Sokku, his son, Master Hwang has long

88   *The Korean War Novel*

been ailing, and 'his failing health was aggravated by his gradual but steady loss of will.' The old patriarch admits to himself that 'he was losing more and more of whatever power he had possessed' (Ahn 1990: 131). In truth, the biggest blow has already been dealt to him in the form of an economic disaster a few years previously, although he has sought to keep it secret. For many generations, Master Hwang has been called 'Rich Hwang' since the Hwang family network has been the wealthiest in the county. However, unbeknownst to others, Hwang has secretly invested his entire family fortune in a gold mining speculation – and has lost it all. In order to pay off his snowballing debt, Hwang has allowed Mr Han, the mill owner, to purchase all of his land, apart from a small hill for the family graves, on the condition that the latter keep the transaction secret until the old man dies. The Hwang family has been reduced to a virtual state of beggary. In other words, in Kumsan, the old man has actually nothing much left in terms of a personal stake to hold onto or to protect, even though he has made painstaking efforts to defend the village from the encroachments of the outside world. From Sokku's perspective, the family has no particular reason to stick around anymore. In fact, he has been considering abandoning his hometown and moving far away before the shameful family secret is revealed (Ahn 1990: 205–6).

At the microscopic level, the disintegration of the village is also mirrored in the total collapse of the Kumsan's boys' club. By ostracising Mansik, Chandol ends up also alienating Kangho, Mansik's closest friend, from the rest of the gang. With one member unceremoniously excommunicated and a second growing deeply embittered, this small society has been silently crumbling too. The apocalyptic end of the boys' club comes in the form of an exploding gun, which costs Mansik his two fingers. The accident appears to be a fitting prelude to the calamity of the massive exodus that soon befalls the village. When the news spreads through the village that Mr Han, the mill owner, has secretly fled south with his family overnight in fear of the advancing Chinese Communist Army, the villagers, who were once hesitant about leaving their hometown because of the ignominy of cowardice, rush to join the flow of refugees. Master Hwang and his family also join the procession southbound.

At the beginning of the novel, five children are seen looking for a legendary secret cave in the nearby forest of General's Hill. According to the local legend, when savage hordes of Mongols invaded the country, destroying all of the big cities and slaying the valiant Korean warriors, the mountain spirits sent the Korean people a general with the power to save the country. This mighty general was born in a secret cave beneath a huge white rock somewhere on General's Hill. This mythic hero's

The UN Ladies' War   89

flight from the rock, says the legend, coincided with the appearance of a silver stallion from the valley attached to the same hill. In a single afternoon, the great general managed to vanquish the invading Mongols. The legend ends with a prophecy: this general will return on his silver stallion if and when Korea suffers a major crisis in the future. For this reason, the five boys from Kumsan have been looking for the legendary cave, hoping that it will be opened so that the hero is able to ride out and help save the country once again. In their naiveté or blindness to the horrific reality of the approaching war, the boys' belief in a local myth parallels their parents' belief in Confucianism. In both cases, a set of anachronistic values is supposed to support a set of vain hopes in the face of the harsh invading forces of the modern world itself.

Of course, the mythic general riding a silver stallion never returns. General 'Megado' was certainly not the mythic hero, arriving with the UN army to wreak havoc on the village, ruining their crops and raping the women, all the while pushing the Communists back. Neither did this messianic figure arrive with the forces of the Chinese Volunteer Army, the expectation of which has caused Master Hwang and the other villagers to 'shudder' in fear. If there is such a figure at all, the heroic general who comes back for Ollye and her ostracised family must surely be Sister Serpent, that smart, adventurous, battle-hardened UN lady. Indeed, Yonghi has been Ollye's tutor all along, even if this does not imply that she has been the most morally ideal one. While charging Ollye rent for a room at the brothel, Yonghi has undoubtedly led her disciple to become both a fully sexual being as well as an independent modern subject. She has awakened her to the intolerable injustices of her old village and introduced her to the new ways of the modern world, including offering her free training in consumer power and financial profit. Under Yonghi's tutelage, Ollye has been able to accumulate a handsome capital, which will come in handy when she resettles further down in the South. It does not take much deliberation to answer the question: Who has the better chances of survival – the traditional villagers, who flew their abandoned village with only their shattered Confucian ideals to protect them or Ollye, this modern *homo economicus*, with her hard-won independence and her financial savings? When the reader considers the novel's outcome in this way, it is possible to suggest that the General on the Silver Stallion returned for Ollye, and for Ollye alone.

Note

1. Following most revisionist historians, Jodi Kim and Daniel Y. Kim hold the view that what might have been a local civil conflict and an attempt to reunify the country was 'superseded' by an international war. See J. Kim, 2008: 288; also D. Y. Kim, 2009: 551.

Chapter 3

Orientalism and the Cold War

In her debut novel, *The Foreign Student* (1998), Susan Choi (1969–) weaves a beautiful tapestry, using her mastery of a nearly poetic, psychology-probing language, concerning the crossed paths of Chang Ahn, a Korean student at Sewanee: the University of the South, and Katherine Monroe, the daughter of a rich family in New Orleans. By interweaving the traumatic pasts and the regularly distraught, yet often romantic, present relationship of this couple, the author creates an interracial romance marked at once by obvious pain and a sense of mystery. The artistic achievement of the novel is scarcely in doubt; it has been rewarded with the Asian American Literary Award and the Steven Turner Award; it was a finalist for the Barnes & Noble Discover Award and was recognised as an *LA Times*'s Top Ten Books of 1998.

The Foreign Student was well received by a majority of critics, who took note of the way that the novel challenged hegemonic Korean nationalist and US imperialist narratives. In the US, Crystal Parikh drew attention to the manner in which the book delineates an 'unruly desire' that 'unsettles the seemingly fixed properties of gender, race, class, and nation' (2009: 62). Similarly, Korean critics see the protagonists as opening up what may be called 'a transnational third space' (Koh and Na 2008: 51) or 'a new site of cultural communication and translational collaboration' (E. Hwang 2013: 173) beyond racial and cultural barriers. Other critics engaged with historical issues, pointing out the status of the novel as a revisionist historiography that contests both the orthodox history of postliberation Korea and its foundational fiction in the US's Cold War narrative of communist containment. The earliest person to strike this critical note was Jodi Kim who reads the novel as part of that set of 'critical Cold War compositions that "discombobulate" the Manichean logics of official nationalist Cold War histories' (2008: 282). For his part, Daniel Y. Kim elaborates on this by noting how the conflicts on the Korean peninsula are narrated from 'the vantage point

92   *The Korean War Novel*

of the Koreans themselves' (2009: 551), although the critic does not necessarily suggest that Choi aims at recovering an objective history. In this view, the Korean War is fundamentally a civil war emerging from the collapse of Japanese colonialism exacerbated by the intervention of the US and other countries. Josephine Nock-Hee Park concurs when she observes that Choi's 'wartime subjects . . . exceed the Cold War politics that integrate and contain them' (2016: 82).

The Foreign Student depicts the tumultuous lives and union of the two protagonists, Chang and Katherine. Both characters are haunted by, and suffer silently from, their respective past traumatic events. Chang had the bitter experience of being left behind by his American superiors while working for the United States Information Service (USIS) in Seoul when the Korean War broke out. He survived the Communist occupation of Seoul, hiding in a secret den at his house. Although he enjoyed freedom with the UN forces' rollback campaign, he boarded a refugee boat bound for Busan upon hearing the news of the UN forces' general retreat but ended up in a refugee internment camp on Jeju (Cheju). Breaking out of the camp, he decided to look for his Communist friend Jaesong Kim there but was wrongfully arrested by ROKA as a pro-Communist spy for the Jeju insurgency that had been rocking the island since the 1 March 1919 Independence Movement Commemoration of 1947. He managed to walk out of the ROKA's notorious torture room without being killed, but only after selling out an American priest who helped him on Jeju. The painful memories of abandonment, betraying and being betrayed and torture would not leave him alone even in his new start in the US. Katherine has been living her own nightmare. At the age of fourteen, she had been seduced to have a relationship with her father's ex-college classmate and professor of English on Sewanee campus, Charles Addison. She had to sacrifice her family ties for her strained love relationship with the much older man. When Chang arrives in Sewanee, Katherine has been living as Charles's closet lover cut off from the rest of the world. Katherine and Chang gradually fall in love with each other, finding a source of consolation within each other. They separate after a quarrel but reunite with each other at the end of the novel.

By re-reading the novel against the revisionist historiographies that the author herself freely draws upon, this study directs critical attention to the import of the author's contestation of the official nationalist or the US-centred Cold War perspectives in her account of post-1945 Korea. It is certainly true that, to some significant degree, *The Foreign Student* gestures beyond the Manichean logics of both Cold War histories and the racialising narratives of the US in the 1950s. The novel criticises both the US occupying forces and their immediate political successor, the first South Korean government; it also exposes both the ethnocentrism of white America and the protagonist's collaboration with this ideology. And yet, for all this, the apparently privileged perspective of Choi's metadiscourse becomes less tenable when considered within the relevant history. Namely, Choi not only fails to encapsulate the wide spectrum of the postliberation Korean politics within her fiction but actually denies her supposed anti–Cold War posture. This unacknowledged alteration generates a contradiction within her text.

This chapter notes another self-cancelling move in Choi's portrayal of an ethnic minority in Chicago, which several critics hailed as an alternative to the self-enclosed realities of Asian minorities in America. Considered contrapuntally in terms of the minority's Midwest settlement history, however, Choi's representation may be said to utilise what I call a form of 'retro-styling'. 'Retro-styling' here refers to a narrative strategy that displaces or projects the past emptied of its problematic substance onto the contentious present. Rendered as such, history is, in Jean Baudrillard's words, 'an invocation of resemblance, but at the same time the flagrant proof of the disappearance of objects in their very representation' ([1981] 1994: 45), an ideological process that bears similarities with what Fredric Jameson calls 'the nostalgia mode' (1988: 18) in that the very act of reviving bygone days serves to eclipse them. Although both Baudrillard and Jameson theorise the notion of retro-styling in relation to postmodernism, the effect of such past-recycling appears to reverberate in Choi's representation of Chicago's Japan Town. In failing to recognise the postcolonial dimension of the conflicts in post-1945 Korea while employing regressive representational strategies which foreclose the 'unruly' racial conflicts in the American scene, Choi compromises the progressive politics almost unanimously attributed by critics to this debut novel.

'A potted history of war' vs revisionist history

In *The Foreign Student*, Chang arrives in the southern US in 1955 to study. In return for his American church scholarship, he occasionally gives a talk on the Korean War to audiences composed of Southern congregants. In his lecture, Chang stretches the time frame of his presentation back to the Japanese colonial rule of Korea. He then proceeds to refer to the Japanese surrender, the division of Korea by the rival US and Soviet occupation forces and the establishment, aided by the two powers, of two rival regimes in the South and the North. One of the

94 *The Korean War Novel*

most cited passages in the novel refers to the lecture that he gives in the following manner:

> Sometimes he simply skipped over causes, and began, 'Korea is a shape just like Florida. Yes? The top half is a Communist state, and the bottom half are fighting for democracy!' He would *groundlessly* compare the parallel to the Mason-Dixon line, and see every head nod excitedly. 'In June 1950, the Communist army comes over the parallel and invades the South. They come by surprise, and get almost all to the sea.' His hands swept: an amazing advance. The UN made a force to fight back, of the South's Republic of Korea army, ROKA, and the United States army, and some other armies, like Britain's. (S. Choi 1998: 51; emphasis added)

According to Daniel Y. Kim, the above presentation aligns itself with the US hegemonic narrative. This is because it 'translates seamlessly into the interlocking frameworks of containment and integration' (2009: 555). In this view, South Korea is figured as a besieged outpost of democracy whereas the US functions as the saviour of the Third World from otherwise inevitable communist subversion. In order to drive home to his American audience the reality of Korea's divided situation, Chang likens the thirty-eighth parallel to 'the Mason-Dixon line' and sees its immediate effect in the form of his audience's excitedly nodding heads. As noted by critics, the use of the American geographical reference in a Korean context originates with Cumings, who uses the phrase in his revisionist readings of the Korean War (Cumings 1984: 3; Cumings 1995: 7). This geographical trope, however, sits jarringly next to the line of thinking espoused by Chang, according to which the Korean War is an example of a free democratic world's rollback of a communist invasion.

In contrast, Cumings sees the Korean War as primarily a conflict among rival groups of Koreans, using the geographical trope in order to emphasise this. In *The Origins of the Korean War 1*, Cumings encapsulates this view nicely by defining the war as 'civil and revolutionary in character, beginning just after 1945 and proceeding through a dialectic of revolution and reaction' (1981: xxi). From this perspective, the Korean War is seen as an extension of the struggles that had been going on in Korea since 15 August 1945, the day of national liberation from Japanese colonial rule. As pointed out by some of Choi's critics (J. N.-H. Park 2016: 90; D. Y. Kim 2009: 556), it is precisely this kind of historical understanding that is absent from Chang's church lecture. In other words, the protagonist employs the revisionist trope without fully realising its historical significance. In failing to establish a connection between the social turmoil of the postliberation period and the Korean War, his presentation mechanically conjoins the two incidents, revealing his own prejudiced or perhaps actually ignorant view. In the novel, the author makes it clear that Chang's historical outlook is distinct from that of the author herself by revealing more than once his sense of failure as an informal historiographer: '[h]e always felt hopeless, called upon to deliver a clear explanation of the war. It defied explanation' (S. Choi 1998: 51). This sense of the protagonist's incompetence and failure is emphasised in the author's comment: '[h]e would *groundlessly* compare the parallel to the Mason-Dixon line' (S. Choi 1998: 51; emphasis added).

The epistemological discrepancy between the author and the protagonist also marks the conversation that takes place during the war between Chang and Miki, the housemaid, about their mutual friend Jaesong Kim, the Communist. After Seoul is retaken by the UN and the ROK armies, Miki, who is in love with Kim, worries about the latter's safety. When Chang emphasises the safety of Seoul under the ROKA's control, Miki sharply retorts by observing that unlike Chang, Kim does not work for the government and is therefore facing danger in the 'liberated' South. Chang tries to correct Miki's view on his employment status:

'I'm not working for the government. I'm working for the Americans.'
'There's no difference.'
'I think there is.'
She shrugged and lifted her bag again. 'Kim would say that working for the Americans you're still working for the divided Korea. He works against it. . . .'
'I reject both sides. I am against this war. I can see that's not your feeling anymore.'
'I reject both sides,' she aped him. 'Oh, no you don't. That's the idealist's role. That's what Kim is doing, wherever he is. You're a pragmatist, like me.'
'Meaning?'
'We're out for ourselves. Taking sides is the only way to do that.' (S. Choi 1998: 184–5)

In this dialogue, Chang positions himself as a pacifist who refuses to support either the South or the North in the war. He seems to believe that the neutral position he carves out for himself places him at a moral distance from the madness of the fraternal butcheries. His disaffection with both regimes derives from his bitter experiences of both sides during the war. Having lived in a hideout for three months under the KPA's occupation of Seoul, he knows well what communism means to the propertied classes to which he belongs; working as a translator at the USIS and also as an unofficial liaison between the US Army and the Korean newspapers, he has had access to the information about what the ROKA has done to the civilians in the recaptured territory. As the

96   *The Korean War Novel*

narrator reports, '[o]nce the army passed through, Rhee's National Police would arrive to hunt out Communists . . . Large numbers of villagers living north of the parallel and south of the advancing front were shot' (S. Choi 1998: 182).

In Chang's view, his employment at what he believes to be a representative organisation of the third party that is the US (USIS) bolsters his detachment from both of the warring regimes. However, the protagonist's complacent view of himself is contradicted by none other than his best friend Kim, albeit through the mouth of the latter's girlfriend. According to the alternative view, 'working for the Americans you're still working for the divided Korea.' Here, the narrator renders a verdict that many critics of the Cold War would agree with, which many right-wing Koreans of today would heatedly deny: the US is responsible for the division of Korea in the first place and is thus an interested party of the war. In the above dialogue, Chang is thus seen as self-deceived in believing himself to be free from the bipolar politics of the divided Korea. The narrator makes an ironic comment on the protagonist's self-professed non-partisanship by having Miki expose the truth that 'We're out for ourselves.'

The author's portrayal of the US military government also indicates her distance from the US's triumphalist narratives. John Hodge, the Military Governor, is described as a tired soldier who just 'wants to go and retire', frustrated at Washington's refusal to provide further logistical support (S. Choi 1998: 66). His troops are seen as 'demoralized, flaccid, and lazy'; they hate and disdain Korea out of a sense of 'overwhelming inconvenience' (S. Choi 1998: 65). Hodge's expedient style of rule is easily inferred from the episode in which the general gives to Chang, his hand-picked interpreter, instructions to help build up the Korean Army: '[m]ake it work and don't tell me about it' (S. Choi 1998: 67). President Rhee fares even worse at Choi's hands, as seen in the sweeping assessment made from the perspective of Americans: '[on]nly after installing Rhee as the Republic of Korea's president did the Americans realize he was unmanageable, bellicose, paranoid, and so undiscouragably [*sic*] determined to declare war on the Communist north' (S. Choi 1998: 64).

Hodge's regional Cold War

According to Choi, Rhee's government plays up Cold War politics in order to justify its brutalities; and Chang serves the regime as a loyal functionary. After the successful campaign against the Jeju Uprising,

Police Chief Ho calls a press conference in the late fall of 1949 as a potential PR opportunity for the new government. In front of foreign reporters, Ho lays particular stress on the fact that the campaign incurred no police casualties. An unconvinced reporter from *The New York Times* presses Chang, the interpreter, for the truth. Their ensuing dialogue runs:

> 'Most guerrillas give up when they face with resistance.'
> 'How can that be? From what we're seeing out there, every day?'
> 'They have no any [*sic*] strength of conviction. You see, they get an order from the Soviet Union. They are poor, and with no any [*sic*] education. They love their country really very much. When they see police, they see they are wrong and they most times surrender.' (S. Choi 1998: 83–4)

Chang's explanation that 'docile', patriotic peasants were misled into a riot engineered by the Soviets stands in need of correction. This is because the comment subscribes to the typical Cold War rhetoric which both the US and the South Korean authorities utilised at the time in quelling popular postcolonial uprisings. Not surprisingly, Chang's reply replicates the actual public statement issued by the National Police, who were themselves under American command: in his 14 April 1948 public statement for the islanders, Cho Pyŏngok, police chief, declared, '[y]ou were all deceived by the evil conspiracy and scheme of the communists who would sell the nation to the Soviets' (qtd in C. Chang 2007: 211–12; author's translation). By having Chang support Ho's absurd story at the press conference, the author exposes both Rhee's government and her protagonist as morally compromised, insinuating that their perspective is not something that the novel endorses.

At the same time, Choi's Korean historiography is marked by an odd failure to look closely into the political causes endorsed by the Korean protesters and insurgents. This causes the occlusion of crucial factors and elements from the narration of the volatile politics of the South in the wake of liberation. A prominent example is the author's report on the Jeju Uprising mentioned above. Although she rejects the Korean government's official report on the incident, the author stops before identifying exactly what it is that it falsifies, apart from the obviously hyperbolic figure for police casualties. As a result, the readers are left in the dark concerning why the insurgency occurred in the first place or what the insurgents fought for.

Immediately after its arrival and occupation of the southern half of Korea, the US Army tried to implement a set of American ideas concerning order and democracy. However, its attempt at cultural translation did not take into account the fact that Korea was not a tabula rasa

98   *The Korean War Novel*

awaiting or inviting foreign inscription. It had both its own proud cultural traditions and its own deep-rooted social grievances too. In the wake of liberation, Koreans were faced with the colossal task of liquidating the colonial legacies that were still making themselves felt at every level of the nation due to almost two generations of Japanese rule. However, ignorance of Korea's socio-economic situation quickly drove the military government into an antagonistic relationship with wider Korean society. Choi mentions Hodge's expedient style of rule by remarking that he planned to run Korean society 'out of the materials at *hand*', assuming that 'what did not fit would be altered by force' (S. Choi 1998: 67; emphasis added). Yet, this commentary characteristically chooses not to specify at this point exactly which 'hand' the general looked to for 'the materials'.

Korean history bears out that it was by turning to his *right hand* that Hodge miscalculated because this chosen instrument turned out to be part of the much-hated legacy of Japanese colonialism. It was his first, and, in retrospect, most crucial, mistake, as discussed in the introduction. It is widely recognised that southern Korea enjoyed peace and order under the CPKI – something that jars with the wholesale attribution of post-1945 social chaos to leftist and pro-leftist activities in Choi's book (1998: 65). As one study testifies, the number of crimes in the wake of liberation, a majority of which comprised destroying Japanese imperial shrines and attacking and ransacking the sites of colonial police stations, reached a high of 278 on 18 August, but then fell off sharply from 21 to 25 August, with the number of incidents falling from 42, to 33, to 7, to 0 and 1 (G.-T. Lee 2006: 14–17). The low level of destruction, even of the hated symbols of colonial rule, speaks for the peace-preserving capability of the CPKI and the KPR interim government. Remarkably, this period of order in the months before US occupation is elided from the book's wholesale portrayal of post-1945 Korea.

More importantly, instead of working with the de facto government, Hodge decided to sponsor the main pro-Japanese rightist group, which was composed of rich landlords and entrepreneurs, by inviting them to accept administrative and advisory positions in his government. This decision is, of course, attributed to the US military governor's fear that the KPR favoured the Soviets, a concern fuelled by the Japanese colonial authorities (Oh 2002: 3). To put it another way, Hodge had taken the decision to start his own Cold War in South Korea. In this aim, the general was one step ahead of Washington. What Hodge did not consider seriously was that by reinstating and even promoting Korean collaborators in his government, he had effectively crushed the desire of the Korean people for decolonisation. The consequence, however, was not something that 'would be altered by force' (S. Choi 1998: 67), which Hodge came to realise too late.

Viewed in this context, the Jeju Uprising, about whose successful suppression Police Chief Ho in Choi's fiction bragged about at the press conference, has multiple factors such as the US military government's administrative ineptitude and its inadvertent act of crushing the local people's postcolonial aspirations. A more direct cause for the clashes between the islanders and the right-wing National Police and paramilitary organisations is, however, the military government's anticommunist policy, which gave the state agents a green light to persecute the islanders in the name of 'reorienting' them.

According to a number of historians (Cumings 1990: 253; S.-K. Hwang 2016: 32–6; H. J. Kim 2014: 20–36; M. Kim 2019: 230–1), the origin of the Jeju incident dates back to the skirmish of 1 March 1947 touched off by the police's firing at some local civilians celebrating the independence movement of 1919. Yet, behind its explosion into a leftist-led armed uprising a year later, an insurgence that then persisted for several years, was the islanders' pent-up resentments against the unchecked terrorism of state agents like the police, the military and the rightist youth groups acting as police deputies, all under American command, that had been indiscriminately carried out under the pretext of purging the island of communists. Before the US military rule, the island kept order and peace under its own local leadership. Even General Hodge was aware of it. As Cummings reports, 'Hodge told a group of American Congressman in October 1947 that Jeju was "a truly communal area that is peacefully controlled by the People's Committee without much Comintern influence"' (1990: 252). Despite his painting of the island 'red', Hodge here acknowledges that before the uprising, Jeju was run peacefully by a local leadership that, emerging in 1945, was moderate left in its political viewpoint and acted independently of external communist influences.

The US military government's brutalisation of the islanders in the cause of 'reorienting' them caused the islanders first to support and later to join the leftist-led uprising. In this regard, the incident was a self-fulfilling prophecy for Hodge. At the time, the Jeju Islanders had set forth three major demands: the purge of pro-Japanese Koreans, land reform and the cancellation of a separate general election in favour of a unitary election (C. Chang 2007: 224). These demands were the same ones taken up by most demonstrations that took place in southern Korea during the years of direct American military rule. Yet, neither this political cause nor Hodge's responsibility for the uprising, not to mention the major differences between the moderate Korean leftists and

100   The Korean War Novel

the card-carrying Communists, receives any attention in Choi's novel. Even in the scene where Chang encounters the insurgents in his sojourn on the island, the latter are not allowed to speak for themselves.

What is left unsaid

The similar set of narrative strategies of occlusion and conflation that shape Choi's depiction of the Jeju incident are at work in her overall portrayal of postliberation Korean history. As a result, the range of oppositional groups with their differing social class and ideological backgrounds, from communism through moderate socialism and centrist to the various forces on the right, are subsumed under the umbrella category of 'leftist peasants'. A look at the author's summary of the social unrest in post-1945 Korea demonstrates this:

> South Korea was a logistical disaster, crowded with junk and angry people who were unemployed at best, but generally homeless and starving. They committed crimes, intended and inadvertent, thefts and arsons, unpremeditated murders and anti-government, proleftist insurrections. And so Hodge used the National Police, and his situation grew even worse. 1948 turned into 1949. Opposition to the partitioning of Korea, then to the stewardship of the U.S. and the USSR, now to the Rhee government, mostly maintained by *leftist farmers' unions*, had been constant since the American arrival, but now, enraged by the increased power of the National Police, this opposition solidified into an armed guerrilla movement, with cells scattered all over the south. Hodge tried to create a constabulary which was not as militaristic as the National Police, but this force was equally despised, and completely ineffectual. Hodge needed more soldiers, not fewer. (S. Choi 1998: 65; emphasis added)

Unlike this report, which points to a single group – 'leftist farmers' unions' – as the agent of social unrest, the vast majority of Koreans initially unanimously resisted both the division of Korea and foreign stewardship. To quote the historian Choi Sang-Yong, '[i]t is noteworthy that both the right and the left wings were against trusteeship, and the Korean provisional government who worked overseas, centred on figures, such as Kim Ku [Koo], who persistently fought for national independence, led the anti-trusteeship campaign' (2002: 16).

In January 1946, this intra-Korean consensus on trusteeship collapsed when the Communist Party in Korea reversed its position, coming out instead in favour of trusteeship, following instructions from Moscow. After this time, the anti-trusteeship campaign was mainly led by the forces on the right (S.-Y. Choi 2002: 16). Figure 3.1 illustrates one of

Orientalism and the Cold War 101

Figure 3.1 A right-wing protest against trusteeship on 23 June 1947. (Source: National Archives photo no. 111-SC-288649)

those right-wing anti-trusteeship rallies, organised in June 1947 by Kim Koo, which staged 'a passive sit down demonstration' in front of the gates of Deoksugung Palace, home of the US–USSR Joint Commission, the organisation tasked with preparing for an independent, unified Korea. It is therefore unclear to which phase of the anti-trusteeship campaign Susan Choi is referring when she states that the leftist peasants opposed the stewardship. If the reference is to the period before January 1946, one may wonder what point it serves to single out a particular group when virtually the whole nation was against it. If the reference is to developments after January 1946, the author's statement ignores the fact that the oppositional campaign, after its abandonment by the leftist forces, was now mainly led by conservative and right-wing nationalists, not left-wing forces.

The 'anti-government, pro-leftist insurrections' and high crime rates, for which Choi holds hungry and lawless South Koreans responsible, are in fact attributable to none other than Hodge's military rule. Among Hodge's grave mistakes was the confiscation of the Japanese-owned farmland and factories that had previously been taken over and were being managed in the aftermath of national liberation by the local People's Committees, the peasants' and workers' unions; and the sudden

102 The Korean War Novel

introduction of a free market in the rice economy, which dealt a staggering blow to the unstable economy. The surplus rice disappeared quickly as a result of massive speculation and hoarding by the brokers and large landlords. The subsequent, spiralling inflation and near starvation brought forth a general economic breakdown (Cumings 1981: 203–4). As a consequence, the colonial rice collection policy was soon reinstated, and 'rice raids' were carried out by government officials and police, while American troops maintained the peace in order to fill the collection quotas (Cumings 1981: 205–6). General strikes for increased rice rations and wages by the urban salaried classes soon swept through the nation. The rural areas were also badly affected since the peasants, who were mostly subsistence farmers, needed their harvest to feed their own families but had been forced to give this up. Ironically, some of the farmers had to rely on rice rations. The peasants' grievances gradually developed into a massive resistance termed the 'Autumn Harvest Uprising' or the 'Taegu Uprising of 1946'. These events were triggered by the police's firing on groups of demonstrators supporting the striking workers (Cumings 1981: 351–8).[1] One crucial factor that escalated the demonstration on Jeju into a full-scale insurgency was the issue of forced grain collection from the impoverished islanders. As Cumings notes, '[u]nauthorized grain collections had been five times as high as official ones in 1947' on Jeju (Cumings 1990: 253).

What makes the novel more misleading is the chronological transgression. Even in the passage quoted above, the politico-economic situation during the period of the military occupation becomes decontextualised and attributed to the later governmental rule of Syngman Rhee. On the same page, Choi is again seen reversing the historical development by depicting Hodge still in power after the establishment of the First Republic of South Korea: 'Rhee's government was repressive, incompetent, and stupendously unpopular. Peasant uprisings throughout the South took the food supply hostage. The trains didn't run. Hodge needed more platoons to make order' (S. Choi 1998: 65). Just as Chang, the protagonist, mechanically conjoins Japanese colonialism and the civil war in his church lecture, Choi here conflates the social events associated with the rule of two distinct phases of government: the cross-class nationwide resistance and the unpopularity of Rhee's government. General strikes, mass protests and peasant uprisings, as seen in the Taegu Uprising and the general strike of 1946, are characteristic of the earlier period of American direct military occupation.

In contrast, Rhee's regime in the early years was only dealing with beleaguered groups of guerrillas in the mountains – that is, after the direct military occupation had already destroyed the wider popular

Orientalism and the Cold War **103**

resistance. As Cumings reports, the Taegu Uprising resulted in 'the effective demise of the local organs that had protected the interests [of the peasants]' (1981: 381). The re-emergence of mass protests has to wait until the later years of Rhee's rule. Thus, with the cause of popular resistance absent and the social strife displaced, the historical account offered by *The Foreign Student* appears somewhat obfuscatory at best.

For most Korean peasants, what happened under the American military government was a form of economic and political déjà vu. Even after national liberation, the peasants still found themselves exploited and deprived, as the rich pro-Japanese landlords became even wealthier. In this situation, being 'pro-American' came to be virtually synonymous with being 'pro-Japanese'. This is confirmed by Hodge himself, who as early as in his report for 6 December 1945, evaluated his reception among the Koreans in the following terms: '[t]he word pro-American is being added to pro-Jap, national traitor, and Jap collaborator' (Cumings 1981: 209). When Rhee was competing for power, this American protégé, following his American predecessor, made an alliance with the same collaborator class who in turn found a strong protector of their interests in him.

What needs to be emphasised here is that without recognising the American military government's policy debacles and the collaboration of both regimes with the wealthy landowner collaborators, the domestic turmoil in post-1945 Korea is likely to be dismissed as a simple matter of rival ideologies. In this context, the anger of both the rural peasantry and the urban workers can be explained as a demand for decolonisation through the purge of colonial legacies and the elimination of foreign influences, which, they believed, would also solve the pressing issues of food shortages and police terrorism. It is this domestic situation prior to the war among others that gives an indelible feature of a civil war to the otherwise regional hot war of the Cold War. When she understands this war as a civil war kidnapped by the Cold War, Jodi Kim shows a similar awareness of what she calls 'the uninterrupted chain of colonial and imperial succession in Korea' (2008: 288). However, though she attributes this critical awareness to Choi's novel, the popular struggle for decolonisation is in fact treated in *The Foreign Student* as the simple ills of a society wallowed in anomie. To visit the narration again: 'South Korea was a logistical disaster, crowded with junk and angry people who were unemployed at best, but generally homeless and starving. They committed crimes, intended and inadvertent, thefts and arsons, unpremeditated murders and anti-government, proleftist insurrections' (S. Choi 1998: 65). Characteristically, the wider anti-government movement, which is labelled as 'proleftist',

104 *The Korean War Novel*

is placed on the same list as the wanton criminal acts of theft, arson and murder.

If the Cold War brought an unending tragedy in the form of national division to the Korean people in the wake of liberation, it also brought a lifeline to the propertied, pro-Japanese collaborators in the South who felt cornered by both local nationalists and the anti-Japanese Communist regime of the North. The Manichean politics of the Cold War endowed this beleaguered group not only with a chance to turn the tables around but also with a handy, efficient weapon of anti-communist bashing, which they wielded freely against their adversaries. To paint and persecute all intractable oppositional forces as Communist is a manoeuvre that Rhee's regime was also well-known for. As the later political history of South Korea also testifies, anti-communism has in turn served the military dictatorships in cracking down the pro-democratic movements.

Despite its progressive posture, Choi's fiction, because of its failure to acknowledge the spirit of decolonisation within the civil strife, ends up endorsing the far-rightist practice of anti-communist bashing, aligning itself with the Cold War framework. The reader is forced to speculate a series of possible scenarios. Is this reverse postcolonial turn simply due to the narrator's or the author's negligence in distinguishing the conflicting, ideological orientations of Korean political forces of the time? Or does it imply that the text is oblivious to the explosive issue of pro-Japanese collaboration? Has the author deliberately chosen to see Korean politics through the Manichean lens of the conservative class? Whichever way one answers this question, there looms the issue of the ideological regression or repression that constitutes what Macherey calls the 'silence' of a text (1980: 85). It is difficult to say whether this is something the author remains unaware of or is simply unable to take into account. Nonetheless, it is this absence or silence that serves to structure the political overview of the text.

In *The Foreign Student*, historical displacement and political misrepresentation are interspersed with actual errors in chronology. Most prominent is the mixing up of the dates of the occupation (8 September 1945–15 August 1948) and the first South Korean regime (August 1948–April 1960). In one of the passages cited earlier, the author reports: 'Hodge used the National Police, and his situation grew even worse. 1948 turned into 1949 . . . Hodge tried to create a constabulary which was not as militaristic as the National Police' (S. Choi 1998: 65). And yet, after 15 August 1948, Hodge was no longer the military governor. In fact, he was no longer in Korea, having left for his new office in the States on 27 August 1948. According to Choi, Hodge had

Orientalism and the Cold War **105**

also tried to create the Constabulary in 1949 as an alternative force to the too-aggressive National Police. But history testifies that Hodge created this force in January 1946 (Millett 2004: 27; M. Kim 2019: 220), much earlier than the novel believes. Another inaccuracy is found in the passage that describes Chang as fifteen in the fall of 1945 (S. Choi 1998: 68). Yet, the novel suggests that Hodge recruits him from Rhee's new Ministry of Public Information and assigns him to assist in the creation of the new Republic of Korea Army (S. Choi 1998: 66–7). Again, not only is Hodge's presence chronologically incompatible with the actual rule of Rhee's government but the creation of the ROKA has to wait until the arrival of Rhee's government to power. Apart from the National Police, essentially a resuscitated version of the Japanese colonial police, the only Korean armed force Hodge created was the Constabulary. However, in late 1945 when Hodge was planning to create this force, Chang is described as a first-year high school student.

Colour blindness, Orientalism and Little Tokyo

In the year that Chang arrives in Sewanee, the American South was going through a deeply divisive, racially charged time of turbulence. Although the 'separate but equal' doctrine had been declared unconstitutional by the US Supreme Court in 1954, this ruling was meeting with strong resistance from white Southerners. African Americans who refused to comply with the laws regarding segregation were being beaten and arrested in 1955; and, in response, black protests and boycotts were starting to be organised throughout the nation. In December 1955, in the immediate aftermath of Rosa Parks' unjust arrest in Montgomery, Alabama, the first significant civil rights movement had started to coalesce. In the same year, the nation had been confronted by the ugly face of white racism in the form of newspaper photos of the brutally mutilated body of a fourteen-year-old African American boy from Chicago, Emmett Louis Till. Emmett had been lynched and killed and his body had then been abandoned in a river in Mississippi in August 1955 for allegedly offending a white woman. Media images of his open-casket funeral had elicited a wave of sympathy and anger across the nation. Rosa Parks testified to the impact of this tragedy on the civil rights movement when, reminiscing of her refusal to move to the back of the bus before her arrest, she stated: 'I thought of Emmett Till, and I just couldn't go back' ('Remembering' n.d.).

The turbulent events of 1955, which shocked the American nation, are entirely absent from *The Foreign Student*. Oddly enough, very few

African American characters, not to mention disgruntled ones, are actually seen in this novel, which is shot through with 'a nostalgic image of postwar America' (J. N.-H. Park 2016: 99). The few black figures who appear fleetingly characteristically belong to a docile servant class: the good-natured university dining hall hands who later embrace the disgraced Chang as a fellow worker; the nameless 'kitchen boys' in Glee's house; Mrs Jackson, Glee's cleaning lady, and a restaurant 'busboy' in Nashville. The absence of discontented black people in Sewanee may be attributable to the latter being a small white-majority university town. However, the situation is no different when Chang visits Chicago, which reportedly had the largest concentration of African Americans on earth in 1950 (Lait and Mortimer 1950: 42). According to one source (Gibson and Jung 2005: Table 14), Chicago's black population in 1950 amounted to 490,000; according to a second (Lait and Mortimer 1950: 42), the number was 750,000 out of a total of 3.6 million. What is remarkable about Choi's Chicago narrative is that Chang does not see a single African American during his entire stay in this northern multi-ethnic city. Or it might be more accurate to say that no African Americans are registered in his eyes, given the fact that he must have run across hundreds of them during his daily commutes on the El after he moved up north. Given his statement that the Roosevelt El station was near his first boarding house (S. Choi 1998: 239), and the fact that this station is only two stops away from the 'Lou' Jones/Bronzeville station, both Chang's workplace and room were not far from Bronzeville, a black ghetto. Yet, there is not a single African American around either Chang's work or his boarding house.

With the protagonist conveniently acting racially colour-blind, such black-and-white conflicts as the white terrorism of the 1950s against the black residents in places like Cicero and Trumbull Park Homes and the resultant mass rallies against white Chicagoans' housing segregation (Hirsch 1995: 522–50), are foreclosed in Choi's text. What is brought up as compensation for such foreclosure is Orientalism, or to be more precise, a sanitised form of Orientalism that appears mild or even innocuous in comparison with the anti-black racism of the 1950s. Readers of the novel have already been given a glimpse of this by certain members of Chang's church audience and a few other, otherwise hospitable, Southerners, including the parents of his friend, Crane. For instance, at the Thanksgiving dinner at Crane's, Chang meets the senior Crane, a Grand Dragon in the Ku Klux Klan. The possibly volatile encounter between this arch-racist and his non-white guest, however, is immediately contained when Mr Crane shows Chang politeness tinged with condescension (S. Choi 1998: 59–60). As pointed out by Daniel Y. Kim

Orientalism and the Cold War   107

(2009: 564), Mr Crane's paternalism allows him even to offer his Asian guest an honorary membership in an imaginary white club, symbolically expressed in his granting the boy the right to choose between white and dark meat.

Another example of condescending Orientalism taking the place of potential racial confrontation is when Chang shows a slide of American platoons marching in the clean, European-style streets of Seoul before the Korean War, one of the disappointed members of his audience questions whether the image she is seeing is really Seoul. Obviously, this member of the church audience has been eagerly waiting to have her preconceived ideas about Korea confirmed. As Chang later says to Katherine, one American at another church has even asked him if Koreans live in the trees, divulging his Orientalist bias. Instead of disabusing his American audience of their ethnocentrism, Chang delivers the much-craved exotic products – that is, photos about 'Water Buffalo in a Rice Paddy' and 'Village Farmers Squatting Down to Smoke' – although there are no water buffalos in Korea. The image of farmers 'in their year-round pyjamas and inscrutable Eskimos' faces' (S. Choi 1998: 52) draws appreciative responses from the audience. By critically revealing Chang and his American audience trafficking in the stereotypical images of Korea as premodern and of Koreans as 'inscrutable Orientals', Choi is able to set her novel epistemologically above her characters.

Yet, in Chicago, Orientalist paternalism and exoticism are exchanged for verbal abuse, as seen in the racist remarks by Fran, the old white lady at Chang's work, who calls him a 'slanty-eyed son of a bitch' (S. Choi 1998: 237), suspecting him of stealing money from his job. This is one of the few moments in the novel when Chang is explicitly racialised, as Parikh also notes (2009: 60). Chang finds himself able to deal with this racism confidently once he moves up north to the Japanese American community in Lakeview. This ethnic minority shows hospitality as well as respect toward Chang, calling him 'Sensei Einstein' for his preoccupation with calculus in public eateries. Chang's adoption by the ethnic Japanese is expressed in the warmest terms:

> In Little Tokyo he was treated like a shabby aristocrat. Doing his shopping at the street market under the El he would be offered cigarettes or bean cakes or cold cans of beer. When there was an eviction notice or a jury summons he was sought out to read it and comment. 'You ought to be a lawyer and quit with these numbers. We need a lawyer, not an Einstein,' they said. But they seemed proud of his pragmatic erudition. (S. Choi 1998: 244)

Chang not only represents the scholarly pride of this community but also is his neighbours' favourite playmate. On the Cubs' game days,

108 *The Korean War Novel*

he and the other hotel residents enjoy the game from the platform of a stadium railway station for the price of a token. On such occasions, for his Japanese mates, Chang translates live radio commentaries, while the whole group can be seen 'eating the bento-box lunches, drinking beer, [and] clambering onto each other's shoulders' (S. Choi 1998: 244) when the action gets hidden by the stands. In this community, Chang acquires a more balanced and confident view about his life: 'It occurred to him, for the first time in his entire life, that he didn't have to be a student. There were endless other ways to live, endless other lives to take, without waiting for the church councils or Dean Bowers or a gracious invitation' (S. Choi 1998: 245). In other words, he realises he can choose the life he wishes to lead on his own. It is this reinforced sense of self-respect that sends him to seek out Katherine in New Orleans, defiant in the face of the expected disapproval of others, including his own family and the school authorities, as well as of the unwritten Southern law forbidding such romantic entanglements.

In his blending into the community of the ethnic Japanese, Chang's Japanese language skills, which he first acquired during the colonial period, play a role. Yet, the protagonist believes that even if these people discover his Korean identity, it will not matter because in this Japan Town, 'Old prejudices were irrelevant and unprofitable' (S. Choi 1998: 245). The camaraderie between Chang and the residents of Little Tokyo has received due attention from Choi's critics. Josephine Nock-Hee Park terms it a 'panethnic solidarity' (2016: 79). Others see in it 'a transformation that engenders a novel sense of interethnic connection' (D. Y. Kim 2009: 568) or even 'a nascent panethnic Asian community' (Parikh 2009: 60). However, despite their general perceptiveness, what these views do not consider is that the minority in question has to bear the marker of belatedness or antiquatedness for Choi's pan-Asian advocacy. In other words, to be reborn as a healing ethnic community that restores to the hero the self-respect and agency to 'make himself, to throw away what he hated and say what he was' (S. Choi 1998: 247), the Japanese in Chicago have to be represented in certain reductive ways, ways that are reminiscent of an Orientalist outlook on the world.

Most of the Japanese residents of Chicago in the 1950s were there as an indirect result of the internment of the Japanese of the West Coast that started in March 1942. Those who wished to resettle inland, moving to such places as New York City and Chicago, were allowed to leave the camp as early as in the fall of 1942. As a result, the number of Japanese Americans in Chicago jumped from a pre-war figure of just 400 to approximately 20,000 after the war's conclusion (Brooks 2000: 1655). *The Foreign Student* confirms the effect of the relocation

Orientalism and the Cold War   109

programme on the Japanese demography of Chicago: 'Many of the families in the neighbourhood who weren't new immigrants had lived in California before being interned during World War II' (S. Choi 1998: 244). The profile of these ethnic resettlers is elaborated in the following ethnographic studies:

> In her analysis of the 1950 census, Thomas found that Japanese Americans who remained in New York City and Chicago had an extremely high level of education compared to those returning to Los Angeles. In these two cities the ethnic population was twice as likely to be college educated as their white neighbors, whereas in Los Angeles, they pursued higher degrees at the same rate as whites. Thomas also noted that many more of those remaining east of the Rocky Mountains moved on to professional jobs than those returning to the West Coast. (Kurashige 2002: 105)

After the war, the majority of Japanese no longer lived in a socially and economically self-contained ethnic community. The evacuation and relocation had destroyed the *Issei*-dominated (first-generation immigrants), petit bourgeois ethnic enclave, although they were to some degree recreated in several West Coast areas. The larger society had become much more receptive to the occupational and assimilation aspirations of the Nisei (second-generation immigrants), most of whom were just beginning their careers. Thus, they were no longer trapped into working in the ethnic economy, and many of them took positions with corporations and government agencies, which were rapidly expanding during the post-war era (Fugita and O'Brien 1991: 81). According to these sources, many of the American-born Nisei chose to resettle in Chicago and New York City, while the *Issei*, their immigrant parents, decided to stay in the camps. Significantly more adventurous, adaptive and competent in English, the second-generation Japanese were able to move out into the white economy, in sharp contrast with the members of the first generation of Japanese immigrants.

Given this profile, Choi's Japanese Chicagoans are a reflection of the *Issei* rather than the Nisei in several significant aspects. The Nisei, who were largely 'born between 1910 [and] 1940' (Kitano 1981: 131), for instance, did not need help with English-to-Japanese translation, unlike Chang's neighbours who turn to him for their translation-related needs (S. Choi 1998: 244). If anything, it was their Japanese language skills that needed practice. As Charlotte Brooks maintains, 'most members of the second generation could speak only basic Japanese. Few had ever worn traditional Japanese clothing except in photographs or for holidays' (2000: 1664). Likewise, Chang's fellow hotel residents, who spend their time mostly gambling in the hotel lobby or loitering and

110   *The Korean War Novel*

smoking on the outside stairs, alienated by their language incompetence from the English-speaking world outside, do not fit the model of the Nisei who 'all looked upon the United States as "their own" and felt little attachment to Japan' (Brooks 2000: 1664). What is noteworthy about this projection of the *Issei*'s ethnocultural characteristics onto the Nisei or, rather, the displacement of one generation by another, is that these immigrants are called back into existence suffering a certain kind of historical amnesia. That is, if the first-generation Japanese are stripped of the resentful memories of their internment of only a decade before, the second generation appear to lose their even fresher memories of the painful, tumultuous process of forced evacuation and relocation.

As affirmed by two sociological studies, the first published in 1948, the second in 1953, the Japanese Chicagoans wanted to 'assimilate into Chicago' quickly and 'move away from the "colored side" of the color line' (Harden 2003: 64). They wanted to give their children 'an opportunity to become "regular" Americans'; and 'American meant white to them' (Harden 2003: 64). In this regard, Choi's advocacy of Chicago's Little Tokyo as a 'panethnic Asian community' is misrepresentative of this ethnic minority. In fact, its members had as a major goal the desire to spread out and blend into white America for their own benefit as well as in accordance with the instructions of the War Relocation Authority. For the same reason, the ethnic Japanese that admire Chang for studying calculus, calling him 'Sensei Einstein', appear to have sprung from a frozen past or from the kind of Orientalist comics that the nameless white boy shares with Chang on a Greyhound bus headed for Chicago (S. Choi 1998: 230). Given these facts, Choi's representation of this ethnic minority is anachronistic at best and, perhaps, even Orientalist at worse by attempting to represent an image of this old-style, unassimilated Japanese to stand in for the American-born Nisei.

At his summer job, Chang gives away a one-dollar bill to Fran, pretending to have found it in one of the used books he has been searching through in order to find the forgotten banknotes of the books' previous owners. In other words, he makes a small financial sacrifice in order to prevent the more serious charge of stealing a large amount of money from being broached. Replicating this strategy, Choi utilises the strategy of Orientalist critique, a relatively minor social issue at that time, in order to deflect attention away from the much more volatile conflicts between African Americans and white Americans in the United States of the 1950s. Only one critic has voiced dissatisfaction with the novel for 'dilut[ing] the significance of the [Southern] setting by including competing narratives of war and interracial romance' (Chung 2013: 59). But the author's rendition of multi-ethnic Chicago as well as of post-1945

Korea invites a similar criticism. The postliberation Korean setting in particular, against which Chang's past is played, demands a deeper examination of the continuing legacy of colonialism.

A flawed anti–Cold War critique

Choi sports her in-depth historical knowledge about the post-1945 Korea and the Korean War, ranging from the social unrest of the pre-war southern Korea through MacArthur's 'scorched-earth policy' (S. Choi 1998: 186) to the vicious Red-hunting perpetrated by the ROKA, the National Police and the rightist youth corps in the recaptured territory of the South (S. Choi 1998: 103–4, 182). However, the overall picture of South Korea and the Korean War that the author paints with her profound knowledge comes out self-contradictory at best in its perspective. If her portrayal of postliberation Korea corroborates, instead of contesting, the Cold War perspective of the US military government she criticises, the author's rendering of the Korean War remains as a civil war only in the sense of a fraternal war, lacking the postcolonial, revolutionary dimension.

In a way, a recognition of the postcolonial dimension of the movements might have undermined the author's vindication of Chang's father as a man of insight and judgement. In the novel, Dr Ahn, the father, is portrayed as a member of a select elite in colonial Korea. He is admitted to the Japanese Imperial University, groomed for a teaching position and then becomes the only Korean to be appointed to a university chair (S. Choi 1998: 69). Dr Ahn justifies to his son his commitment to colonial education as a means of preparing for the future of the nation: '[t]ake the police. They have the power now, but when the Japanese leave, what do they have? The hatred of the people, and ignorance. We'll have the knowledge' (S. Choi 1998: 243). After liberation, he then comes to teach at Yonsei University as an English professor. This scene seems rather superfluous to the storyline since Chang, like some Joycean hero, has by then disowned his family. Yet, by inserting this scene in the novel, the author appears to point to the rashness of the sweeping judgement of the postliberation era that served to publicly disgrace and penalise many prominent pro-Japanese figures as national traitors.

Choi's novel intervenes in the South Korean politics of today, whose ideological fault-line is marked by what appear to be such anachronistic terms as 'pro-Japanese' and 'pro-Communist' or 'pro–North Korean'. Today, the polarised political camps hurl these vituperative terms at each other, continuing or actually reanimating the legacies of the

112   *The Korean War Novel*

Cold War. In this political arena, 'pro-Japanese', the term referring to right-wing conservatives, also means 'blindly pro-American', a rough equation that reflects the history of the pro-Japanese collaborator class's alignment with the Hodge military government. It was this government, or so the argument is made, that crushed the Korean people's decolonising hopes in the wake of the latter's liberation from Japanese imperialism. This equation makes sense when it is considered that the conservative politicians did tend to glorify Syngman Rhee, America's protégé, as the founder of the nation. For his part, Rhee chose to work with members of the pro-Japanese, propertied class, while ignoring the significance of the earlier provisional government led by nationalist figures like Kim Koo. The liberal or left-liberal politicians, on the other hand, are often referred to as 'pro-Communist' because of the tendency to adopt a non-aggressive approach to the North Korean regime. This label was confirmed in the eyes of their opponents by their adoption of former President Kim Dae-jung's 'Sunshine Policy'. President Kim believed that economic and cultural interactions were the best means of reducing inter-Korean tensions and inducing the North to abandon its nuclear ambitions.

Placed within this context, Choi's apologia for Dr Ahn may be seen to undermine the cause of many liberal South Koreans who feel that the wider ramifications of Japanese rule have never been properly addressed. President Moon Jae-in spoke for these people when, in his address to commemorate the 100th anniversary of the 1 March Independence Movement in 2019, he pledged, '[t]his new 100 years will be the century for completing a true country of the people' while emphasising that the need for 'eradicating the vestiges of "*chinil*" (i.e., pro-Japanese activities) is an undertaking that is long overdue' (Paik 2021). According to Paik Nak-chung, a well-known South Korean literary critic and pro-unification activist, 'it was [Syngman] Rhee's alliance with former collaborators in the new era of Korean independence that allowed the "vestiges of Japanese colonial rule" to evolve beyond the actions of individuals and become more deeply entrenched in South Korean society' (Paik 2021).

Choi's failure to recognise the postcolonial cause of the anti-government movements appears to have left her little choice but to represent them as 'leftist' or 'pro-leftist' insurgencies. Yet, the connection between the reascendance of the pro-Japanese collaborators and the post-1945 anti-government struggle would appear to be unmistakable, at least for one familiar with the revisionist histories of the Korean conflict. This perspective is well encapsulated by the historian whose work the author herself refers to at one point in her novel:

The Americans staffed the military, the police and the bureaucracy mostly with Koreans who had had experience in the colonial regime; they thought they had no other choice, but in so doing the regime took on a reactionary cast that weakened it in its competition with the North. The Americans immediately ran into monumental opposition to such policies from the mass of South Koreans, leading to a sorry mess of strikes, violence, a massive rebellion in four provinces in the fall of 1946, and a significant guerrilla movement in 1948 and 1949. (Cumings 1995: 35)

While Cumings' revisionist historical insights have been attributed to the novel, *The Foreign Student* remains somewhat oblivious to – or perhaps deliberately avoids addressing – the postcolonial dimension of the anti-governmental struggle after 1945, despite containing critiques of both the Rhee and the American military regime. The author's choice of a Manichean logic that bipolarises Korean politics into a contest between communist subversives and an inefficient government bureaucracy ends up consolidating the Cold War perspective of the US Occupation and the first Rhee government.

Note

1. It is worth noting here another historical report which, pointing to Cumings' tendency to see the uprisings of the time in the South as spontaneous, argues that the workers' strike was planned by the leftists but it was the police's firing into the strike's supporters that sparked popular uprisings that took place region after region in the southern provinces, demanding the eradication of the colonial legacies, land reform and more rice rations (I. Kim 2004: 152–4). According to Kim Haknoh, the fact that these uprisings did not take place simultaneously but one after another indicates that there was no masterminding leadership in this incident but the starving people angry at the pro-Japanese collaborators, the vicious police force and the government officials' rice raids (2022: 11–16).

Chapter 4

The Politics of Neutrality

Growing up during the years of the Great Proletarian Cultural Revolution (1966–76), which shut down schools and humiliated professors, Ha Jin (Xuefei Jin, 1956–) did not receive much of a formal education. Instead, while serving in the People's Liberation Army, he read Russian literature and learned English by listening to an English program on the radio. At the end of the Cultural Revolution, Jin enrolled at a Chinese university and studied English literature for his BA and MA. He then took the decision to go to the United States, where he received his PhD in English from Brandeis University. He first taught at Emory University in Atlanta, Georgia, and then at Boston University, in Boston, Massachusetts.

Jin's literary achievements are nothing short of stellar. For his debut book of short stories, *Ocean of Words* (1996), he received the PEN/Hemingway Award, while his second collection of short fiction, *Under the Red Flag* (1997), was awarded the Flannery O'Connor Award; *Waiting* (1999) won the National Book Award and *The Bridegroom* (2000), a collection of short stories, received the Townsend Prize for Fiction. What is more, *War Trash* (2004) received the PEN/Hemingway Award and was nominated for the Pulitzer Prize. Many of his works portray the lives of Chinese people during the Cultural Revolution. Jin's experiences while growing up during that era are depicted in *Under the Red Flag*, while his period of army service, for which he volunteered at the age of fourteen, is reflected in *Ocean of Words*. Both the novels *Waiting* and *The Crazed* (2002) also reflect the embittered lives of ordinary people during the harsh years of the Chinese cultural and political purge of the late 1960s and early 1970s.

In contrast to their warm reception among Western critics, Jin's works have not been well received among Chinese scholars. For instance, *Waiting*, the author's most commercially successful novel, triggered great controversy in mainland China. This novel revolves

The Politics of Neutrality   115

around Lin Kong, a military doctor, who has to wait eighteen years to divorce his wife, Shuyu. At the beginning of the novel, through a family arrangement, the main character has to marry a traditional rural woman with bound feet; but he never loves her. He finally gets a divorce and marries Manna Wu, a fashionable urban nurse whom he falls in love with at the hospital. Yet, by a quirk of fate, he then finds he has to beg his ex-wife to receive him back after his new wife develops heart trouble after giving birth to twins. According to *The New York Times*, in the year 2000, Liu Yiqing, a professor at Beijing University, penned an angry review entitled 'Bartering Away One's Honesty: Ha Jin and His *Waiting*' in which the reviewer accused Jin of a form of self-Orientalism. The reviewer contended that the female protagonist's foot-binding represented an anachronistic device of the plot intended to 'emphasize the backwardness of China' (Eckholm 2020). In 2014, Yan Ying, writing in the Chinese-language journal, *Foreign Literature Review*, criticised the author for feeding his American readership with 'self-colonializing discourses' that feature 'a shameless whore, a foot-binding woman and asexual or impotent men' (qtd in Su 2012: 14). According to this line of Chinese criticism, in his fiction, Jin has set out to vilify China deliberately in order to promote his literary career in the US.

Placed in this context, the author's early views on the role of a writer read as though he had already taken stock of some of the criticism that was to come. In the preface to his first published work, *Between Silences: A Voice from China* (1990), for example, Jin pledges to speak for the underdogs whose voices are silenced in China. He suggests that his mission is to 'speak for those unfortunate people who suffered, endured, or perished at the bottom of life and who created the history and at the same time were fooled or ruined by it' (1990: 1). In this regard, the project of self-Orientalism in Jin's work might be interpreted as an attempt to offer a voice to the previously silenced Chinese subaltern class.

Interestingly enough, Jin's resolve to champion 'those unfortunate' echoes Richard E. Kim's espousal of advocating 'small histories' of those who are 'destroyed in the end by a ruthless, heartless "grand history"' (1985: 48). Like Kim's *The Martyred*, Jin's *War Trash* describes the life trajectories of the unfortunate through the eyes of the protagonist and disinterested chronicler, Yu Yuan, something noted by many critics. In the opinion of Xie Xinqiu, for example, '*War Trash* is a form of history, a historiographical metafiction whose aim is to preserve – as history is supposed to do – through a creative process in order to pass on collective wisdom' (2012: 39). For Jodi Kim, '*War Trash* helps us grapple with how the biopolitical space and the geopolitical territory constitute each other' (2017: 580). For his part, the historian Bruce Cumings has praised the novel, suggesting that '*War Trash* rings true on every page' (2010: 75). For Sunny Xiang, the protagonist's documentary style succeeds in distancing him so thoroughly from his memoir that he seems to be not so much an embodied speaking subject but rather a mere 'hand (*manus*) impersonally reproducing documents' (2018: 75). In this way, the novel's strategy of self-effacement enables 'a politics of unintelligibility' in a post-Cold War racial context (Xiang 2018: 89).

And yet both Xiang's idea that Yuan serves as an impersonal 'hand' operating 'beyond the polarizing ideological choices' (2020: 151) and Cumings' idea that Yuan is portrayed as an 'interested, fair, discerning observer' (2010: 75) are debatable propositions. What is more, the view of the protagonist as a disinterested documenter of facts does not really hold up. In this chapter, an opposing set of propositions is articulated: in Jin's *War Trash*, the protagonist's decision to include certain historical facts and withhold others is neither politically disinterested nor the mark of a truly objective chronicler of the truth.

This chapter, then, will analyse the ways in which the microhistories that may be recovered from a reading of *War Trash* engage with the official narratives of the Cold War. By illuminating the Chinese Civil War that unfolded in the US-run POW camps during the Korean War, Jin aims at debunking both the US Cold War view of the Korean War as an anti-communist crusade and the Chinese Communist Party's view that the Korean War illustrates a war of liberation from imperialist oppression. Nonetheless, the author's anti–Cold War project is paradoxically compromised by the political orientation that emerges in his attempt at documenting the events in the POW camps in a 'neutral' manner. Jin's attempt to carve out a neutral space within the fierce ideological battlefield of a POW camp ends up promoting to the reader the quite specific ideological form of Western liberalism.

This chapter reads the protagonist's liberal individualism as it veers towards a form of solipsism in his attempted intellectual journey to political autonomy. In probing this issue, I will compare Jin's Korean War novel with one of its sources, *Wo de Chaoxian zhanzheng: yige zhiyuanjun zhanfu de zishu* (My Korean War: A Volunteer Army POW's Memoir, 2000) by Zhang Zeshi.[1] Both Jin's novel and Zhang's memoir challenge the US's national image as a world champion of justice, but the two works part with each other in their position on Chinese Communism. The conclusion of this chapter is that the microhistory recuperated in *War Trash* is as deeply enmeshed in politics as the grand histories generated by the two ideological rival camps. In this way, the author's attempt at an 'anti–Cold War project' comes to grief.

History and objective truth

Because of the position it takes on the writing of novels, *War Trash* occupies a special place in Jin's work. In a 2004 interview, he speaks of his aim in writing the novel and offers some strikingly bold claims:

> *All I tried to do was be objective* . . . In this country, Korea [*sic*] is very much a forgotten war, but it is not forgotten in China. The difference is that in China people cannot write honestly about the war. As I wrote this book, I kept thinking how we always talk about heroes in war, but there are many soldiers, like Yu Yuan, who suffered greatly during war and are now forgotten. *This book is not my personal perspective about the Korean War. I just wanted to tell the truth*, and it may outrage some people, but that's okay. (Rightmyer 2004: 48; emphasis added)

In this interview, the author rejects the idea that the novel offers his 'personal perspective' in favour of the strong position that *War Trash* contains *the truth* about the Korean War, suggesting that the novel is about the war's forgotten soldiers rather than the heroes memorialised in the official historiographies.

In his later 2008 essay, in which he expresses his changing view of the writer's role as a public intellectual, expressing greater hesitancy about the wisdom of such a position, Jin still emphasises the mission of the writer as a conscientious voice in society: '[t]here is no argument that the writer must take a moral stand and speak against oppression, prejudice, and injustice, but such a gesture must be secondary' (2008: 29). What seems to have changed then is the issue of where a writer should place his or her primary emphasis. For Jin, the first consideration is that a writer must prioritise artistic values and ensure the autonomy of art. In this way, if the writer chooses to serve a public cause, he should do it on his own terms, not dictated by whims of others or even the society at large. In Jin's own words, a writer should 'stay above immediate social needs and create a genuine piece of literature that preserve[s] the oppressed in memory' and 'combat[s] historical amnesia' (H. Jin 2008: 30).

Nonetheless, the claim that this novel carries the truth about the Korean War is a daring one. There can be no denying the importance of writing alternative histories against the truncated accounts of official or hegemonic ones, but the reader cannot help asking what is really at stake when a writer sets as his task the restoration of facts supposedly missing from the accounts of a certain period of history. This issue invites consideration of the questions raised by Hayden White and other historical philosophers on the possibility of retrieving what can be called 'raw

118   *The Korean War Novel*

facts'. This line of inquiry is based on the idea that historical writing always involves interpretation and is organised by literary means such as narrative modes and figures (White 1973: 29–34). In this view, 'the past does not come pre-packaged in narrative form . . . It is the historian who imposes a narrative order on the past and in this sense "makes history"' (Gunn 2006: 30). In a similar context, Fredric Jameson distinguishes history in the form of writing from history as the brute record of what has taken place in the past. According to Jameson, the latter is 'inaccessible to us except in textual form, and . . . our approach to it and to the Real itself necessarily passes through its prior textualization' (1981: 35). A set of literary works may refer to the same past historical events, and yet the events represented in these works may end up being as divergent as those works themselves. The reason for this is not difficult to discern: upon being introduced in literature, those past events are subject to interpretation. Commonly referred to as 'history', this interpretation of the past is more than a simple, inert background against which the plot of a literary work unfolds.

Jin's claim to have written a novel that embodies the objective truth is based on a belief in the possibility of historical accuracy. To achieve this outcome, the author consulted many historical sources in the process of writing *War Trash*. Curiously enough, this fidelity to his textual sources also opened him up to the charge of plagiarism. According to Chen Li and other critics, Jin appropriated as many as 10,000 words from Zhang's *Personal Records in the American Prison Camps*, one of that writer's five war memoirs about the Korean War (See Tsu 2010: 108–9).

Although neither Zhang's text nor Jin's novel dwells on the Chinese Civil War (1927–49), this protracted period of Chinese history has a tremendous impact on the lives of the protagonists. After the fall of the Qing dynasty in 1912, except for a brief period of rule by Yuan Shikai (1912–16) and two periods of unsteady Nationalist–Communist power-sharing (1924–7, 1937–45), China was torn by bitter social conflict. This extended period of uncertainty and social strife was only ended by the final victory of Mao's Communist Party in 1949. Jin's narrative starts with a glimpse at this civil war. According to the first-person narrator, before the civil war comes to an end, he is attending the Huangpu Military Academy, the Kuomintang's (the Chinese Nationalist Party) prestigious military educational apparatus. When the Communist Army arrives, the cadets of the military academy readily surrender because of their strong aversion to the corruption of Chiang Kai-shek's Nationalist government.

There are striking resemblances between Zhang's memoir and Jin's narrative of the life of Yuan. For example, both receive an English educa-

The Politics of Neutrality   119

tion from missionaries at an early age. When Communist China decides to intervene in the Korean War, both Zhang and Yuan are placed in the same division of the Chinese Communist Army and later captured by American soldiers around the same time. Each of them works as a translator at POW camps and fights for the rights of the Communist POWs against the anti-communist terror of the pro-Nationalist POWs. Each has a fiancée waiting for him at home, and each chooses to return to China during the repatriation interview. However, unlike Zhang, Yuan has never been a member of the Chinese Communist Party, even though he is no supporter of Chiang's Kuomintang either. He has enrolled in the Huangpu Military Academy, but it is simply because the academy offers free tuition, and his family is too poor to support him through college. In addition to creating a politically neutral background for his hero, Jin bolsters his claim to objectivity by employing a documentary style in his novel: the account takes the form of a memoir that Yuan, at the age of seventy-four, writes for his grandchildren in the United States.

One problem which a scribe like Zhang runs across when representing himself as an individual without flaws (in this case, as a model Communist) is that such an idealised portrayal tends to call into question its probability. One strategy of imparting plausibility to such a model of writing is to reveal at times what the writer is really thinking or feeling at a given moment, without embellishment or excuse, however inappropriate it may sound – but then to rectify these thoughts or feelings later in the form of self-criticism. A prominent example of such self-correction is found in one of the early combat scenes. Here, a butterfly bomb from the US Air Force suddenly goes off, breaking an arm-thick tree branch above the protagonist's head. At this moment, Zhang is so fear-stricken that he wonders if he could even march to the thirty-eighth parallel ([2000] 2009: 11–12). Although the experience of fear is not something a card-carrying Communist ought to express without embarrassment, the presence of such spontaneous responses in the war memoir lends it the quality of genuineness. At the same time, Zhang circumvents the charge of wavering loyalty by subsequently acknowledging the inappropriateness of his initial reaction. In the passage that follows, he testifies to the fact that he was able to 'overcome his weakness' after witnessing the dire consequences of the US Air Force's indiscriminate bombing of the areas he is marching through. He pledges to 'shoot the bastards to death by even crawling to the thirty-eighth parallel' (Zhang ([2000] 2009: 12). In this way, the writer extricates himself from the possible accusation that he is a cowardly reactionary.

Since he is writing primarily for a Western readership, Jin does not have to deal with Zhang's constant need to prove his loyalty to the

120 *The Korean War Novel*

Communist Party. If Zhang seeks to win approval from his Communist readership through a set of textual strategies designed first to entertain and then to overcome the scepticism an individual may naturally feel about undertaking dangerous combat tasks, Jin seeks approval from a Western readership by learning to distance himself from both Communist and Western voices. Thus, if Zhang's memoir moves toward the end point of ideological fortification, Yuan, the protagonist in *War Trash*, moves toward the intellectual telos of political autonomy.

Stories withheld in an anti–Cold War critique

By focusing on the POW camps, which were the site of furious ideological warfare, Jin tells the reader a story quite different from the official narratives with which readers on both sides of the Pacific have become familiar. As David Cheng Chang asserts, the struggles in which the Chinese inmates found themselves in the US POW camps seemed like a form of déjà vu of everything that they had just finished going through:

> While physical deprivation and hardship made prisoners' lives miserable, incessant strife – between the Communists and the anti-Communists, between various anti-Communist factions, and between a Sichuanese secret society and the Nationalists – rendered their lives precarious. The civil war continued in POW camps. (D. C. Chang 2020a: 191)

Like the Korean War, the Chinese Civil War involved the US supporting the Nationalists in their war against the Communists. Yuan finds that the same civil war is raging in the POW camp.

In this way, the story that Yuan relays about the sufferings of the Chinese POWs is meant to counter the grand histories of the two polarised Cold War camps; it aims at dislodging the centrality of both the US-centred narrative and the official Communist narrative of the Korean War. If Jin's unadorned portrayal of the US-backed pro-Nationalist terror waged against the Communist POWs belies the 'moral victory' of the US over the Communists, then that narrative also calls into question the Chinese Communist myth of political comradeship. This is done by means of the hero's slow awakening to the ugly realities of the allegedly egalitarian ideology. However, Jin's criticism of the two rival forces is not solely the upshot of the recovery of the pertinent historical facts that lie buried beneath the two official narratives. Instead, it is articulated by making certain historical facts salient – while concealing a number of others. In its mobilisation of the rhetorical tactics of both amplification and exclusion, Jin's criticism ends up depending almost as much on what

The Politics of Neutrality   **121**

it does not say as what it does. As a consequence, Jin's 'documentary' is both asymmetrically focused and weighted: it includes textual silences that serve to articulate the author's anti–Cold War critique.

Following Zhang, Jin makes a pointed disclosure about the pro-Nationalist or pro-Kuomintang terror carried out against the Communist inmates over the issue of repatriation screening. For instance, in his original war memoir, Zhang relays in detail the grisly facts concerning the disembowelling of the Communist inmates, Lin Xuebu and Yang Wenhua, by Li Da'an, the pro-Nationalist ([2000] 2009: Ch. 11). In his novel, Jin describes those same murders in equally graphic detail, with only the names of the victims and the victimiser changed. One of these murder scenes is described by Jin in the following graphic manner:

> Liu Tai-an stabbed him in the chest and twisted the dagger. Without another word Lin Wushen dropped on the floor. Immediately Liu bent down and cut his stomach open while the dying man's feet were still kicking. His blood and intestines spilled out, and a few men at the front began retching. With a sidewise slash, Liu slit his chest, then pulled out his lungs and heart, all the organs quivering with steam. He cut out the heart and skewered it with the dagger. Raising the heart, he brandished his bloody free hand at us and said, 'Look, this is what I meant when I said we wouldn't let you leave unscathed. If anyone wants to go back to the mainland, I'll have to see the true color of his heart first.' He turned to give the corpse a kick. (2004: 107–8)

In this extraordinary passage, the author exposes the living hell of the pro-Nationalist-run compounds. Any inmate who supports repatriation is liable to become the object of public terror by Liu. On another occasion, after cooking it on a kerosene lamp, Liu consumes a piece of flesh he has just cut off the body of a Communist inmate in front of horrified witnesses in order to intimidate the Communists into renouncing repatriation to the mainland (H. Jin 2004: 111–12). The pro-Nationalists also resort to the forced tattooing of anti-communist slogans on the bodies of the Communist inmates so that they have to give up the idea of returning to China, for fear of affronting the Communist Party and receiving punishment for this.

Such brutal tactics were widespread in both the pro-Communist and anti-Communist Chinese and Korean POW compounds. Figure 4.1 displays a North Korean Communist inmate on whose body anti-Communist inmates forcibly tattooed the image of a South Korean national flag as well as an anti-communist slogan as punishment for alleged spying. While his left arm is inscribed with the politically neutral phrase 'patriotism', his right arm sports the words 'eradicate communism', a tattoo that would undoubtedly cause him future unpleasantness

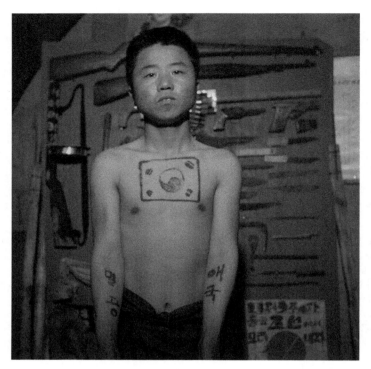

Figure 4.1 A North Korean prisoner forced to undergo tattooing in a photo taken on 18 July 1952. (Source: National Archives photo no. 111-C-9290)

if the Communist regime were to be informed of its existence.[2] Yuan himself falls victim to these barbaric practices. After knocking him out, the pro-Nationalists inscribe the phrase 'FUCK COMMUNISM' on the abdomen of the unconscious protagonist. When he wakes to find the tattoo etched on his body, Yuan blacks out again in shock and despair (H. Jin 2004: 97–8).

What is noteworthy about the anti-communist terror tactics is the location. For example, Liu's murder of Lin takes place in the classroom of the Civil Information and Education (CIE), the new camp organisation set up by the Truman administration for the purpose of indoctrinating the Communist inmates.[3] Liu's practice of cannibalism takes place in the open space outside Yuan's tent. Yuan describes the attitudes of the US guards towards these terror tactics using matter-of-fact language: 'The Americans had adopted a let-alone policy and didn't care what happened in the compounds as long as the POWs remained behind the barbed wire' (H. Jin 2004: 69). By exposing the fact that anti-communist brutalities were carried out with the tacit endorsement of the US POW

The Politics of Neutrality   **123**

Camp Command, the author gives the lie to US Cold War propaganda. In truth, what these events would appear to signify is the descent of the Free World into primitive barbarism, not an unambiguous sign of its moral superiority.

By way of contrast, the anti-Nationalist terror practised by the Communist inmates does not receive as much attention in Yuan's report. It is also not emphasised in Zhang's memoir. Zhang's oversight or prejudice on this issue is not surprising since he is writing from the perspective of a 'good' Communist. And yet perhaps another reason for this is that such acts of barbarity were not as widespread in the POW camps as the acts of anti-communist persecution, given that the Chinese Communists were in a defensive position vis-à-vis the aggressive and relatively more empowered pro-Nationalists. Within these POW camps, the Chinese Communists were besieged by the triangular forces of the pro-Nationalists, the US guards and the CIE program. Because it faced a number of separate challenges from a variety of sources, the Communist Party leadership resorted to certain violent counter-measures in order to keep the inmates in line. For example, the leadership organised death squads, euphemistically termed 'security forces', the job of which was to kill Party members whose loyalty they suspected. In this way, they were able to rid themselves of traitors and consolidate the ranks by force of intimidation. One of the most notorious mass executions was committed in September 1952 on Jeju Island as a means of uniting the Communist inmates before the 1 October National Day celebrations. As David Cheng Chang recounts, the Communist leadership on Jeju had as many as seventeen 'traitors' executed by Communist Solidarity, a secret security squad (2020a: 310). Nonetheless, this slaughter receives attention neither from Zhang nor from Jin. Although Jin introduces a single instance of murder by the Communists – the scene in which Ding Wanlin, Yuan's good friend, is killed on suspicion of betraying Pei Shan, the Commissar – the author is more interested in highlighting the criminal brutality of the pro-Nationalists. In this respect, it might be because Jin does not think it seems fair to censure those who were more sinned against than sinning. Whatever the reason, Jin appears to have started writing the novel with a strong sense of which side constituted the principal villains in regard to the intra-camp terror.

According to David Cheng Chang's study, until the Communist prisoners were transferred to separate compounds, there were a number of violent clashes between the two factions in the US-run POW camps over dominance, including the showdown of 9 October 1951 that took place in Compound 86 between 'Sichuan's Gowned Brothers', a pro-repatriate league, and the anti-repatriate band of Chinese inmates.[4]

124   *The Korean War Novel*

Although he does not dwell on the Communists' anti-Nationalist terror in his narrative, Yuan backhandedly acknowledges its existence when he compares the torture methods of the American guards with those of the Chinese and the Korean inmates:

> In the art of inflicting pain, the Chinese and the Koreans were much more expert than the Americans. When GIs beat you, they would kick and hit you, and they would break your ribs or smash your face, but they seldom tortured you in an elaborate way . . . But the Chinese prisoners, especially some of the pro-Nationalist men, were masterful in corporal punishment and even took great pleasure in inflicting pain on others. They knocked your ankle-bones with a special stick that had a knurl on its end; they shoved a water nozzle into an inmate's anus and then turned on the hydrant (one man was killed this way); they tied your hands up and rubbed chili powder into your eyes; they forced you to kneel on sharp-edged opened cans; they slashed your flesh with a knife and then put salt on the wounds . . . In contrast to the pro-Nationalists, the Communists were less creative and more blunt. If you were in their way, they either beat you half to death to teach you a lesson or just killed you. They would knock you down and drop a sandbag on the back of your head to smother you. They did everything secretly, perhaps because they were in the minority and had less power in the camp. (H. Jin 2004: 86)

In this comparison, the pro-Nationalists come out worse than their counterparts. They are portrayed as sick masochists who take 'great pleasure' in torturing others using a variety of creative methods; in contrast, the Communists appear the more practically minded: they carry out the necessary punishment in a merely efficient way. What is more, the pro-Nationalists appear to become personally invested in terror. One may easily conjecture that this personal investment may have something to do with what they have had to undergo in Communist China, but this conjectured reason is not mentioned in Yuan's account.

Jin's preconceived ideas about the pro-Nationalists are detectible not only in what he decides to say about them but also in what he chooses to withhold. There is a moment in the novel when the author allows one of the violent pro-Nationalist leaders, Chief Wang Yong, to shine in what appears to be an entirely human light. Shedding his usual thug-like manners, Wang humbly invites Yuan to a drinking party apparently in order to share his secret worries about his future with him (H. Jin 2004: 97). According to Wang, uneducated, 'coarse' men like him and his cronies, who have no future in China because of their pro-Nationalist background, 'will be dumped to the bottom' of Taiwanese society. He believes that unlike him, Yuan will certainly rise to the top ranks in the Taiwanese army due to his prestigious credentials as a Huangpu cadet

The Politics of Neutrality   125

and thus will be able to look after him in Taiwan. In this speech, Wang entreats Yuan to renounce repatriation and become his and his men's patron in Taiwan. However, after this sad story has been related, Wang and Yuan, with tears in their eyes, briefly toast each other before Yuan goes to leave and gets knocked out and forcibly tattooed by Wang's men. In the end, it is difficult for the reader to decide whether Wang's sobbing entreaty was a hoax or a last peaceful attempt to convince Yuan before the resort to brute force. At any rate, in this episode, the author obviates his reader's sympathy for the pro-Nationalist inmates by portraying them as cunning, treacherous and violent.

Jin's withholding of the back stories of the zealous pro-Nationalist inmates is most salient in the scene in which the UN Command announces the imminence of repatriation screening. The announcement is made in this way:

> The U.N. Command can offer no guarantee whatsoever on the ultimate fate of those of you who refuse to return to your own people. Therefore, before any of you decide irrevocably to resist repatriation, you must consider the consequences of your decision for your family. If you fail to go back, your government may hold your family accountable. On top that, you may never see them . . .
> Hearing those words, POWs became tearful. Some men drifted back into their tents and buried their heads in blankets, weeping. Wang Yong flew into fury. 'Fuck the Americans!' he cursed. 'If I had a grenade, I'd blow up that sound truck.' (H. Jin 2004: 101–2)

Somewhat surprisingly, the UN Command's announcement strongly discourages the POWs from renouncing repatriation by accentuating the grave consequences of non-repatriation. It attempts to drill into them the complex message that while the future awaiting them is uncertain if they choose Taiwan, what cannot be doubted is that their families at home will face certain retribution from the government for their traitorous acts. The announcement would appear to sabotage the non-repatriation campaign the UN Command has vigorously pursued by the simultaneous offer of both the whip and the carrot, the CIE's civil work and the threat of anti-communist terror. In this respect, the reader can understand Wang's angry response and, at the same time, perhaps find it hard to understand why the other pro-Nationalist inmates respond to the same news with such intense grief.

The problem is that, due to the contradictory policies of the UN Command, the pro-Nationalists cannot be sure of their safe relocation to Taiwan. David Cheng Chang elucidates the UN Command's ambiguous policies on the pro-Nationalist inmates in this way:

> The UNC's [UN Command] self-contradictory POW policy of prisoner reindoctrination only heightened the prisoners' fear. First, ... the UNC indiscriminately treated willing defectors and the captured as POWs. Anti-Communist prisoners felt they had been misled by UNC propaganda ... They began to lose faith in the Americans.
>
> Second, throughout their long captivity, the UNC made no explicit guarantee that prisoners would be relocated to Taiwan. Washington might repatriate most – if not all – Chinese POWs to China in exchange for UNC prisoners. To declared anti-Communists, repatriation would mean death or severe persecution, which many had witnessed in land reform or various other violent political campaigns under the Communists. The stakes for anti-Communist prisoners were extremely high. They had lived in constant fear and uncertainty. (2020a: 204)

In Chang's opinion, it is contradictory on the part of the UN Command both to indoctrinate the inmates to renounce communism and then to withhold the guarantee of non-repatriation to those who declare themselves to be anti-communist. Thus, the back story of the pro-Nationalist inmates that is withheld in the earlier scene concerns their anxiety about the uncertain future, which is different from the uncertainty Wang earlier alerted Yuan to when they were drinking together. If Wang's first anxiety was about his future in Taiwan, this second source of anxiety concerns his future in China – that is, what he may face if he is forced to go back to China. By carrying out an aggressive anti-repatriation campaign in alliance with the CIE, the activist pro-Nationalist inmates have as much as signed their own death warrants. This would not matter as long as the pro-Nationalists are sure of eventually being relocated to Taiwan.

According to David Cheng Chang, when, following the start of the armistice negotiations, the news about the Communist delegates' insistence on an all-for-all POW exchange, a policy in line with the Geneva Convention, reached them, the pro-Nationalist POWs were shocked and appalled. Since the UN Command was suddenly not in a position to ensure their safe relocation, the pro-Nationalists, feeling abandoned and panicky, had to take drastic actions to attract the attention of the Taiwanese government to their predicament. They resorted to tattooing anti-communist slogans on themselves, as seen in Figure 4.2, and collecting letters of petition written in blood in order to demonstrate their determination to go to Taiwan. Although these letters were sent to the US Command, there was no response (D. C. Chang 2020a: 205). It was because of this dire need to prove their unswerving loyalty to Taiwan that the pro-Nationalist inmates conducted their brutal anti-repatriation campaign. In this way, it is possible to suggest that the pro-Nationalist reign of terror in the POW camps is attribut-

Figure 4.2 Anti-communist slogans tattooed on the arms of pro-Nationalist prisoners. (Source: National Archives photo no. 306-N-54-822)

able to the US Command's ambiguous policies regarding the Chinese inmates.

When the UN Command repeatedly implied before the commencement of the repatriation screening that the future for non-repatriates was uncertain, it may be thought natural that this would raise the intense fear of compulsory repatriation in the hearts of professed anti-Communist inmates like Chief Wang. But the reader is only offered Wang's angry response to the UN Command's self-sabotage: there are no comments concerning his fear for his own safety. Nor is his fellow mates' anticipatory grief about the fate awaiting them at home given a voice. In this way, Jin's withholding of the personal stories of the pro-Nationalists and their anxiety about the precarity of their future prevents the reader from reacting in an emotional way to their plights. A somewhat similar textual strategy of distancing is found later in the novel when Yuan participates in the collective struggles of the Communist Compounds. This distancing creates the impression that he is being even-handed in withholding insight into the stories of both

128   *The Korean War Novel*

the pro-Nationalists and the Communists. However, Yuan's criticism of the Communist inmates is personally motivated. That is, it derives from his realisation that he too has to make a contribution to the common good of his fellow mates in the form of an act of self-sacrifice. In this regard, Yuan's eventual maintenance of his distance from the Communist camp, following his earlier critique of the pro-Nationalist camp, does not necessarily guarantee his political neutrality. This time, the narrator not only withholds the back stories of the Communist prison leadership, but he projects his own story or psychology onto them. In so doing, this chapter argues, he emerges as someone firmly anchored in a particular ideology.

The emergence of a liberal capitalist

Posing as an objective historian, Yuan would appear to be speaking for the author when he declares in the prologue, 'I am going to tell my story in a documentary manner so as to preserve historical accuracy' (H. Jin 2004: 5). At the end of the novel, the protagonist reinforces the objective status of his story in the following manner: '[D]o not take this to be an "our story." In the depths of my being I have never been one of them. I have just written what I experienced' (H. Jin 2004: 350). The referent of the first-person plural pronoun in the phrase 'our story' is to the Communist inmates in the US POW camps. Commissar Pei Shan, the main leader of the Communist inmates in the US-run POW camp, initially asked Hao Chaolin, the vice-Chief of a Chinese Communist Compound, to write their story down, but the latter entreats the protagonist to do this instead, excusing himself from the task because of his failing eyesight and confused memories. Although the protagonist often regards Pei respectfully, Yuan, at the conclusion of his memoir, dissociates himself from his fellow Communists. By setting himself apart from the Communists, Yuan buttresses the point that this story is not only politically neutral but also truthful.

In Yuan's earlier ideological comparison sheet, however, the Communist regime initially comes out as a winner by a landslide:

> I had seen how my country had been ruined by the Nationalists. Inflation, corruption, crime, poverty, all the evil forces had run amok in the old China . . . How could common people have continued to live under that regime? By contrast, shortly after the Communists came to power, people in dire poverty were relieved, usury and market cornering were banned, and criminal gangs disappeared. For better or worse the Communists had brought order and hope to the land. (H. Jin 2004: 122)

The Politics of Neutrality   **129**

According to the passage, Communist rule transformed a corrupt and impoverished China into a hopeful place for ordinary people. The old social ills of crime, poverty and corruption were eradicated. The difference between the two regimes is also detectible in their militaries. The sight of the squad and platoon leaders in the Communist Army fetching hot water to bathe their men's sore feet deeply impresses Yuan, who is used to a strict hierarchy among the ranks. He cannot help comparing the fraternity that he sees in the ranks of the Communist forces with the abuse of power in the ranks of the Nationalists, where even junior officers commonly mistreat their subordinates (H. Jin 2004: 17). Communist egalitarianism is also witnessed later when, captured in combat, the protagonist is sent to the US POW camp on Geoje (Koje) Island, the second-largest island located on the southern coast of South Korea. In the Communist-dominated Compound 602, the sizes of all the tents are the same and the same meals are provided, regardless of the inmate rank – in stark contrast with the situation in the pro-Nationalist-run compounds (H. Jin 2004: 116). Yuan is so attracted to the democratic methods of the Communists that he resolves 'to abide by its principles, because [he] believe[s] in socialism' (H. Jin 2004: 122).

However, Yuan's enthusiasm for Communism fluctuates, in a significant way, both depending on how he himself gets treated at particular moments and whether or not he is required to make sacrifices for other inmates. For example, his initial excitement suffers a minor period of deflation when he learns that his application for membership in a Communist prisoners' political organisation has been turned down by the Communist leadership. He suspects that despite his recent devotion of himself to their cause, his fellow Communists do not entirely trust him, believing that this may be due to his 'reactionary' past as a Huangpu cadet. This initial rejection significantly deflates his new enthusiasm for Communism. In his subsequent dialogue with Commissar Pei about his membership application, the protagonist goes on to reveal that he has certain lingering reservations about Communism:

> The Communists treat every person just as a number. One plus one equals two. One hundred people have united, then you get the power of one hundred men, as though humans are horses. For me, this is too simple. I believe there is a power much larger than an individual, like a multiplier. If you tap that power, you can multiply yourself. You can become one hundred or one thousand, depending on what the multiplier is. (H. Jin 2004: 125)

For the protagonist, what stops him from embracing Communism wholeheartedly is the fear that it represents a form of what might be termed 'mechanical egalitarianism'. In this view, Communism not only

130   *The Korean War Novel*

pursues equality in economic and political terms but also operates on the assumption that human ability may properly be measured in terms of the equation, '[o]ne plus one equals two'. Such a mechanical view undergirds Communist society's 'treat[ing] every person just as a number'; in this way, individuals may end up being reduced to mere component parts of the whole.

However, the Communist society Yuan criticises for treating humans as undifferentiated cogs in a gigantic wheel is not something the first theorists of communism endorsed. In *The German Ideology* (1845), Karl Marx suggested that:

> in communist society, where nobody has one exclusive sphere of activity but each can become accomplished in any branch he wishes, society regulates the general production and thus makes it possible for me to do one thing today and another tomorrow, to hunt in the morning, fish in the afternoon, rear cattle in the evening, criticise after dinner, just as I have in mind, without ever becoming hunter, fisherman, shepherd or critic. ([1932] 1978: 160)

The communist society envisioned by Marx is one that allows people to enjoy being versatile; it is one in which individuals may take their pick among a variety of tasks and occupations one day and change this choice the next, with the only consideration being their own particular interests. Stated in this way, Marx's vision comes close to the vision of freedom and choice that underpins capitalist ideology, whereas capitalist cultures tend to fall far short of their own much-vaunted ideals. Recognising this, the protagonist's criticism of human beings being reduced to standardised units of a whole is more applicable to capitalist societies where individuals are treated as replaceable or interchangeable units of the workforce, as Marx and other critics have long recognised (Marx [1867] 1990: 739). What is significant as far as the novel is concerned, however, is that the narrator's earlier experience of early Communist China contradicts his view of communism as a standardising, mechanical kind of egalitarianism. The new Communist regime of China, for instance, treats the protagonist differently from others: it offers him the privilege of continuing his studies at the newly established Southwestern University of Military and Political Sciences when it might just as well have punished him for his affiliation with the Nationalist Military Academy. It also commissions him as an army officer. In contrast with Yuan's criticism, the new Communist regime appears to support meritocracy rather than mechanical egalitarianism.

The notion of 'multiplier' utilised by Yuan in his criticisms of Chinese Communism deserves further attention. As he states: 'If you tap that

The Politics of Neutrality   131

power, you can multiply yourself. You can become one hundred or one thousand, depending on what the multiplier is.' If this theory highlights the importance of collective causes or collective beliefs, an identification with which can draw out the best in an individual, it simultaneously reverberates with the ethos of investment capitalism. Here too, there are individuals who seek out a 'multiplier' to 'tap' in order to multiply their capital 'one hundred or one thousand' times (H. Jin 2004: 125). Yuan's basic idea that one can increase value and power exponentially through a discovery of the right cause is not very far from the spirit of a venture capitalist or speculative investor who constantly aims at dramatically increasing his fund by discovering the scarce commodity or recent startup in which to invest. Over and over again, Yuan demonstrates the ethos of the individualistic capitalist when he is called upon to participate in POW camp collective struggles against the US Command. For example, the protagonist meticulously calculates the possible gains and losses for himself, which the investment of his time and energy in the collective cause may incur: he speculates about the risk, measures the possible outcomes against the expected sacrifices and above all conscientiously tots up his share in the rewards. Such a thorough reckoning turns him against what he finds to be the high-risk, low-return ventures he encounters. For this reason, when the leadership of the Communist inmates decides to stage a protest, which appears to run a high risk of failure in the eyes of the protagonist, Yuan starts to harbour resentment.

On one occasion, Yuan feels excited, thinking that he has found the 'multiplier' in Communism. The temporary revelation takes place following the kidnapping of General Bell, a fictional character based on the real-life military figure, General Francis Dodd, by North Korean prisoners. In the account by Yuan, which is one closely modelled on Zhang's recollections of the incident, the North Korean inmates in Compound 76 conspire to abduct the US Commander and force him to confess to the crimes committed within the camp, including the brutal methods of the US guards, the forced nature of the repatriation screening and the use of terror tactics by the pro-Nationalists against the Communist inmates. The kidnapping is motivated by the resistance of the North Korean inmates to the US Command's policies; and the plan involves gaining some leverage for the Communist delegates during the truce negotiations by ensuring that the Americans are forced to take responsibility for the crimes committed in the prisons. After they succeed in detaining General Bell, the North Koreans invite the leaders of the Chinese Communist inmates to the negotiation table. Yuan initially feels highly elated to become part of such a great, historical event:

132   *The Korean War Novel*

> I felt for the first time that I was a useful man, and that my life had finally been shaped by a goal. How small an individual was. Only when you joined a cause greater than yourself could you expand your individual role by a multiplier. For the time being, maybe the struggle against the American imperialists was the multiplier I had been seeking. (H. Jin 2004: 171)

It is important to note that the Chinese Communists have previously offered a form of assistance to the North Koreans by causing General Bell to lower his guard when dealing with the prisoners. When the Chinese inmates had an earlier interview with the camp commander and resolved their grievances in a peaceful manner, General Bell lost whatever wariness he otherwise might have felt about holding face-to-face talks with the POWs. Profoundly touched by the success of the North Korean POWs in forcing the camp commander to sign the agreement they offer to him, Yuan becomes convinced that he can entirely commit himself to Communism. From now on, Yuan believes, he will know how to conduct himself in order to realise his maximum returns.

However, Yuan's exultation, along with his belief in the concept of the 'multiplier', quickly lapses, when all the prisoners, including himself, end up paying a heavy price for the abduction of the senior military officer. In the ensuing clash, the company of American troops, who move into the prison compound, backed by the force of forty tanks and armoured vehicles, wound or kill about 200 of the North Korean inmates. In the end, the North Korean leaders, along with the heads of the other compounds invited to take part in the negotiations with the POW camp commander, find themselves locked up in a special war crimes prison on Geoje Island. In the aftermath of this major loss, Yuan's scepticism rises to the fore once again:

> At heart I was starting to doubt the wisdom of abducting General Bell. True, we had created a piece of international news and provided ammunition for the [North] Korean and the Chinese governments, but at what cost? Our living conditions had definitely deteriorated, and hundreds of men in Compound 76 had been killed or wounded. Why hadn't we thought about the consequences beforehand? Was any news story worth so many lives? Who would get credit for the victory? Of course the Communist leaders here, not those men buried underground . . . Lonesome and miserable, I felt I had been used too. (H. Jin 2004: 190)

Incarcerated in a special prison and later tortured, Yuan comes to look at the recent 'victory' in a completely different light. On his new balance sheet that compares individual losses against collective gains, the whole venture is deemed a great failure since the prisoners paid too dearly in the end for some temporary success. What deserves mention here is that by reviewing the whole incident from an individualist perspective, the protagonist is able to play up the losses of the inmates, while writing off as uncertain the repercussions of the international propaganda and the leverage the Communist delegates wield at the peace talks. According to Rosemary Foot, however, at the armistice negotiations, as well as in their publicity, the Communist delegation made good use of General Dodd's acknowledgement of anti-communist brutality and the existence of violent screening procedures. They publicised both as hard facts that 'demonstrated the hollowness of the U.N. Command's stand on nonforcible repatriation' (Foot 1990: 119). Interestingly, however, this slice of history is significantly absent from Jin's novel.

Like many liberals who 'regard appeals for the common good warily' (Raeder 1998: 520), after the fallout from the abduction incident, Yuan comes to view the collective prison population in a new light. Schematically, he begins to divide the prisoners who united and fought together into two groups: those who do the leading and those who allow themselves to be led. From this polarising perspective, most of the prisoners are seen as the subjects of exploitation in situations where their leaders claim all the credit for success themselves. Nonetheless, in making such a blanket accusation, the protagonist does not consider the fact that credit for the success of a collective struggle is rarely distributed equally, regardless of whether the regime those individuals live under is a capitalist or a communist one. This inequality stems mostly from the fact that any complex undertaking involves major differences in the roles performed by individuals. As a consequence, the organisers of the events usually receive a greater share of the spotlight and more credit than the other participants. Yuan's assessment of the post-abduction situation, in which he criticises the unequal system of Communist rewards, contradicts the meritocratic standards he advocated in his earlier rejection of Communism as a form of uniformist or mechanical egalitarianism.

The criticism of the alleged mechanical egalitarianism of the Communists also collapses when the protagonist expresses resentment against the decision of Pei, the leader of the Communist inmates, to send him – instead of Chang Ming, the Communist inmate working closely with Pei – to Busan. When the US Command orders Chang Ming to report to Busan for re-registration, the Communist leadership in the POW camp suspects that this order masks the desire on the part of the US Command to separate Ming from his fellow inmates for interrogation or forced repatriation. As a consequence, Pei decides to send Yuan instead, counting on the fact that the US POW Camp Command will not know what Ming really looks like. Yuan becomes infuriated by this decision:

134　*The Korean War Novel*

> I was angry about the commissar's decision, my throat aching. Indeed Ming was his interpreter, secretary, code man, and signalman, yet I could easily have replaced him without interrupting the regular work and communication . . . Then the thought crossed my mind that probably this was because I was not a Party member. (H. Jin 2004: 279)

What Yuan appears to forget is that Pei's decision is based on the standard of comparative merit. From Pei's point of view, Ming's many work skills, which include being the commissar's secretary, interpreter and code man, are not easily replaced, contrary to what Yuan suggests. Most likely too, the information that Ming has acquired from his close interactions with the commissar is too valuable to be put at risk. As the protagonist eventually realises, most importantly of all, Ming is a Communist Party member whose proven loyalty is a greater asset to the Party than is the untested fidelity of a non-member like Yuan. In this regard, Pei's decision is sagacious and even strategic, made after due consideration of the different values of the range of individuals under his command. His highest motivation consists of his need to protect the interests of the entire collective in the best manner possible. Read in conjunction with this episode, Yuan's earlier criticism that a Communist leadership treats each individual 'just as a number' does not hold. The claim that he might easily substitute for Ming contradicts Yuan's own belief in the differences among individuals in terms of ability and value, the overlooking of which invokes the perspective of the uniformist egalitarianism that the protagonist attributes to Communism. Yuan's angry reaction to the possible sacrifice required of him in the name of the common good is traceable to his unstated belief in the liberal doctrine that would categorically object to the deliberate sacrifice of any one individual person in the name of inviolable human rights and interests.

Yuan's reaction also contradicts his previously expressed conviction that people need a collective cause in order not to be reduced to the level of the animals. Watching his fellow inmates gambling and fighting over trifles, he deplores them in striking language: 'Why should they behave like brutes? . . . How easily could humanity deteriorate in wretched conditions? How low could an ordinary man fall when he didn't serve a goal larger than himself?' (H. Jin 2004: 69). Here, Yuan recognises that a collective cause is necessary for the sustenance of a healthy society, but he cannot accept that a collective cause may thereby sometimes require the sacrifice of a particular individual's self-interests; indeed, he explodes with rage when he finds that he has to bear the brunt of the collective burden. And yet, the society whose collective well-being never requires any form of sacrifice on the part of its members does not need to posit

The Politics of Neutrality   135

the idea of a collective cause: that society must already be an ideal one. A similar critique was once made of John Rawls, that great liberal theorist who rejects the concept of sacrifice and emphasises the inviolability of the individual: '[h]is theory does not apply to sacrificial situations. It is an "ideal" theory that is only valid for a society already governed by the Rawlsian principles of justice!' (qtd in Palaver 1995: 46). Yuan's philosophy, one which prioritises individual interests before everything else, even while acknowledging the need for a collective cause, runs into similar problems. This philosophy may work in an ideal, democratic society. And yet, by categorically denying that there is ever a genuine need for individual self-sacrifice, it would seem next to impossible to bring about change in any society that is less than ideal, never mind in the context of a POW camp during wartime.

Yuan's positioning of himself as a liberal capitalist may come as a surprise when the reader considers that he has been continually surrounded by Communist inmates and exposed to the disciplinary practices and system of indoctrination conducted by the Communist leadership during his captivity. Nevertheless, it is not entirely unwarranted, given that the protagonist has been subject to much the same discipline and indoctrination, but to the very opposite purpose during the CIE programme in the POW camp. Monica Kim explains the aim of the CIE programme in the POW camps in this manner:

> [A]t the heart of the [CIE] program, like many of the American education projects in Asia during the Cold War, was the assumption that if one could train the Asian to behave in a certain manner – an idealized American manner – then surely his political consciousness would develop and follow (American) suit. The Asian subject would learn to renarrate himself, embed his life trajectory into a larger American global and local story about *liberal freedom* and the desirability of *free market capitalism*. (2019: 242; emphasis added)

According to Monica Kim, the CIE programme aimed at the interpellation of the Communist inmates as model American citizens. From this point of view, the ideological requirement for an Asian to become a model American involves subscribing to the 'desirability of free market capitalism' and the supreme value of 'liberal freedom'. Driven by the protagonist's need to develop a counter-ideology which will validate his scepticism about individual sacrifice, Yuan, in his criticism of the Communist inmate leadership, ends up articulating what may be read as a defence of liberal capitalism. And it is the protagonist's alliance with liberal capitalism that compromises the author's claim to historical objectivity.

An individualist's ventriloquism

When the repatriation issue drives each and every inmate into the crazy, violent turmoil of the proselytising campaign, Yuan feels threatened too. However, he finds it impossible to make the choice of Taiwan his own, regardless of ideological orientation. The rationale is articulated when he makes an appeal to one of the pro-Nationalist camp leaders. Here, he emphasises that his choice of mainland China does not imply that he is a Communist; instead, it is a choice made for entirely personal reasons. According to Yuan, he is not the only one whose repatriation decision is without ideological or political conviction:

> The pro-Nationalists, who were determined to go to Taiwan, believed that whoever intended to return to mainland China must be a Communist or a pro-Communist. In fact, *most of us* wanted to go home not for political reasons at all; our decision was personal. (H. Jin 2004: 65; emphasis added)

Here, Yuan takes upon himself the task of speaking for all those prisoners who have decided to go back to China. According to him, the decision to be repatriated to China, one that has been taken by 'most of us', is one that is motivated by personal considerations. Given the historical report that 5,640 out of the 20,720 Chinese POWs were repatriated,[5] 'most of us' here refers to one-quarter of the Chinese POWs. In other words, a quarter of the Chinese inmates who chose repatriation did so for personal, not political, reasons. In his own case, Yuan chooses repatriation because he has both a fiancée and a widowed mother waiting for him at home. When read in conjunction with the US Command's celebration of the results of repatriation polling as a moral victory, the protagonist's explanation has no small repercussions for the international politics of the Cold War. It is because it may suggest that 'most of us' – most of the POWs in favour of repatriation – do not particularly care about politics and, by extension, that Communism is extremely unpopular, even among the Chinese Communist inmates. Even when the reader considers that a large number of the Chinese People's Volunteer Army were ex-Nationalist soldiers who consented to Communist conscription in exchange for exoneration of their reactionary pasts (D. C. Chang 2020a: 205), Yuan's explanation that 'most of us' had nothing to do with communist ideology still radically reduces the number of loyal Communists among the Chinese POWs.

In the context of Cold War politics, Yuan's underestimation of the number of loyal Communist inmates may be used to reinforce US propa-

The Politics of Neutrality   **137**

ganda about the superiority of Western democracy to Communism. And yet Yuan, this liberal individualist, characteristically uses it for his own purpose. By attributing the choice of repatriation by a large group of his Communist inmates to purely personal reasons, Yuan serves in part to justify his own decision. What is more, by describing this group of inmates as politically indifferent, Yuan is able to use this as ammunition to discredit the Communist inmate leadership when he later becomes fully disillusioned about Communism.

The same practice is found at work in the protagonist's commentary on the incident where the Communist inmates decide to fly their national flags in the Jeju POW Camp. Following Pei's order, the Communist inmates make some red flags and plan to raise them in commemoration of the 1 October National Day, the anniversary of the inauguration of the Republic of China, preparing themselves for the anticipated clash with their American guards. Some of Yuan's fellow inmates pledge in blood their resolve to protect the flags; many of them volunteer for dangerous tasks for the expected armed struggle. And yet, according to Yuan, these inmates are acting neither out of love for their mother country nor out of a sense of bravery. To quote the protagonist's words: '[o]n the surface we appeared courageous, but in reality our resolve was mixed with desperation' (H. Jin 2004: 235). If the reader compares Yuan's analysis of the psychology of the inmates with his description of the war preparations, however, there appears to be a marked difference:

> Now Commissar Pei's order gave them a chance to vent their pent-up emotions, and many men couldn't wait to fight. Some even believed it would be better to fall in *a heroic, if ill-fated, battle* than to be jailed like animals. So all at once the compounds turned hectic – the prisoners were busy preparing to confront the enemy. They picked up stones and piled them in places, filled bottles with urine, gathered wooden sticks and cudgels, made knives out of the steel sheets torn from oil drums, forged and honed daggers . . . The inmates seemed *suicidally blind* to the resources the enemy had. I was agitated but dared not say anything, fearing the accusation of cowardice. (H. Jin 2004: 235; emphasis added)

For those who are said to have prepared for combat out of 'desperation', the inmates would appear to act with too intense a sense of enjoyment and fervour. As the narrator indicates, 'many men couldn't wait to fight': these inmates appear to be burning with the desire to engage the enemy. Although the ready resolve of the inmates to lay down their lives to defend their national flags may indicate unwavering loyalty to the mother country, the protagonist dismisses this merely as a sign of their 'desperation' and their being 'suicidally blind' to the enemy's superior

138 *The Korean War Novel*

firepower. At this point, the reader may question whether the commentary that attributes battle preparations solely to 'desperation' derives from the psychology of the prisoners or the psychology of Yuan himself who clearly lacks the patriotism and enthusiasm exuded by most of his comrades.

In this regard, it is both interesting and illuminating to compare Yuan's description with the account offered in Zhang's *My Korean War*. Since he was not among those relocated to the new prison facilities on Jeju, Zhang does not provide a detailed record of these events; instead, there is merely a brief summary of what transpired and some emotional reflections on what he heard. Nevertheless, his memoir does contain the record of similar events in the Geoje POW Camp, where the Communist inmates also raised red flags to protest the US Command's policy of forced repatriation screening. Zhang begins by first describing in detail the making of the red flags. After the preparation of two separate sets of cloths, the first dyed red using mercurochrome and the second, star-shaped cloths, dyed yellow using quinine sulfate, all the inmates seem eager to get on with the job of stitching the stars to the flag. In order to solve this problem, Zhao, the leader of the Communist inmates, suggests that they share equally in the process of stitching the cloths together. The narrator describes the way these inmates take on their task using the heartwarming language of genuine patriotism:

> When Commissar Zhao, taking the initiative, walked to the flag, knelt on his knees, and stitched the edges of an octagon-shaped star to the flag, one person started singing the national anthem . . . My comrades, one by one, walked forward, knelt on their knees, stitched the stars, and kissed the flag with their ardent love, worship, longing, and loyalty for their country. In the meantime, the sound of our sobbing grew in volume; the sound of singing and sobbing mixed with that of wind and rain flew away to a distant land. (Zhang [2000] 2009: 176–7; author's translation)

Still undetected by the guards, the Communist inmates finally raise the flag. However, when they start singing the national anthem in front of the fluttering flag, the attention of the US guards is drawn to this unusual activity. At this point, the guards threaten to shoot them if they do not lower the Chinese Communist flag:

> Wu Xiaozong, beating his chest, shouted, 'How dare you! If you want to shoot, shoot me here!' The machine gun on the watch tower made firing sounds and South Korean soldiers fired too. Immediately Wu Xiaozong fell, clutching his abdomen. Ren Guiquan and Sun Changqing also fell in a bloody massacre and the machine gun left a string of bullet holes on the flag. My comrades were infuriated. Some ran towards the wounded, looking

The Politics of Neutrality   **139**

after them while many readied themselves with rocks to throw at the guards. Waving his arm, Ma Xingwang, the battalion commander, gave an order in a loud voice: 'Don't move. Communist Party members move to the front and protect the inmates!' Upon hearing this, the Communist Party members swiftly moved to the front of the ranks and took one another's hands, creating a human wall. (Zhang [2000] 2009: 179; author's translation)

Even when it is considered that these descriptions are from a memoir written for a predominantly Communist readership, it is nevertheless revealing to compare the two passages with Jin's fictional account of similar events. In Jin's account, the incident of the flag-flying is designed by the Communist leadership to allow a group of desperate inmates to 'vent their pent-up emotions' (H. Jin 2004: 235); in Zhang's, the demonstration is driven by unalloyed patriotism.[6]

According to the first fictional account, the lives of 'suicidally blind' inmates are placed at risk solely for the benefit of their leaders; in the second account, which is found in the memoir, the Party members put their own lives at risk in order to protect the lives of the other inmates. What Yuan does not consider in writing off the flag-raising incident as absurd is its significance for the inmates. For many Chinese Communist prisoners, men who had been constantly harassed by their US guards, raising their national flag and singing the national anthem on enemy territory had a symbolic value that they believed was worth the risk of their lives. Viewed in this light, the most salient difference between Yuan and the other inmates is that these inmates identify unproblematically with the national symbols of their native land and draw moral sustenance from it. In contrast, Yuan does not.

When Yuan, in his account, belittles the Communist inmates' risking of their lives for the sake of a red flag, he is obviously not with them. To put it differently, when he comments that the combat preparations of the Communist prisoners derive from a sense of 'resolve . . . mixed with desperation', the analysis speaks more of his own conflicted psychology: he wishes to purge himself of the stigma of being mere 'war trash', a term referring to disgraced soldiers who have failed to uphold their pledge to resist capture by means of death, by participating in the commemorative act of patriotic loyalty, while, at one and the same time, he despairs at the futility of the symbolic action, which appears to him to be 'suicidally' self-defeating. One of the reasons why the flag-raising incident appears this way is that Yuan views collective struggle through a thoroughly individualist set of lenses, discounting the effects of publicity in the international arena. For one who shares neither the enthusiasm nor the loyalty of his comrades, and who, perhaps as a result, is opposed to individual sacrifice for a collective cause, the entire incident, deemed

140   *The Korean War Novel*

'heroic' by most of his comrades, comes across as merely desperate or even insane.

The history of the Korean War suggests that the 1 October demonstrations on Geoje and Jeju possessed a dual importance. On the one hand, these incidents aided the repatriation agenda of the Chinese delegation during the truce negotiations. In fact, the US delegation, in order to justify voluntary repatriation, had repeatedly claimed that the Communist POWs did not want to be repatriated. The flag-raising incidents, whose main purpose was to protest against the forcible repatriation screening, served to counter this claim. These incidents also helped the Communist leadership on Jeju to unify men who, since being relocated, had felt lost, completely cut off from the outside world. Most importantly, the Communist inmates on Jeju volunteered for the self-sacrificial task not simply because they had been duped by their leaders or had become blindly desperate but rather because, to quote David Cheng Chang, 'the worsening condition in the prison convinced many of the need for immediate action' (2020a: 305). It seems undeniable that the collective and international dimensions of the flag-flying incident have been completely edited out of Yuan's self-centred narrative.

Solipsism

In critically assessing prison politics, Yuan tends to project, consciously or unconsciously, his own hopes or despair onto his fellow inmates. In turn, this projection serves to reinforce the protagonist's belief in liberal individualism. It is this self-justifying process that defines Yuan's individualism as somewhat solipsistic. The protagonist's solipsism is best seen in his psychological or psychologising probing of Commissar Pei's motives concerning the prisoners' collective struggles. When the US camp authorities inform the inmates of Compound 602 of their decision to relocate them to Jeju Island, the inmates become worried. Their anxiety is escalated by the rumour that the Taiwanese Nationalist Army is receiving combat training on Jeju before its entry into the war. For the Communist inmates, this news means that they will soon be completely at the mercy of the pro-Nationalists. To make things worse, the US Command, having found out about the commissar's existence, has been searching for him. However, since many Chinese POWs, including Pei, have used aliases during their captivity, the US authorities are having difficulties identifying the commissar. For this reason, the Communist inmates have become anxious at the prospect that the guards might try to separate them from their main leader, by taking advantage of the

The Politics of Neutrality   **141**

confusion involved in the relocation process. At a compound meeting, a majority of the leadership committee proposes that they resist relocation, while Pei finds himself alone in advising against it. Pei defends this position out of a sense of prudence, pointing out that as yet they have no definite information about the situation on Jeju. When other leaders insist on the importance of immediate collective struggle, the commissar suggests a compromise: no one should move unless the guards decide to move in first and that no blood should be spilt, if possible. This peaceful plan of resistance initially impresses Yuan deeply:

> I was impressed by the compromise plan he had made. Then the thought occurred to me that he might have argued for peace for *personal reasons*. A full-blown confrontation would have put him at a disadvantage. If he fell into the Americans' hands, they might punish him more for the resistance he had masterminded. Enraged, they could cripple or even kill him and then blame it on an accident. In other words, *he must have been fearful, worried about his personal safety*, knowing that without his thousands of men around him, he would be at the enemy's mercy. (H. Jin 2004: 198; emphasis added)

In this psychological analysis, Yuan places Pei in a catch-22 situation. According to Yuan, if he decides to put up a fight against the evacuation plan, Pei can be criticised for sacrificing his men for personal interests. Contrariwise, if he opts for a peaceful resolution, as he eventually does, Pei opens himself up to the criticism that he is simply putting his personal interests first. This is because by not provoking the American guards, Pei maximises his chances of avoiding harsh punishment. Yuan's construal of the supposed ulterior motives of the commissar is based on his surmise that Pei 'must have been fearful, worried about his personal safety'. In formulating this conjecture-rich analysis, the protagonist may be seen to be speaking of himself, the individualist preoccupied with saving his own skin, even if he dares not express this concern openly. An example of this kind of thinking is revealed in an earlier sentiment of Yuan: 'I was agitated but dared not say anything, fearing the accusation of cowardice' (H. Jin 2004: 235).

Later when he decides to raise the red flag on Jeju on Chinese National Day, Pei opts for armed resistance against the expected intervention of the US guards. Once again, Yuan is hard at work, trying to ascertain the commissar's ulterior motive:

> By now I was certain I had divined Commissar Pei's motives, which also revealed his weakness. He seemed to have lost his composure and patience and could no longer wait. He wanted to be considered by our negotiators at Panmunjom without further delay. There was another element in his anxiety which wasn't easy to discern, namely that like a regular prisoner here, he

142   *The Korean War Novel*

> too was at sea about what to do. The POWs all looked up to him, depending on his directives and believing he was their backbone; what they didn't know was that he needed a lot of backing himself . . . Another thought also occurred to me about Pei's fear. He must have been afraid that his captivity had tarnished his image in the Party's eyes. Probably he needed a battle to achieve something that would change the Party's opinion of him. (H. Jin 2004: 237)

It is an open question whether the various motives that Yuan ascribes to Pei's decision to opt for active resistance have any substance. Regardless of whether each ascribed motive is true or not, each one of these conjectures is meant to justify the protagonist's own individualist outlook. One method for assessing Yuan's own motives is to re-examine each of the scenarios he rehearses. In the first scenario, the commissar, chafing under the strain of prolonged captivity, may have decided to attract the attention of the Chinese Communist government to the dire situation of the POWs by means of armed struggle. This would seem a fairly natural response, and to that extent may well be plausible. However, it would seem doubtful that such a motive can be called either ulterior or personal. This is because if the signal, whether sent out from motives of distress or loyalty, moves the Chinese government into action, the fruits of this action will be enjoyed by all the Chinese POWs. In the second scenario, the commissar, despite appearing to be calm, has been secretly worried about and wants to redeem his tarnished reputation as a POW. This is also not an improbable situation. Indeed, the commissar has good reasons to be worried about his future. This is because, following their return to China, the Chinese POWs will be treated as 'war trash' and party members like Pei will receive even harsher treatment than non-party members. Finally, Yuan conjectures that the commissar may have become anxious and restless because he has not received fresh instructions from his superiors. However, the protagonist does not offer any evidence for this conjecture. In sum, whether true or not, each of the conjectures that point to the commissar's anxieties about the abandonment, isolation and uncertainty of his post-repatriation future in China speak no less of the protagonist's own emotions. That is to say, the proffered psychological analysis reveals more about the working motives of the analyst than it does about the projected motives of the analysand.

Indeed, the tendency of Yuan to project his emotional turmoil onto Pei is detectible in several other episodes of the novel as well. For example, when neither the international press nor the Chinese government appears to take notice of the US prison authorities' massacre of sixty-three Chinese POWs during the Chinese National Day commemoration, Yuan becomes restless. He feels as if 'this island were a deserted corner forgotten by the world', believing that 'our country had forsaken us' (H. Jin 2004: 244). Typically, he projects his own anxiety onto the commissar: 'Pei too was apprehensive, probably more so than they [his men] were, because he had no superior to rely on' (H. Jin 2004: 244–5). Indeed, the protagonist's abandonment anxiety may be traced to a deeper source. Earlier, when Compound 72 was being run by the pro-Nationalists, Han Shu, the Chief of the POW regiment, waged a psychological campaign against all of the Communist inmates, including Yuan. Han Shu reminds his Communist audience of the miserable fate awaiting them in their mother country: 'you must prepare to go through denunciations, corporal punishment, prison terms, and executions once you're back in our homeland' (H. Jin 2004: 103). This speech shakes the audience up because it taps into their nagging fears about post-repatriation life in China. The Communist prisoners painfully recollect that they broke the pledge they had made that they would keep their honour by death rather than be captured by the enemy; and they become greatly scared of the prospect of the severe punishments waiting for them. Given the gravity of this 'original sin', the Communist POWs have every reason to suspect that their mother country may find it unworthy to bring home the 'war trashes' whom it considers traitors; and Yuan is poignantly aware that he is not an exception to the fate of this unworthy lot. Also, Yuan has another serious reason to worry about his future that most of his fellow Communist inmates do not share: his 'reactionary' past as a cadet at the Huangpu Military Academy. In this regard, the protagonist is haunted by an agonising anxiety that whatever he does, whatever sacrifices he makes, he may not be accepted by the Communists as one of their own.

As Xiang maintains, in recording his inmates' behaviour and activities, Yuan 'becomes openly ethnographic' (2018: 88). He observes his object closely but remains emotionally distant from it and practises a form of psychological profiling on his fellow inmates. However, in the process, Yuan equally reveals his own psychological profile. This is because Yuan habitually projects his own motives onto others. His psychological reporting serves as an alibi for his own individualistic desires: it serves to justify his urge for repatriation and his reluctance to participate in high-risk collective struggle. In this sense, both Cumings' and Xie's view of the narrator as a 'fair, discerning observer' with a 'detached perspective' (Cumings 2010: 75; Xie 2012: 39) seem misplaced.

There are many similarities between the account offered in Zhang's memoirs and Jin's novel. What is just as interesting are some of the ways in which the two literary texts differ. In Jin's opinion, the Chinese Communist government betrayed the POWs who chose to repatriate by

144   *The Korean War Novel*

labelling them 'traitors' and destroying both their lives and the lives of their immediate families. Back in China, for instance, every one of the returnees is discharged dishonourably; every Communist loses his Party membership. Pei is treated as 'war trash' and sent out to a rural provincial area to live as a rice farmer, while Ming begins earning a living by carrying water buckets for a bath house. Zhang's memoir, by contrast, tells its readers nothing about the harsh treatment of the repatriates by the Chinese government. Even though the sixteenth chapter of Zhang's memoir describes his life after repatriation, it says nothing about how all the returnees, including himself, were deprived of their Party cards and other privileges. It was left to another writer to reveal the difficulties that Zhang underwent once he returned to his motherland. According to Jin Daying, '[i]n 1959, [Zhang] was labelled a member of the rightist traitor clique and thrown into jail because he and his comrade-in-arms, Jiang Reifu, along with several others, wrote a letter complaining of the unfair treatment of the 6,000 POWs. Because of this, his beloved girl friend [*sic*] deserted him' (1993: 396). The staunch Communist inmates who resisted with their lives the advance of the US tanks in order to protect the red flags in the POW camp were no exception to this treatment. Peng Lin, one of the inmates who had protected their national flag during the Communist demonstration in the Jeju POW Camp, died by suicide after being labelled 'an American spy' and having 'his property confiscated' (D. Jin 1993: 397).

The politics of writing small histories

In *War Trash*, Jin tells his readers about the Chinese Civil War that continued between pro-Nationalist and Communist inmates in the US-controlled POW camps. The central issue around which this war revolved was the repatriation of the POWs. The issue had dramatic political repercussions in the international arena, keeping the truce talks going for nearly two years. The armistice negotiations began in the city of Kaesŏng on 10 July 1951, with the two delegations swapping their mutual POW lists on 18 December, five months later. However, the US and China were unable to sign a proper treaty until 27 July 1953. The negotiations were drawn out over the issue of the prisoner exchange as a result of two interrelated issues: the first was the great disparity in the number of the POWs held by the South (132,194) when compared with the number held by the North (11,559). Obviously, in an all-for-all exchange, this would have offered the Communist forces a huge advantage in military strength;[7] the second issue was the unbridgeable line

The Politics of Neutrality   **145**

of division between the US proposal of voluntary repatriation and the Chinese one of repatriation by force.

With the majority of the Chinese POWs refusing repatriation, this issue became the site of a moral war in which both the US/South Korea and China/North Korea competed to prove the superiority of their political systems. As Foot maintains, victory in this competition offered itself as compensation for the military victory that neither of the two sides could win on the battlefield (1990: 220–1). With an overwhelming number of the Chinese inmates renouncing repatriation, the US, in the words of Allen Dulles, the director of the Central Intelligence Agency, congratulated itself on 'one of the greatest psychological victories so far achieved by the free world against Communism' (qtd in Foot 1990: 190).

This moral war had major repercussions for both regional and global geopolitical dynamics. To quote Monica Kim, the issue of repatriation held out large benefits in terms of the ideological rivalry on the Korean peninsula:

> The presence of two states on the Korean peninsula, one created under Soviet military occupation, the other under US military occupation after liberation from Japanese colonial rule in 1945, literally created a competition between [*sic*] which type of putative decolonization was valid, effective, and democratic. After the 1948 elections in the south, the United States and the United Nations declared the southern Republic of Korea the only sovereign state on the peninsula. For the United States, to have prisoners of war choose to not repatriate to the northern Democratic People's Republic of Korea would be to validate the US project of liberation through military occupation in the south. (2019: 9)

From this perspective, the exact number of North Korean inmates who renounced repatriation was important: a large POW cohort turning their back on communism would serve to justify US military actions dating back to the US occupation of the Korean peninsula following the defeat of Japan. For China, the issue of repatriation was somewhat similar, except that losing this numbers game would be a setback in its competition with Taiwan for national legitimacy. No less importantly, a psychological victory in this war would serve the US administration's interests by deterring a future war with the Soviet Union. The Soviet leadership would see only too clearly that it too might suffer a similar kind of troop defection in the event of battle (Foot 1990: 198–9). In short, the issue of repatriation had become an integral 'part of America's containment policy' (Foot 1990: 198–9).

It is in the context of international politics that Jin's critical rewriting of the Korean War as a Chinese Civil War resonates most strongly,

146   *The Korean War Novel*

with a significance not limited only to the Korean peninsula but affecting much of East Asia. By focalising Yuan as an 'outsider' within the ranks of the Chinese Communist inmates, the author carries out his project to neutralise the politics of the Cold War, by both exposing the hypocrisy and inhumanity of Communism and criticising the US Command and its allies for their sanctioning of anti-communist terror. In the words of Daniel Y. Kim, in this novel, '[t]he ultimate finger of blame is thus pointed at all the foreign soldiers'; it is necessary not only to criticise the governments of the United States and the People's Republic of China but also to question severely the motives of the soldiers, the 'war trash' themselves (2020: 240). While his analysis of US Cold War propaganda is legitimate, Yuan's debunking of the myth of communist comradery appears to be jeopardised by his unquestioningly individualistic outlook.

At another level, Jin's *War Trash* is a novel that deals with the protagonist's *bildung* as a critical, autonomous individual. Paradoxically, this does not mean that the story does not espouse a political position for itself. It does. The protagonist's prioritising of personal interests over collective causes aligns him with the doctrine of liberalism whose credo is to maximise an individual's rights without impinging on the rights of others. This ideology separates itself from both communitarianism and communism in its flat denial of the idea of sacrifice for the common good. In the narrative of Yuan, the novel consistently takes the side of a protagonist who projects his personal motives onto others, convincing himself in the process that everyone else shares a similar set of motivations. In consequence, the Communist POW leadership appears reduced to an accidental grouping of self-seeking individuals. In a similar line of argument, the struggles of the inmates under Communist leadership appear as forms of exploitation in which the men receive no benefit or are obliged to aid leaders who are pursuing their personal interests at the expense of the collective. It is in this characterisation of the Communist Party that Yuan sheds his political neutrality. As a narrator, he offers only a caricature of Communist motivation, depriving the characters of all sense of political conviction and advocating in its stead the apparently no-nonsense ideology of liberal individualism.

When he declares that all he wanted to do in *War Trash* was to deliver 'the truth' about the Korean War, Jin implies not only that the past that is recalled in this novel is historically accurate ('I changed the names, but the situations all happened as I wrote about them' [Rightmyer 2004: 48]) but also that his work delivers 'the truth' by offering a series of small histories that have largely been silenced or overlooked. Nonetheless, in the novel, the claim to know and speak 'the truth' must reckon with the idea that the past is rarely available in a transparent form. Since it is a form of writing that does not exist apart from its literary modes of narrative, history, in this sense, comes into being only through and after interpretation (Jameson 1981: 81). It is always the task of the author to organise and interpret that set of historical facts. In the terms of Hayden White, as the author does this, they must necessarily draw upon, whether consciously or unconsciously, their own set of generic, explanatory and ideological preferences (1973: 29–34). In *War Trash*, this reconfiguration of the 'raw data' into novelistic form is most conspicuous when Yuan, believing himself to be politically neutral or disinterested, nonetheless views the collective struggles in the POW camp through the lens of liberal individualism. Believing that liberal individualism is politically neutral or disinterested involves accepting, perhaps unconsciously, this Western ideology as the default epistemology of the world. In the event, the historical context against which the work of any artist unfolds will be a narrative designed to satisfy a set of political and formalistic needs. In a historical novel like *War Trash*, the truth a writer conveys is a truth that they have already half-created. Regardless of the set of historical facts that writers seek to marshal, the act of (re)interpretation is unavoidable.

Notes

1. Jin claims that in writing *War Trash*, he used *Personal Records in the American Prison Camp*, a memoir by Zhang Zeshi. To Chen Li's accusation that he pilfered around 10,000 words from Zhang's work, Jin replied that Zhang 'contributed a chapter on the abduction of General Dodd' (Xie 2012: 41, note 2). In total, Zhang published five memoirs that have similar content. In this book, I used for comparison a Korean translation of Zhang's full-length war memoir, *Wo de Chaoxian zhanzheng: yige zhiyuanjun zhanfu de zishu* [My Korean War: A Volunteer Army POW's Memoir] (Beijing: Shishi chubanshe 2000). This memoir was translated by Son Chunsik in 2009: *Chunggukkun p'oroŭi 6·25 ch'amjŏn'gi* [A Chinese POW's Memoir of the Korean War] (Seoul: Institute for Military History, Ministry of Korean Military Defense, 2009). For more details about the plagiarism issue, see Tsu 2010: 108–9.
2. The note on the photo taken by G. Dimitri Boria reads: 'With the idea of spying in mind, this young North Korean Communist POW joined the anti-Communists in their compound on Koje-do, Korea. After five months had passed, he requested of US officials to return him to his "real" friends in the Communist compound. Upon hearing of this the non-Communist POW's, in lieu of executing him, tattooed the South Korean flag on his chest, and "anti-Communist" and "Against Russia" on each of his arms before returning him to the Communist compound'.

148   *The Korean War Novel*

3. As David Cheng Chang reports, the CIE programmes were called 'anti-Communist schools' by the Communist inmates, whereas they were termed 'schools of democracy' by the anti-Communists. The CIE schools in Compounds 72 and 86 were 'indoctrination program[s]' aiming to 'inculcate a more favorable attitude among POWs toward western and democratic ways and to instil [a] distrust of communist ideology' (2020: 201).

4 In this incident, the Brothers attacked the pro-Nationalists, and the ensuing melee mobilised more than 1,000 prisoners who fought against one another with clubs and rocks. The battle was ended by the intervention of the US guards, but the Brothers paid a heavy price later, in the form of arrests by the US guards and torture at the hands of the pro-Nationalists (D. C. Chang 2020: 197–8).

5. In Min Kyung Kil's account, this number refers to the group of POWs who were repatriated in Operation Big Switch of September 1953. It excludes the 1,030 sick and wounded Chinese POWs who returned earlier to their home country in the earlier Operation Little Switch of April 1953, along with the 469 inmates who later switched from non-repatriation to repatriation (Min 1997: 4). In Rosemary Foot's slightly different account, a total of 16,000 out of the 21,000 Chinese POWs chose Taiwan, while only 5,000 were repatriated. For more details, see Foot 1985: 175.

6. A more direct comparison is provided by another work of literary reportage by Jin Daying, which records the flag-raising event on Jeju in the following terms:

> The POWs were in tears as they looked up at the Red Flags. As they saw the Red Flags waving in the dark POW camps over the foreign soil, they felt as if they had seen their own motherland and relatives. The National Flags have been dyed red from the blood of the POWs. While constructing the National Flags, they were short of red dye. The POWs cut open their arms and beat upon their noses with their own fists. Thus the red dye was their own blood. (D. Jin 1993: 284–5)

7. According to Stueck's count, the numbers are estimated as 150,000 versus 10,000 ([1995] 1997: 212). In the view of the US Command, an all-for-all exchange would have restored the enemy's military strength back to when they started the aggression. Returning all the prisoners, some would argue, would give the enemy 'an advantage of 12 divisions' (D. C. Chang 2020: 219).

Chapter 5

Beyond the Cold War?

Choi In-hun (1936–2018) was born in Hoeryŏng city in North Hamgyŏng Province, a region that now forms part of North Korea. When the Korean War broke out, he fled with his family to South Korea. In 1952, Choi entered Seoul National University as a law major, but dropped out in 1956. From 1958 to 1963, he served as an interpreting officer in the South Korean army; and it was during this time in the military that he started to publish his stories. *The Square* (1960 in Korean, 2014 in English), the first work to earn him fame as a writer, was published during this period. This novella, which was first serialised in the Korean literary magazine *Saebyŏk* (Dawn) in November 1960, received general critical acclaim. Critics praised him for his scathing critique of the social realities of both the Communist and the democratic regimes that were then ruling a divided Korean peninsula. Choi expanded the story into a full-length novel, revising it as much as ten times.[1] He received many literary awards, including the Tongin Literary Award, the Isan Literary Award and the Best Playwright Prize of the Hankook Theatre and Film Awards. Choi is considered one of the first Korean writers who 'capture[d] the ideological battles that took place during the second half of the twentieth century' ('Author Choi In-hun' 2018). Besides *The Square*, *A Grey Man* (1963) and *House of Idols* (2003) are among his many works that are available in English. Many of Choi's works, from *The Square* and *A Grey Man* to *Keyword* (1994), probe the nature of the ideological confrontations that swept the Korean peninsula into tragic turmoil.

Choi's *The Square* interlaces two narratives: the first concerns the protagonist's voyage to India, the country he has chosen at the POWs repatriation screening during the Korean War; the second is the back story that revolves around his decision to defect to North Korea. In the late fall of 1948, Lee Myong-jun is a junior college student majoring in philosophy. Ever since his mother passed away, Myong-jun has been

150 *The Korean War Novel*

living with the family of Mr Pyon Song-che, his father's good friend. After national liberation, Lee Hyong-do, the protagonist's father, one of the two founders of the Namno Party (the Communist Labour Party in the South), goes to the North, disappearing for a time. When later a speech by Myong-jun's father is broadcasted as propaganda in the South, the Korean National Police come after the son, accusing him of spying for the Communists. After being brutally tortured by the police, the protagonist seeks comfort in an intimate relationship with Yun-ae, a young woman that Mr Pyon's daughter Yong-mi introduces to him. Without breathing a word about his intentions to his new-found love, he surprisingly defects to the North, reunites with his father and starts a new life as an editorial staff member at *The Labour Daily*. Nonetheless, he soon becomes disillusioned with the Communist regime. Once again, he finds solace in an intimate relationship with a young woman, this time a ballerina named Un-hye who works for the National Theatre. When the Korean War breaks out, Myong-jun is conscripted as a political officer. Captured by the UN army, he is thrown into the US POW camp. At the repatriation screening, he opts to sail for a neutral third nation. The novel ends with Myong-jun's suicide during the voyage to India.

In *The Square*, Choi focuses on the ideological trajectory of his hero. The focus shifts from his early critique of the capitalist South for its uncritical adoption of the hegemonic ideology of the United States, through his subsequent disillusionment with the Communist North, to his final apparent decision to live in a neutral third country at the repatriation screening. By portraying the protagonist turning his back against the repressive regimes of both the South and the North and of his regression into the 'private chamber' of two personal relationships, the author attempts to explore the dysfunctional status of the 'political square' both south and north of the thirty-eighth parallel. However, in the novel, the protagonist is not depicted as a simple victim of political tyranny who deserves the reader's unreserved sympathy. This political victim also turns out to be a tyrant. That is, within the privacy of his bedroom, Myong-jun reproduces the tyranny of the political square. Choi questions the practice of automatically associating the political victim with righteousness, as saliently witnessed in the ideology of 'victimhood nationalism'. The novel also explores the origins of the subsequent deadly confrontation between the two Korean regimes in the larger superpower conflict between the US and the Soviets. *The Square* is also fundamentally critical of the Cold War. It gropes toward an alternative space beyond its ideological boundaries. In his choice of exile in a neutral third country, the novel's protagonist upholds the vision of

Beyond the Cold War? **151**

a decentred Cold War, an escape from the political binarism that still traps his fellow countrymen. Nonetheless, the author highlights the difficulty of this choice in the image of the protagonist's suicide during his voyage toward an apparently freer life.

Life in a coffin

The Square takes place over the course of about five years, from late 1948 to early 1954. At the beginning of the protagonist's back story, in the late fall of 1948, Myong-jun appears haunted by a sense of inner emptiness, the feeling that his life does not genuinely belong to him. He feels that something important is missing, but he cannot pinpoint what this is, no matter how hard he tries. Even when he diverts himself with Yong-mi's amiable companionship, a young woman for whom 'life seem[s] synonymous with fun' (I.-H. Choi [1960] 1985: 13), Myong-jun finds it impossible to prevent himself from experiencing a lack of fulfilment:

> Usually he went wherever she [Yong-mi] asked. But at the same time, no matter where they went, he couldn't bear the sense of being out of place which he felt. It wasn't the weariness that comes after eating one's fill, but rather from the outset it was an impatience which said *It can't be like this, it isn't like this* . . . [H]e sensed very clearly that the life he saw around him was not what he was looking for. (I.-H. Choi [1960] 1985: 14; emphasis in the original)

As a university student, he has no great complaints about his life, particularly because he is being supported by the generous patronage of Mr Pyon, the banker. Indeed, he enjoys the hospitality of Mr Pyon's family, especially the friendship of his two children, Tae-sik and Yong-mi. And yet, he is painfully aware that the life he is currently living is not exactly the one he wants. What is even more frustrating is that he cannot figure out the kind of life that would make him happy. He only knows that something crucial is wrong with his life and that this provokes the constant feeling: '*It can't be like this*'.

At first, the protagonist turns to books for wisdom in an effort to find guidance for his restlessness, some solace to fill 'the emptiness inside him' (I.-H. Choi [1960] 1985: 22). In consequence of his spending on books, Myong-jun soon finds himself in possession of a major collection, a treasury of about 400 classic texts. According to this university student, the experience of reading the old masters gives him both a sense of 'gratifying victory' and a sense of security '[l]ike armour protecting

152 *The Korean War Novel*

his naked body' (I.-H. Choi [1960] 1985: 22). Nonetheless, if he initially feels that reading books better equips him to deal with life, the sense of accomplishment and security he acquires does not last long. Each time, the unfailing return of emptiness prods him to seek new adventures, fresh diversions. It is while he is experiencing the need for new spiritual fulfilment that Myong-jun visits a certain Mr Chong. His purpose in visiting is to view the Egyptian mummy that is on display at Mr Chong's house. He is obviously attracted to the idea of seeing this surviving human relic from an ancient civilisation. When he finally views the mummy, the remains of what was, according to Mr Chong, a once noble lady, he cannot help trembling. Myong-jun explains his own response by observing that he felt 'as if moss-grown majestic time had flown with a cry into his body' (I.-H. Choi [1960] 1985: 31). Myong-jun's observation highlights the flight of the 'moss-grown majestic time' or, perhaps, the idea of time travel itself as the reason that the sight of the mummy impacts his senses with such force. This suggests that the protagonist's main interest in the human relic is triggered not so much by his idle curiosity about past ages as by his desire to escape from his own personal frustrations, the cause of which he cannot pin down.

The final edition that Choi oversaw, the one that was published in 2010, registers an intriguing change from the earlier editions used by his translators, Kevin O'Rourke and Kim Seong-kon. In the final edition of the novel, the protagonist does not in fact view the mummy in Mr Chong's house. Instead, Myong-jun finds a coffin in the shape of a human form, with a picture of the embalmed person drawn on the surface of the casket. When Mr Chong eventually opens the lid, Myong-jun finds that it is empty (I.-H. Choi [1960] 2010: 58). By means of this careful revision, the author highlights the symbolic resemblance between the protagonist and the mummy, this figure of an ancient time traveller. In this rewritten version, the protagonist and the absent noblewoman mirror each other in the way in which they find themselves stuck in the wrong place at the wrong time. The casket has nothing to show but a human lookalike painted on the outer casing to represent what remains of her. In his examination of his own empty-shell-like existence, Myong-jun regularly attempts to reach inside himself, only to find emptiness. As seen in Kim Seong-kon's translation, the figural resemblance is reinforced when the protagonist meditates at a later point on his life in the US POW camp on Geoje Island:

> In fact, all of his private chambers had been empty since Eun-hye [Un-hye] left for Moscow. All the empty rooms seemed to stem from the empty mummy's coffin he saw at Chung [Chong]'s house. It was like the Russian

Beyond the Cold War? **153**

nesting doll, which had another doll inside, and another inside of that, and so on to infinity.

Geoje Island, which was located in the south of the peninsula, was also like a coffin. It was the coffin where dead soldiers labeled as prisoners of war lay down and fell asleep every night, like sardines in a can. Myong-jun was simply one of the helpless fish tied up in a pack. Inside his body, lay coffins within coffins. Nestled in the infinite depths was the mummy's coffin he saw at Chung's house. Beyond the emptiness of the mummy's coffin was yet another coffin – the one in the deepest place in his mind. Suddenly he realized the empty casing was his. *Was this bleak coffin the final destination of my life?* He wondered. (I.-H. Choi [1960] 2014: 136–7; emphasis in the original)

By likening the US POW camp to a gigantic coffin that holds 'dead' bodies, the author lays stress on the confined, demoralised state of the KPA inmates. At the same time, given the protagonist's criticism of the North Korean leadership, Choi implies that these KPA soldiers are not committed revolutionaries who have freely chosen their destinies but rather zombie-like beings conditioned to act on Party orders. Like his fellow inmates, Myong-jun feels that inside him there are only 'coffins within coffins'. If the coffin he saw at Mr Chong's was a mere simulacrum of its owner, carved in the shape of the dead and with an accompanying full-length image drawn on the casket, the protagonist now suggests that each inmate is no more than a sum of multiple icons in human form like 'Russian nesting [dolls]'. If the reader expands this metaphor of POW camp as coffin, it is possible to imagine that the Korean peninsula itself takes the shape of a giant coffin too, with each one of its citizens trapped in the death house of the regional hot war of the Cold War.

In this and other passages, Myong-jun emphasises his sense of inner 'emptiness'. What is odd, however, is that while he stresses feeling hollow inside, he simultaneously insists that he does not lack a sense of self. Indeed, his belief in his sense of self is expressed at one point in clear Cartesian terms:

The word *self* did not contain such things as food, shoes, socks, clothes, blankets, a place to sleep, fees, cigarettes, an umbrella . . . Rather, self was what was left when all these things were taken away. However, after doubting everything, there was one final thing left which he couldn't doubt. This was the self which he could feel. This was meaningful to Lee Myong-jun, conceptual philosopher's egg. His father was not a part of the make-up of self. His mother couldn't be a family member of self. Myong-jun was alone in the room of self. Self was not a square. It was a room. (I.-H. Choi [1960] 1985: 39; emphasis in the original)

What is worth noting here is the way in which Myong-jun conceives of himself in spatial terms; that is, as a private room. When Mr Pyon

154   *The Korean War Novel*

speaks of Myong-jun's father, someone about whose existence he has all but forgotten, the protagonist does not feel himself related to him in any way. He thinks of his 'self' as 'a room' that lets in no one but himself. Even the immediate members of his family are not entitled to enter this space. Nonetheless, if it is a sacrosanct place necessary for an individual, it is also a lonely and confining one: Myong-jun compares it to a 'solitary confinement for a prisoner which permits no revenge' (I.-H. Choi [1960] 1985: 39–40).[2] It is this duality of the self – at once both a solitary cell and a bulwark against outside interference – that places the protagonist in an ambivalent relationship with the world. He selectively allows certain outsiders – his lovers, for example – to enter this otherwise solitary room. And while, as long as life lasts, the Other may help to fill out the dimensions of this solitary space, not even love can solve for good the profound feeling of being 'out of place' or of experiencing that other sense of the self as a series of shell-encased experiences of emptiness.

The reason for Myong-jun's obsession with being 'out of place' may actually be found in his earlier conversation with Mr Chong. The protagonist asks Mr Chong, who is twice as old as he is, for some advice about 'living a full life' (I.-H. Choi [1960] 1985: 31). Their dialogue naturally turns to what it is like to live in South Korea. At this point, the protagonist confides to Mr Chong his candid, almost sardonic views, which have become famous among Korean critics and readers. These views concern the major public sectors of the South or, to frame it using the terms he would employ, the political, the economic and the cultural square. In the opinion of this philosophy major, human beings cannot live inside closed chambers. They need broad squares in which the public may come out and freely participate in interpersonal or communal transactions. But only closed chambers exist in the South: each of these squares has lost its function as a healthy public realm. There are reasons why these public squares have disappeared:

> In the Korean political square dung, urine, and garbage are heaped on piles. Things that should be for common use like roadside flowers are picked and put in a flower-pot at home, or the tap is taken from a fountain and installed in one's own washroom, or a pavement is dug up and put down as a floor in the kitchen.
>
> When Korean politicians come into the political square they bring a gunny-sack, an axe and a shovel, their faces hidden behind a mask. They are coming to steal of course. If a good passer-by tries to stop this, gangs . . . suddenly spring out of the lane, which leads from the square, and destroy him with a single thrust. (I.-H. Choi [1960] 1985: 32–3)

Beyond the Cold War?   **155**

In Myong-jun's opinion, the political square in the South is under the control of corrupt politicians in collusion with thugs. It is only natural that with public thievery and rightist terror rampant, the political square has been deserted. Running away from the source of terror, men hide in private chambers for mere survival. The economic square is not much different. According to the protagonist,

> The square of economics is overflowing with stolen goods. All stolen goods. There is a bag of potatoes there which was taken from a farmer who refused to let go and had his thin arm slashed off at the wrist with an axe. There is a cabbage stained with blood there. A dress hangs there that was stripped from a raped woman's body; it is torn and stained with semen. (I.-H. Choi [1960] 1985: 33)

For Myong-jun, South Korea is not even a proper capitalist society because its economy is run on the basis of violent, mass-scale thievery by the powerful. The cultural square receives as biting an assessment from the hero: 'there the cultivation of opium flowers is at its peak' (I.-H. Choi [1960] 1985: 33).

At the end of his conversation with Mr Chong, Myong-jun emphasises again that the square in the South is 'dead' while elsewhere 'secret rooms abound' (I.-H. Choi [1960] 1985: 34). That is, both rightist terror and naked exploitation shut down the public sectors that are sustainable only by means of the genuine, voluntary participation of the people. Myong-jun's diagnosis of the death of the public realm in the South points to the possibility that his fixation on feeling trapped inside a shell or being 'out of place' may be related to a flawed process of his ideological 'becoming'. This is particularly true when the reader considers that an individual's sense of identity is created through their interactions, public and private, with others rather than in a socio-political vacuum. In a commentary on the subjecthood of the black Caribbean, Stuart Hall propounds the idea of identity as a process of historical becoming. According to Hall, 'cultural identity is not a fixed essence at all, lying unchanged outside history and culture. It is not some universal and transcendental spirit inside us on which history has made no fundamental mark' (Hall 1990: 226). The idea of identity as an upshot of a ceaseless series of social interactions casts light on a certain lack in Myong-jun's upbringing.

According to the novel, as a child during the Japanese colonial period, Myong-jun was living in Manchuria. Probably as a result of his father's involvement in the independence movement, his family had to move semi-periodically from city to city. His father would be gone for months at a time and then reappear suddenly out of nowhere (I.-H. Choi [1960] 1985: 40-1). As a result, for the majority of his formative years, the

156   *The Korean War Novel*

protagonist lived like a drifter, unable to make stable connections with the social environment, never mind being able to form a place-based identity from out of them. The convulsive nature of the society that emerged in the South during the period of the US military occupation and the first term of the Rhee regime proved themselves unable to provide a stable point of identification for the protagonist either. Myong-jun's early experience of paternal abandonment, his subsequent life as a social drifter, the failure of the protagonist to be provided with a symbolic father in the form of the dictatorial government of Syngman Rhee: each of these experiences appears to have disrupted, rather than assisted, the protagonist's ideological or political becoming, making him feel 'out of place' and even rebellious. Lacking a stable point of identification, Myong-jun is like a rebel without a cause.

The links, however nominal or fragile, that Myong-jun might have forged with the hegemonic ideology of the South are completely shattered after he is subjected to brutal anti-communist persecution at the hands of the South Korean National Police. Before he is tortured, Myong-jun believes that he will be allowed some privacy, however circumscribed, as long as he stays out of politics and occupies himself instead with small things, such as '[c]ultivating flowers at the window, hanging soft curtains, having a shiny, polished desk and bed' (I.-H. Choi [1960] 1985: 40). After he is tortured, however, he comes to realise that private chambers in the South lack walls that seal them off from the outside world. The protagonist discovers too late that the private chamber has a door that allows the terrorists who gather in the political square private access: '[t]he door of self which he had believed so strong had been opened discourteously without a knock and the ruffian who had intruded with muddy shoes had beaten him at will' (I.-H. Choi [1960] 1985: 46).

The square populated with marionettes

Following the police interrogation, Myong-jun comes to realise that the individual's right to a private chamber is not guaranteed, even when that individual abdicates his right to take part in the activities of the public square. When an individual gives up his right to participate in public manifestations, he loses the right to a secure private chamber also. This line of thought leads Myong-jun to contemplate how society might best be changed. At this point, he shares with Mr Chong his cherished idea of becoming 'the trumpeter who gathers the citizens into th[e] completely empty square' (I.-H. Choi [1960] 1985: 35). At the same time, he wonders if he is made of sufficiently heroic material to carry out this proposal or, to quote his own words, asks himself whether he has inside of him 'the seeds of living the hero's life and dying the hero's death' (I.-H. Choi [1960] 1985: 53). Sadly, he feels almost immediately that these 'seeds could not flower in a dark square lit by a black sun' (I.-H. Choi [1960] 1985: 53).

Although he eventually chooses to play the role of a trumpeter, Myong-jun raises his trumpet in a different square, the political square of the North. Later, while talking with his father in Pyongyang, he explains his reason for defecting to the North:

> Frankly, it wasn't because of an unbearable longing to see you, Father, either. Nor from fear of interrogation by an ignorant detective. At my age, not having a father doesn't mean one can't live, does it? Also, no matter how they disliked me, would they have killed me just because you were active up here? *I wanted to live.* I wanted to put my youth on fire with a sense of things achieved. *I wanted to live life as it should be lived.* (I.-H. Choi [1960] 1985: 87; emphasis added)

Here, Myong-jun attributes his defection to his desire to 'live'. In the South, he 'wanted to live life as it should be lived' but found it impossible to pursue the dream in 'too dirty gruesome a square'. If this account indicts the regime of the 'free' South for its police brutality and lawlessness, it also explains the reason for the eerie feeling that has haunted him all along, the feeling that has kept whispering to him, *'It can't be like this, it isn't like this'* (I.-H. Choi [1960] 1985: 14).

However, only six months after smuggling himself across the thirty-eighth parallel, the protagonist reaches the sad conclusion that the North has no need of a trumpet player like him. Because he speaks and fights for what he believes, when he is assigned to the editorial department at *The Labour Daily*, he stays late in the company library, reading books about the history of communism. But his attempt at living a new life soon runs aground. What he does not know is that in the North, the Party does all the thinking on behalf of the people. In fact, the Party does this in such a way that nobody can later alter it. All the people need to do is to follow the Party's leadership. For this reason, each time Myong-jun speaks his mind, he accidentally transgresses the bounds of what is considered acceptable Party thought. As a consequence, the chief editor admonishes him for not having yet shed the last vestiges of the reactionary habits of the bourgeois intellectual:

> 'Comrade Lee Myong-jun, you talk as if you alone were thinking of the Republic. If one does as the party orders, this is for the Republic. Put away individualism.'

158   The Korean War Novel

'Ah, ha, the party is telling me not to live. I feel this in everything. That I am not the hero, the party is the hero. Only the party gets excited and intoxicated. It tells us just to repeat and follow. The party will do the thinking, judging, feeling, sighing; all it asks us to do is to repeat and follow ... Everything is left as something once said by an illustrious comrade.' (I.-H. Choi [1960] 1985: 89)

The Communist Party monopolises not only the right to speak but also the right to interpret what it says. In prohibiting people from thinking, the Party, the protagonist feels, might as well order people to cease to exist. Although the revelation comes too late, Myong-jun realises that people in the North are no better than automatons. The protagonist came to the North to fight alongside the other revolutionaries in the political square; instead, he finds 'only placards and slogans' there; the 'new, unstained square' on which he once looked forward to working is actually a 'playground buried beneath a tedious mass game' (I.-H. Choi [1960] 1985: 107).

The economic square of the North is no better. Myong-jun is at first surprised to find that many farmers in the North are not excited about receiving the land confiscated from large landlords. He soon figures out the reason. Since all farmland belongs to the state, individuals cannot buy or sell it; they can only till it. At the same time, they are being constantly pressed to exceed the harvest goals set by the planned economy. In short, both tilling the state-owned land and meeting the ever-increasing production goals mean that the farmers' lives are no better than before. As the protagonist cynically observes, '[t]hey had just changed from being tenants of a landlord to being tenants of the state' (I.-H. Choi [1960] 1985: 95). If capitalist greed has turned the economic square in the South into a jungle where the powerful feed on the weak, the state's taboo on the desire for personal gain has made the square in the North a place where complete indifference has replaced initiative and diligence. As the protagonist sarcastically observes, 'When there is no prize even for first place, who is going to run? Even when they run because the party says run, it's just a pretence of running, a minimal effort' (I.-H. Choi [1960] 1985: 95).

Myong-jun's verdict on the North is scathing: 'in the square there were only marionettes, no people' (I.-H. Choi [1960] 1985: 95). The Communist republic he finds there is a great lie, in which imitation and mockery have usurped whatever was genuine. In the economic square, pretended diligence parades in the name of pretended production quotas. In the political square, likewise, pretended slogans defend a pretended social revolution. Here, even the notion of the revolution is a fake. To quote Myong-jun's derisive remarks: '[n]ot a revolution, but

Beyond the Cold War? **159**

an imitation of a revolution. Not excitement, but an imitation of excitement. Not belief, just a rumour of belief' (I.-H. Choi [1960] 1985: 86). A grim irony for the protagonist is that, although he fled to the North, looking for an alternative to the corrupt capitalist South, he now finds it hard to tell the regime of the North apart from its southern counterpart.

Myong-jun realises that the regimes of both the South and the North are a far cry from their vaunted cries of democracy, with their real ugly faces revealed by their vicious persecution of mere suspect individuals as well as genuine political nonconformists. For instance, in the South, the detectives in the police interrogation room know no legal bounds when they threaten to kill Myong-jun. They carelessly boast that they can easily 'kill a Red bastard' like him (I.-H. Choi [1960] 1985: 44). The unabashed threats of terror on the part of law enforcement officers cause the protagonist to wonder in a language smacking of Agamben's thesis on *homo sacer*: 'Am I outside the law?' (I.-H. Choi [1960] 1985: 44). In the allegedly free nation of the South, those who transgress, or who are merely suspected of transgressing, the ideological boundaries drawn by the anti-communist regime are persecuted up to and even beyond the limits of the law. Deprived of any legal protection, Myong-jun is reduced to what Agamben calls 'a bare life' (Agamben 1998: 9).

But the North does not hesitate to persecute nonconformity either. When Myong-jun writes a field report for his newspaper *The Labour Daily* detailing the difficult lives of the diasporic Korean farmers on a collective farm in southern Manchuria, he is brought in by his card-carrying Communist colleagues to a self-denunciation session. Although he appeals to them that his report is strictly based on the facts he has gathered, his seniors censure him for picking out small faults in order to insult both the heroic farmers and their great cause of 'creating a new history and moving forward towards a shining future' (I.-H. Choi [1960] 1985: 98). On the verge of protesting, Myong-jun realises from the 'angry, hate-twisted, sadistic faces' (I.-H. Choi [1960] 1985: 98–9) of his interrogators that they are not interested in reasoning with him; instead, they require complete obedience. Lacking alternatives, Myong-jun caves in to their demands. In the North, the protagonist undergoes a kind of déjà vu during which he returns to his earlier experience in the police interrogation room in the South. The thought police of both totalitarian regimes make it a rule to break down the door of the citizen's private chamber, trampling on everything in the course of their investigation. The two regimes, in other words, are virtually indistinguishable in the strict curbs they set on the right of the citizen to think for themself, prescribing both what is tolerated and what is forbidden. The only difference is that, in the North, Myong-jun is not subject to

160   The Korean War Novel

physical brutality. But the reason is not that the regime in the North is gentler; it is instead because the protagonist's father is a high-ranking member of the Communist Party.

The parallel between the two opposed regimes runs further than the fact that both attempt to police the thoughts of their citizens. What Myong-jun learns about the North is that exactly the same work ethic is required of the people in this communist state as in the capitalist South. After being rebuked for his newspaper report being out of line with the Party guide, the protagonist ruminates on the editor's advice:

> 'You seem to misunderstand. The idea that you must take the Republic on yourself and be responsible for it, that's wrong. If you carry out the work demanded by the party in the area assigned to you, that's all that is required. The party does not demand heroic emotions. What we need are people who are as strong as steel and effective in putting things into practice.' It was exactly the same as saying, become one of those people who day by day lose their human pliability in the vast industrial order of capitalist society. (I.-H. Choi [1960] 1985: 105–6)

Here, the work ethic required in both the South and the North, regardless of ideological orientations, is to behave like a cog in a wheel. The individual is not allowed to think, or raise questions, about the overall direction in which the society is going but is instead supposed to work steadily on a narrowly defined set of tasks. In the name of rationalisation, both regimes, capitalist and communist, place their citizens in a Weberian 'iron cage'. According to Myong-jun, in this gigantic bureaucratic machinery that is structured after 'the vast industrial order of capitalist society', individuals, stripped of their 'human pliability', are reduced to mere replaceable units of the total labour force. There are still a group of people called revolutionaries in the North, but they are like salespeople who 'sell the revolution and draw salaries' (I.-H. Choi [1960] 1985: 106). Myong-jun's father is an excellent example of these 'professional revolution-monger[s]' (I.-H. Choi [1960] 1985: 106).

Myong-jun is very surprised to find that social success in the North is determined by a person's network of personal relationships and individual charm rather than by their revolutionary efforts. After the self-denunciation meeting at work, the dejected protagonist compares himself with some of the other staff at the newspaper office. He feels that these people are 'lazier' and play the 'humbug' more than he does (I.-H. Choi [1960] 1985: 93). However, to his dismay, these imposters all manage to get along with the fussy, querulous editor. Myong-jun finds it hard to believe that his work-related difficulties are all attributable to the issue of his ideological faithfulness. Instead, he suspects that

Beyond the Cold War?   **161**

it is the fault of his character: his inability to be obsequious towards his superiors has caused him to fall out of favour with them. At this moment, the protagonist indicts the society of the North for its nepotism. Myong-jun's final ruling on the North is that it is 'the same old bourgeois society wearing a mask of revolution and the people – the strutting of snobs, party members avoiding the effort which would give initiative to their emotions – no different than the basic nature of bourgeois salarymen' (I.-H. Choi [1960] 1985: 93).

The critique of the neocolonial state

In *The Square*, Myong-jun does not use the term 'puppet regime' in reference to the rival Korean political systems. However, in his analysis of the political situations of both the South and the North, the protagonist notes the relationships between the two regimes and the two superpowers that have led to the Cold War. Myong-jun begins by turning to a consideration of the nature of South Korean politics during the pre-Korean War years:

> Is there any difference between Korean politics today and the disposal of refuse from the mess-halls of American army camps? Pick out the cans and make sheets of galvanized tin, take out the timber and put down wooden floors in fine houses, and raise cattle with what's left over. With these we are to put up smart-looking roofs, lay floors that glide beneath shoes dancing a Strauss waltz, and start farms which would put Denmark to shame? (I.-H. Choi [1960] 1985: 32)

In this passage, Myong-jun muses on the formation and operation of South Korean politics using the language of economic recycling. It is reused garbage from the US military camps that has helped to construct the modern houses and farming facilities in the South. Translated into political terms, this means that the nation-state of the South is dependent on US militarism for both its genesis and survival. This revelation sheds light on the ideological composition of the Rhee government, whose origins can be traced back to the US-led Cold War. Seen from afar, the First Republic of South Korea may appear to have the pleasing appearance of a newly independent, 'modern' nation, but the architectural materials used in its construction are, the protagonist bitterly points out, not procured locally. The absence of local materials in the vast effort at nation-building symbolises the regime's passive mimicking of the US-led Cold War politics. It reveals a lack of courage to devise its own set of policies in accordance with the needs and hopes of the

162   *The Korean War Novel*

Korean people. Korean history bears witness to the Rhee regime's zealousness in adopting the episteme of the US-led Cold War. As a result, the US military government and the succeeding local government were virtually indistinguishable in terms of state apparatus as well as in ideological orientations, as discussed in the introduction. In this light, one might observe that the US military government in Korea successfully completed its task by creating the South in its own image.

Myong-jun points to the colonial legacy in the Southern state apparatus as a crucial factor to explain his disillusionment with the regime. As he notes, while he is sitting for the second time in the police interrogation room, the protagonist overhears one of the detectives telling his colleague about his past experience with the colonial police:

> It was a story about dealing with the Left during the days of the Special Police under the Japanese occupation – the best days of his life, he said. He spoke as if the Special Police was the former self of the Korean Police. There was pride in his voice . . .
> Listening to his story from the old days, Myong-jun was gripped by the feeling that he was in the Special Force Section of the Japanese Police. To this extent his story was a mixture of past and present. It was perfectly clear that as far as catching Reds was concerned there was no difference between the present and Japanese times. Japanese times were anti-communist. We are also anti-communist. So, the conclusion of the syllogism is that both are the same. (I.-H. Choi [1960] 1985: 47)

The detective's conflation of the past and present situations is suggestive of the conflictual double time within the nation-building efforts of the South – that is, the attempt to square the legacy of Japanese colonialism with the new nationalist politics of the South. This disjunctive sense of temporality is justified in the name of anti-communism. Or rather, in the eyes of the detective, the temporal discrepancy does not exist in the first place. As he maintains, 'as far as catching Reds was concerned there was no difference between the present and Japanese times.' The problem with the South is that the National Police is not the only state apparatus which re-employs pro-Japanese collaborators instead of penalising them for their anti-national crimes. As Myong-jun points out to his father, '[f]or some completely unknown reason these fellows, who held official posts under the Japanese and caught and killed patriots like you . . . now sit in jobs like directors of bureau, heads of departments, heads of government offices, and give orders to the people' (I.-H. Choi [1960] 1985: 88).

Although Myong-jun pleads ignorance here as to why collaborators are being re-employed for high-ranking offices in the South, the Korean history of the US occupation and the First South Korean Republic

Beyond the Cold War?   **163**

suggests that each regime required pro-Japanese collaborators. These regimes both needed allies in pursuing the aims of the Cold War and in consolidating their grip on power. This need was particularly crucial, given the challenge represented by the huge popularity of the moderate and the radical left with the South Korean people (Oh 2002: 3). By introducing this episode involving pro-Japanese collaborators who effortlessly assume positions among the ruling elite of the postcolonial South, the author calls into question the presumed postcolonial nature of the first South Korean government. Similarly, by revealing how the nation-building project of the Rhee regime is largely determined by the US's Cold War strategies, the author raises some important issues concerning the alleged sovereign power of the First Republic of Korea. As Kim Dong-Choon maintains, viewed through a postcolonial lens, the First Republic emerges as 'a kind of half-state' (2000: 34), the claim of which to postcolonial nationhood is undermined both by its lingering vestiges of Japanese colonialism and its emergent neocolonial dependence on the US.

Myong-jun's verdict on the politics of North Korea is no less damning. He attributes the failure of communism in the North to the fact that the revolution was not achieved by the sacrifices of the northern Koreans themselves:

> The people's government had not been established by having the hammer and sickle of the people dyed with blood . . . There was none of the intense feeling of the Bastille, none of the excitement of the sudden attack on the Winter Palace.
>
> No Korean people had witnessed the blood that flowed from the guillotine, no Korean people had carried torches to set fire to the emperor's bedroom, rushing up marble steps and breaking statues and sculptures to pieces with hammers. They had merely heard the rumor of the revolution . . . It was a tragedy that the people of North Korea had not experienced a revolution in which they were the central figures. A revolution ordered by an official notice. From above to below. This is not a revolution. (I.-H. Choi [1960] 1985: 106)

In the North, during the immediate postliberation years, the local Korean Communists lacked a significant voice until the Red Army arrived with its hand-picked Communist leader, Kim Il-sung. It was then that the Communists, newly organised by Kim in the North, found themselves striving with the nationalist Christians for political power. Naturally enough, it was the vast military power of the occupying Red Army that enabled the Communists to win this power struggle. In other words, the communist revolution in the North was executed with the help of the brute force of the Red Army and carried out according to the Red Army's diktats. In this regard, Myong-jun's verdict that revolution

164   *The Korean War Novel*

in the North was 'the *gift* of the Red Army' (I.-H. Choi [1960] 1985: 106; emphasis in the original) captures the essence of the political situation in the postliberation North: the revolution can only be explained by setting it within the wider international context of Soviet expansionism.

Decoupled from both the communist anti-capitalism and the anti-communist capitalism of the two rival regimes, Myong-jun finds himself at a complete loss. Particularly after his self-denunciation session following his penning of a supposedly reactionary field report for the newspaper, he experiences for the second time an internal collapse:

> He heard a collapsing sound reverberating in his heart. He had heard this sound long ago when he licked his puffed, swollen lips with his tongue on the small hill behind S Police Station. It was the sound of the door of his heart being broken down.
>
> This time it was louder. But it was a far away [*sic*] sound. A loud but dull ringing sound, like the sound of statues toppling over in the square. If only it were possible, he wished he could fall down where he was and cry . . . All his inner organs were empty, and there was a wind blowing in the empty cave-like shell of his body. (I.-H. Choi [1960] 1985: 99–100)

Here, Myong-jun's disillusionment about the Communist regime of the North completely shatters his only recently formed ideological identification. Inside himself, he feels a void as if his body were an 'empty cave-like shell'. If he were attracted to the mummy at Mr Chong's house because of the situational similarity of being stuck in the wrong place at the wrong time, the protagonist, this time, experiences the sensation of being transformed into an ancient relic himself, feeling disembowelled, as witnessed in his following sensation: '[a]ll his inner organs were empty'. Just as his earlier scholarship on the ancient Western philosophers could not properly equip him to cope with the corrupt politics of the South, his later exploration of Marx and Lenin fails to provide him with a guide to deal with the sham revolutionary square in the North.

From victim to saboteur – and victimiser

Having lost all hope of working alongside the revolutionaries in the North, Myong-jun chooses to fall back on the consolation of romance. This is not the first time he has taken shelter by means of an intimate relationship with a woman following an instance of worldly disappointment. When he was feeling distressed about his future in the South after the police investigation, for instance, Myong-jun took the decision to begin an affair with Yun-ae. As he confessed then, '[a]t such times he longed for a woman' (I.-H. Choi [1960] 1985: 49). Although Yong-mi introduced Yun-ae to him some time before, Myong-jun did not take an active interest in her. However, because of Myong-jun's now awakened interest in her, the pair fall for each other quickly and spend time together. Nonetheless, soon afterwards, he leaves for the North without saying a word of goodbye to her. The reason for this betrayal is that he feels that he cannot trust her entirely since she would not submit herself fully to him. At times, Yun-ae refused his amorous advances without specific reason; at other times, she yielded herself to him entirely. Myong-jun feels this 'incomprehensible' caprice may drive him crazy. When she pushes him away, he feels 'insulted' (I.-H. Choi [1960] 1985: 64); he views her as 'some stubborn animal which he couldn't understand' (I.-H. Choi [1960] 1985: 82). According to him, it is this frustration that causes him to go north without notice (I.-H. Choi [1960] 1985: 105).

A central problem with Myong-jun's amorous relationships is that he always wants to have things go his way. His demand for Yun-ae's unconditional compliance with his sexual needs sets limits to their courtship, while his view of women as a form of war 'spoils' (I.-H. Choi [1960] 1985: 60), the object of acquisition and possession, prevents him from seeing the relationship from his lover's perspective. Even in the initial stages of their relationship, the protagonist sees Yun-ae as an object for possession rather than as a human being that requires reciprocal feeling. For example, when they go out on a date together, he finds 'the thought of conquering this woman entic[ing] him' (I.-H. Choi [1960] 1985: 57). In his view, Yun-ae is not an equal partner with whom he will share tender feelings of love and respect but, more simply, a 'thing that [is] surrounded by soft flesh like a wall' (I.-H. Choi [1960] 1985: 55). In these words, the aims of the protagonist are characterised as a military conquest, one which involves breaking down the 'wall' in order to plunder the treasure that is hidden inside. The prize in this campaign is not merely sexual intimacy but actual control of the other person. When he is faced with dogged resistance from Yun-ae, Myong-jun resorts to entreating her to give up her 'pride' in order to 'save' him. Although this desire is articulated in the imploring language of a humble lover, what Myong-jun demands of her is that she should give up her will as a sovereign being. Yun-ae proves to be smarter than this, as is evident from her cold response: 'What am I that I can save you?' (I.-H. Choi [1960] 1985: 83).

What Myong-jun appears to want from women is the sense of sheer power over another rather than the experience and pleasure of loving someone truly. If he seeks refuge from the trauma of his social

166 *The Korean War Novel*

experiences in love, he is nonetheless intent upon turning personal ties into power relationships in which his will always dominates that of the other party. In the North, when his social life is shipwrecked once again, the protagonist seeks out a second relationship to help him cope with the failure of his social life. After his self-renunciation session at work, Myong-jun comes home to mourn alone but finds instead Un-hye, the ballerina, waiting for him. In that moment, he is shocked to discover the powerful attraction of Un-hye's body. The discovery of the possibility of a personal salvation by way of the contemplation of Un-hye's body is expressed in a manner that smacks of a consumer:

> *I will always love you, I will always love* you, Myong-jun muttered to himself. No one could take away this quiet emotion which was springing up from the depths. If it was necessary to sell all the soviets [*sic*] that extend from Europe to Asia for these legs, he would do so. That is, if it was possible to sell them. He felt as if now in this place he was fingering the wall of truth for the first time since he had been born into this world. He reached out his hand and touched her legs. *This is really certain truth. This smooth feeling. Warmth. Lovable elasticity. Can this be doubted? Even if every square returns to ruins, this wall at least remains. Leaning on this wall man can sleep an uneasy sleep until the morning when a new sun rises. These two living pillars.* (I.-H. Choi [1960] 1985: 100–1; emphasis in the original)

Here, Myong-jun eulogises Un-hye's legs, marvelling at these 'two living pillars' that are worth more than 'all the soviets' put together. By calling her legs a 'wall' that is placed between him and the harsh outer world, he is seeking to fortify his compromised self-confidence. Characteristically, however, Myong-jun seeks to confirm his power over Un-hye in practical terms: he demands that the ballerina give up her upcoming performance tour of Moscow and other European cities. Only when Un-hye submits to the unreasonable demand, Myong-jun, intoxicated with 'an overflowing excess of happiness', finds her 'lovable' (I.-H. Choi [1960] 1985: 107).

Although by providing a kind of anchor for his restless, despondent life, this sense of mastery over another human being helps heal his wounded ego, Myong-jun's personal relationships contradict the political ideals he wishes to see triumph in the North. This is because he has managed in this way to turn his private chamber into a miniature copy of the political square of the North. The square that he once believed to be crowded with revolutionaries has turned out to be a stadium capable only of staging 'a tedious mass game' (I.-H. Choi [1960] 1985: 107). If '[i]t was only show' (I.-H. Choi [1960] 1985: 93), it is nonetheless a show performed by a large number of marionettes masterminded by a single puppet master, the illustrious leader. When he invites first Yun-ae

Beyond the Cold War? **167**

and then Un-hye to his private chamber, Myong-jun reproduces the same kind of order. By imposing on them his own will, he is also staging a kind of private theatre. If the public square is host to a spectacular public show celebrating revolution, the latter is host to a humbler private show that celebrates a complete control over a beautiful marionette. By suggesting the parallel between the public and the private, the author emphasises the way in which dictatorship and power politics may corrupt the personal relationships between individuals. Myong-jun's pursuit of a kind of mastery of the soul is only a reflection of the workings of the authoritarian society itself. At the end of the novel, he will be forced to pay a high price in guilt for this attempted shackling of the souls of the two women he loves.

A greater surprise that his life has in store for Myong-jun takes place when Un-hye, whose docility he never doubted, betrays him by leaving for Moscow. However, Myong-jun is not allowed to wallow in self-pity for very long: the outbreak of the Korean War sees him conscripted into the Political Security Bureau. With the KPA's occupation of Seoul, officer Lee Myong-jun stands once again in the political square of the South. This time, he finds himself in a position that allows him to wield absolute power over the citizens who have chosen to remain in Seoul. At this point in the novel, by a peculiar quirk of fate, Myong-jun discovers that Tae-sik, Yong-mi's brother, has been arrested on charges of espionage and is now imprisoned in the S Police Station, which the Political Security Bureau is using as its office. In the interrogation room of the police station, Myong-jun comes face to face with Tae-sik, the son of Myong-jun's generous former patron, a man who was formerly his good friend. Despite these previous connections, Myong-jun acts toward Tae-sik in exactly the same way as the savage detective acted when Myong-jun was interrogated three years before. He punches and kicks his old friend in such a brutal manner that he feels as if 'the detective had come and was sitting in his body' (I.-H. Choi [1960] 1985: 117). What is still worse, when Yun-ae, who is now married to Tae-sik, comes to visit her detained husband, the protagonist sexually harasses her. His devilry, however, stops short of rape. Although he soon relents and eventually helps secure their release, the guilt of persecuting the couple haunts him. Interestingly, in one of his revisions to the novel, the author recasts this episode as a dream that the protagonist has while imprisoned in a POW camp ([1960] 2014: 132–5). In this way, Myong-jun's guilt in the later versions is exclusively the result of issues relating to Un-hye and her unborn baby.

During the Battle of the Busan Perimeter, Myong-jun runs into Un-hye, the former ballerina, who has since volunteered to work at the

168 *The Korean War Novel*

warfront as a military nurse in order to be close to her lover. She asks for forgiveness for breaking her promise to be with him because she could not forgo the precious opportunity to visit Moscow. However, Myong-jun is simply thankful to see her again. He takes Un-hye to a cave he has discovered in the mountains near the troop headquarters so that the two of them can be together whenever the opportunity presents itself. But what starts off as a quiet, romantic escapade soon takes on political significance when the protagonist expresses the significance of resuming this relationship:

> If you try to deceive us in the name of the people, we will take a corresponding revenge . . . If you cheat us out of a penny, you will certainly be cheated out of a penny. In the place set by you for us to watch tanks and artillery we are going towards the primeval square. (I.-H. Choi [1960] 1985: 130)

Here, a series of romantic encounters in the middle of a fierce battle is supposed to symbolise in the mind of Myong-jun his revenge on the North Korean regime for cheating the ordinary workers and peasants, including both him and his lover, of the promise of a genuine revolution and for pushing them into a deadly war with the South. In Kim Seong-kon's translation, Myong-jun articulates more clearly the sense in which he holds the northern regime responsible for the perilous situation in which he and Un-hye find themselves: '[h]is temper flared and grew more heated as he thought about the party putting Eun-hye [Un-hye] and himself [*sic*] in needless danger for the sake of martyrdom' (I.-H. Choi [1960] 2014: 130).

By abandoning their respective duties at a critical moment of the war, Myong-jun tries to pay back the deceitful Communist regime in kind. At one point, Un-hye arrives at the cave in a somewhat absent-minded manner, with a pair of scissors in her hand. Myong-jun also drops by the cave in the course of his delivery of a report from the war front to KPA headquarters, and so is delayed in his mission as a courier. Even though the couple is aware that the pair of scissors might be used to sew up the wounds of a number of wounded soldiers and the report's timely delivery might save thousands of lives, neither appears to care: Un-hye decides not to run back to return the scissors and Myong-jun decides to set aside his courier mission. The two war saboteurs instead spend time together as if for the last time. Curiously enough, their intuitions turn out to be right as Un-hye is killed the next day by the massive strikes carried out by the US Air Force.

Beyond the trap of the Cold War

Before he stands at the repatriation screening, Myong-jun briefly considers the comparative merits of life in the Communist North and life in the capitalist South. He first ponders the fate of the early Marxist thinkers, regretting that the revolutionary spirit of their words has now become mere dogma. The deplorable state of the North is described in the following terms:

> [T]he goodwill and fervour of its [Marxism's] originators disappeared a long time ago. Just as Hegel's philosophy had been an attractive opium and a decisive toxin for the life of faith of Europeans. For Lee Myong-jun, the experience of living in Bolshevik society was something which could not be erased. Because he saw clearly the fact that they were serving idols in that temple. It was a place controlled not by inspiration but by ritual. It was a place controlled not by creative fervour but by iron command. Not love and forgiveness, but hate and revenge. (I.-H. Choi [1960] 1985: 134)

In Myong-jun's view, the ritual of revolution has been substituted for its genuine spirit, and the followers of revolution become the worshippers of new icons. Instead of pursuing the utopian vision of an egalitarian, classless society, Communists now endeavour to build a new class society ruled by 'iron command', one that thrives on 'hate and revenge'. While it is clear that Myong-jun rejects the life-denying North, the South does not appear as a viable alternative: '[i]f [the] religious fanaticism [of the North] was frightening, the lack of an ideal was sad. If South Korea could be said to have a strong point, it was just that there was freedom to become corrupt and freedom to be idle there' (I.-H. Choi [1960] 1985: 134).

Perhaps unsurprisingly, then, Myong-jun's final decision is to choose neither the North nor the South. And Myong-jun's destination is not the United States either but rather the Republic of India. Viewed within the context of the international politics of the Cold War, Myong-jun remains true to the spirit of a saboteur by means of his refusal to assist the cause of either of the two rival regimes. The testimony by Ju Yeongbok, who was one of the seventy-six real-life Korean POWs to opt for a neutral third country at the repatriation screening, bears an uncanny resemblance to the attitude displayed by Myong-jun:

> We were neutral elements because we believed President Rhee and his government were worse criminals than the Communist Party. And as for Kim Il-sung and his government they were opportunists even more detestable than Capitalists and anti-revolutionists. (qtd in M. Kim 2019: 265)

In this passage, the ex-KPA major summarises his condemnation of both regimes with two key words: criminality and opportunism. It is in these terms that he justifies his choice of a neutral third country. When Choi's novel was first published, the political imagination underlying Myong-jun's choice came as a major shock. Living through the 1950s, the novel's readers and critics had been bombarded by a Cold War discourse that valorised liberal democracy over communism. Since the time of national liberation in 1945, most people felt that they had been forced to choose the first ideology. As Choi In-hun himself acknowledged, the publication of the novel benefitted greatly from its timing: it came out during the liberating, sanguine intellectual atmosphere that followed the student-led uprising of 19 April 1960 that toppled Rhee's dictatorship. To quote Choi's preface: '[w]riting this kind of novel would not have been allowed during our previous military regime, built on Asiatic totalitarianism. ... As a writer, I am pleased to live in the new republic made possible by the student revolution in April 1960' ([1960] 2014: 5). However, the political spring of the South turned out to be short-lived: it was violently terminated by the military coup led by General Park Chung-hee on 16 May 1961, just a year or so later.

It is only when it is located in the historical context of the post–Korean War South Korea that the political significance of Myong-jun's taboo-breaking choice can be fully appreciated. For those Koreans who were liberated from colonial rule by the American forces and, then five years later, fought off the invasion of the Communist North, with American help, the United States was not simply an ally. Political, military and cultural friendship with the US constituted the foundations for the subsequent nation-building efforts. Without this friendship, the nation of South Korea would not have come into being. In this regard, pro-Americanism became interchangeable with anti-communism in South Korea. To quote Kwon Boduerae:

> The originary fictionality of South Korea is still haunting us . . . [W]e have to come to terms with the issue about the origin of South Korea that would not have been possible without the US. Pro-Americanism is the ontological secret of South Korea. It was such a parochial foundation that it made Koreans even exclude the line of right-wing nationalist Kim Koo from our nation building. Our impoverished consciousness, as indicated in our having to keep secret even a commemoration of Kim Koo as a symbolic figure that possibly maximises the historical possibility of the nation, bears witness to a time when our perspective could not go beyond the boundaries of the free world. . . . To speak accurately, the US, not capitalism, nor liberalism, is the foundation of South Korea. (2012: 271–2; author's translation)

Beyond the Cold War? **171**

In this passage, the author suggests that the policy of pro-Americanism has had such a strong grip on the South Korean people that any political position that diverges from it, including even the conservative nationalism of the nationalist hero, Kim Koo, thereby becomes a target for state persecution. Since national liberation, pro-Americanism, the twin brother of anti-communism, has dominated the political imagination of South Korea. It is within this fundamental context that Myong-jun's choice of a neutral third country is an invitation to his readers to think beyond the political or cognitive landscape set by the twin hegemonic ideologies of the Cold War.

At one time during his voyage on the *Tagore*, Myong-jun imagines his life as an exile in India. In this foreign country in which no one will recognise him, Myong-jun romanticises leading a humble but honest life as a hospital guard or a fire station attendant or a theatre ticket-seller. He even considers the possibility of giving up his name in order to remain completely anonymous: 'I even want to give up my name. I would be satisfied as one nameless man among countless millions of human beings' (I.-H. Choi [1960] 1985: 143). At another point, he feels relieved to realise that no one will be out looking for him: '[n]ot only would there be no one who knew what kind of man I was, but there wouldn't even be anyone trying to find out' (I.-H. Choi [1960] 1985: 138). If the protagonist's fixation on the possibility of a future life of complete anonymity reflects his desire to break with his past and shed his guilty conscience about the abusive relationships he once had with Yun-ae and Un-hye (according to the earlier editions) – or his failure to protect Un-hye and her baby (according to the last edition) – it also signifies, at another level, his unconscious reaction to the time he spent as an inmate at the POW camp. To put it differently, his wish for complete anonymity should be understood in the light of the fact that he has had to wear the hyper-visible badge of a POW during his entire captivity. It is this which once placed him in a conflicted dual position: he was, presumably, the object of both the psy-ops of the US Command and the vicious non-repatriation campaigns of the anti-Communist inmate leagues, but at the same time, he became the object of a similarly brutal consolidation campaign by the Communist leagues. Social invisibility for people like Myong-jun would mean a guaranteed exemption from any possible future ideological confrontations.

As much as he wishes to distance himself from the ideological rivalry that exists between the two Koreas, Myong-jun wants to see 'Korea' prospering in the future. At one time during his voyage, he imagines reading an article about 'Korea' in a local Indian newspaper:

172   *The Korean War Novel*

> *On the spot complaints by citizens to the Korean Tourist Association that due to the annual increase in foreign tourists, children busy following them around are neglecting their studies, reflected so strongly on the government authorities that the cabinet has collapsed.* (I.-H. Choi [1960] 1985: 139; emphasis in the original)

The picture the protagonist draws of his home country at a moment in the future is a rosy one. With its booming tourist industry, the country appears to be prospering. With so many foreign tourists around, the local children find it hard to concentrate on their studies. It is worth noting here that the protagonist uses the term 'Korea', not South Korea, with the implication that the country he imagines some years in future is a unified one (Kwon 2012: 266). In conjunction with this rosy view of the future, Myong-jun's provocative choice of a neutral country resonates with the political discourse that sees Korean neutrality as a political alternative. Rather than submitting to its fate of being a helpless pawn on the geopolitical chessboard of the Cold War, 'Korea' here asserts its sovereign choice in favour of independence from all superpower rivalries. This utopian ideology is one that blossomed briefly in South Korea during the heady months between the fall of President Syngman Rhee and the reassertion of authority by the army under the command of General Park Chung-hee (Kwon 2012: 288–9; Hughes 2012: 171).

The Square ends with Myong-jun's suicide: he jumps off the Indian ship, the *Tagore*, that is transporting the released POWs to Kolkata. The protagonist's suicide is partly driven by guilt about certain events in his past life, particularly his relationship with Yun-ae. When a fellow ex-POW named Mr Kim makes an obscene joke about the released POWs' desire to disembark in Hong Kong, Myong-jun is reminded of a horrific episode he once heard about from a fellow inmate in the POW camp. There, the inmate shared with his sex-hungry fellow prisoners a shocking discovery he had made on the eastern warfront: a dead girl with 'a stick stuck ... between her legs' (I.-H. Choi [1960] 1985: 76). The luridness of the episode stings Myong-jun's guilty conscience, making him interrogate himself about his past behaviours towards Yun-ae:

> Yun-ae, I loved you. No matter how clumsy the method, I left you and ran away because I loved you. Even if I tried to rape you, I never practiced flower arrangement like the soldier did to the woman along the road. Only those who violate women are animals. (I.-H. Choi [1960] 1985: 77)

Before his defection to the North, Myong-jun abandoned Yun-ae after they had been together for a number of months; later, when she comes to see her husband while he is detained by the Bureau, Myong-jun is on the

Beyond the Cold War? **173**

verge of violating her. Here, however, the protagonist seeks to lessen his guilt by differentiating his own behaviour from that of those whom he calls 'animals'. Since he did stop himself before he actually raped Yun-ae, Myong-jun is not strictly a rapist. Nonetheless, this mental attempt to differentiate his conduct from these other men fails to exonerate him and brings no comfort. Before he kills himself, Myong-jun imagines that the seagulls that have been following his boat since the beginning of the voyage are actually the incarnations of Yun-ae and Un-hye. It is this serendipitous discovery that finally tempts him to join them: '[i]f he went there, wouldn't he be able to meet them?' (I.-H. Choi [1960] 1985: 152).

This episode gets rewritten in the 1989 and later editions. In the 2010 edition, for instance, Myong-jun's near rape of Yun-ae takes place only in his dreams. As a consequence, the protagonist needs to have fewer guilty feelings about the young woman. In these later revisions, a baby bird stands in as substitute for Yun-ae. From the time he boards the *Tagore*, Myong-jun is haunted by the strange impression that he is being watched by someone or something. At a certain point, he decides to use the captain's rifle to shoot one of the two seagulls that have been hovering around the *Tagore*. However, he then discovers that the one he is aiming the rifle at is only half the size of the other bird. It is, indeed, a baby bird. When his eyes meet the eyes of the baby bird, he realises that it is this creature that has been watching him all along. The sight of the mother and the baby bird sitting together on the mast of the boat brings back to the protagonist the cherished memory of his last meeting with Un-hye in the cave near the Naktong River. Before she dies, Un-hye tells him that she is pregnant and that she is sure it is a baby girl. This recollection stops Myong-jun from firing the rifle. After he takes the decision not to shoot, he thinks that the two birds flying gracefully around the ship are whispering to him. Although his guilt for not protecting Un-hye and her unborn baby from the war eventually drives him to die by suicide, the novel requests the reader to recognise that this is not a sad ending. Calling out to Un-hye, 'Myong-jun nearly wept in relief'; and the face he sees reflected in the water before jumping off is 'smiling' (I.-H. Choi [1960] 2014: 157).

Myong-jun's suicide may also be attributed to his frustration at his fellow ex-inmates on the boat. At first, the ex-inmates who have made the same choice at the repatriation screening stick together. They feel bonded together by their choice and share a common anxiety about their uncertain future. However, as time passes, they begin to move away from each other. According to Myong-jun, their sense of camaraderie is compromised over time as each of them attempts to come to terms with his own past or, to borrow the protagonist's words, to 'unravel alone

174 *The Korean War Novel*

and silently the knots in his heart before they [reach] their destination' (I.-H. Choi [1960] 2014: 8). In addition, Myong-jun's relationship with his fellow travellers sours when he fails to acquire permission from the Indian authorities for them to go ashore and enjoy themselves in Hong Kong, during the boat's second stopover. Some of them start to hold a grudge against the protagonist, with Mr Kim, in particular, accusing him of making a deal for personal gain with the authorities. This leads to a fistfight breaking out between the two. This incident serves not only to alienate him from the rest of the ex-prisoners but dampens his optimistic outlook on the future. Myong-jun comes to the tragic recognition that even those who have opted collectively for exile and renounced both Koreas are really no different from those he has left behind. They harass him by the collective power and consider it of little consequence to break regulations in order to gratify their base desires. Nearing Hong Kong, the protagonist is distressed by their view that women exist simply as the means to gratify their sexual desire, as revealed by their plan to have 'a taste of a woman' (I.-H. Choi [1960] 2014: 74). If this small select group with which he shares a sense of comradeship turns out to be hopeless, this means that the protagonist can hold out no further hope for a meaningful life. It is then unsurprising that the protagonist wonders, 'why am I so empty?' on a voyage that supposedly takes place on 'a road to a new life' (I.-H. Choi [1960] 2014: 144).

The history untold

Because he dies in the middle of the voyage, Myong-jun cannot testify to the kind of life that awaits the former prisoners in India. And yet, the history of this overseas settlement reveals that the prospect of enjoying both hospitality and anonymity in this new society is most likely only a dream. Due to the protagonist's untimely death, among the things missing from the narrative is any sense of the precarious nature of the life the ex-inmates, with their virtual statelessness, would have had to endure. Although some of them expressed the wish to go to specific neutral countries before their release, all eighty-eight of the non-repatriate POWs were sent on the British transport *Asturias* to India after the four months of 'explanation'[3] were over. This was mostly because there were no other countries, neutral or otherwise, that stepped forward with offers to accommodate them. As Monica Kim and others have noted, upon their arrival in Madras on 21 January 1954, the ex-POWs realised that it was solely their responsibility to choose and be accepted by a suitable country (M. Kim 2019: 288–300; H.-I. Kim 2016;

Beyond the Cold War? 175

S.-W. Lee 2013). Switzerland and Sweden – the two countries in which many of the ex-POWs were initially interested – had already rejected them, and Mexico, Peru and Poland – countries which had proposed to host these ex-POWs before they had been released – all subsequently withdrew their offers (H.-I. Kim 2016: 64–5). For this reason, these ex-inmates, with little choice but to wait for positive responses to the letters of petition, found themselves stateless refugees flung indefinitely into what Agamben would call 'bare life' (1998: 9). Situated just beyond the protective borders of nation-states, hovering uncertainly between the status of national traitor and abandoned refugee, the death of Myong-jun symbolises the limbo-like status accorded the real-life POWs upon their release.

According to Monica Kim, most of the released POWs had to wait in India as much as two years before they received their official permission to stay; a few of them, including Hyon Donghwa and Ji Kichol, waited more than three years to no avail. They eventually chose to settle in India because Argentina and Mexico, the countries of their choice, repeatedly rejected their petitions. Surprisingly, the stated reason for the rejection was that these two ex-inmates had served as officers of the KPA. As a consequence, they were required to send extra letters in which they tried to 'render themselves politically transparent', by displaying their anti-communist zeal (M. Kim 2019: 294–6). Sadly, this fate signifies the fact that, although these ex-POWs chose to move to the 'free' world in order to escape the binary death-trap of the Cold War, even the outside world, including the supposedly 'neutral countries', was implicated in its logic. Growing tired of waiting endlessly as refugees, some ex-inmates requested that they be repatriated to South Korea, but the Indian government rejected this in favour of an offer of a return to the North. These non-repatriates knew better than to accept the offer, knowing full well, even if the Indian officials did not, the fate that awaited 'traitors' in the Communist state. In the end, the Indian government offered them the right to remain in India, but most of them rejected it, arguing that 'they would be treated as the Untouchable as long as they live in India'.[4] Only eleven out of the eighty-eight non-repatriates ended up staying in India, while the majority of them, fifty-five ex-inmates, were finally admitted to Brazil, after a wait that lasted more than two years. According to the 1958 census of the non-repatriated ex-POWs, among the seventy-six Koreans, six returned to North Korea, forty-nine were admitted to Brazil, twelve to Argentina, nine remained in India. As for the twelve Chinese POWs, two eventually opted for the People's Republic of China, six were admitted to Brazil, two to Argentina, two remained in India (D. C. Chang 2020b: 230). However, even after they

176   *The Korean War Novel*

were resettled, many of the Korean ex-POWs in particular found themselves ostracised within the overseas Korean community due to their background as members of the KPA (S.-W. Lee 2013: 347). Once again, they were caught up inextricably in the battle between communism and anti-communism, unable to avoid the inevitable battle-lines of the Cold War.

At a symbolic level, Myong-jun's tragic ending presages the fate of his utopic vision of Korean neutrality, a vision to which the protagonist's choice of a third country strongly alludes. The vision he entertains during the voyage about the future of a prosperous neutral Korea was one shared by many intellectuals in the wake of the 19 April Revolution. After this college student-led uprising toppled Rhee's authoritarian, anti-communist regime, progressive intellectuals enthusiastically discussed the option of neutralising the Korean peninsula as the necessary first stage toward eventual reunification. This was not the first time when 'a third way' as a future for the two Koreas became a live issue. Immediately following the final ceasefire of the Korean War, the US actually considered the possibility of a neutral Korean peninsula.[5] However, the Rhee government rejected the proposal outright. For many Koreans who still had fresh memories of Communist invasion, the proposal of neutrality held out the offer of a 'free ticket' for a second Soviet incursion. In an article published in a political science journal of the time, this general scepticism was summed up in the form of a rhetorical question: '[l]et us assume also that the general population in both parts of Korea favoured the neutralist proposition. Would the North Korean Communists be willing to dismantle all the revolutionary changes they have instituted in North Korea and relinquish their control?' (C.-S. Lee 1964: 232). In the mass media of the time, the untrustworthy nature of the Communist regime was repeatedly emphasised as the major obstacle to a politically neutral Korean peninsula.[6]

For a brief moment, the political spring ushered in to the political square of the South by the fall of the Rhee regime appeared to open up a new chapter in South Korean politics and, perhaps, in turn, in the dynamics of inter-Korean politics too. For example, the proposal of peaceful reunification, a proposal which had first been raised by Cho Pongam, the man who was then summarily executed by President Rhee under false pro-Communist charges, resurfaced in the wake of the 19 April Revolution. However, all talks of possible alternative political futures were brought to a sudden halt by the military coup that took place on 16 May 1961. A renewed political winter soon set in, one that was to last until late 1979, when the anti-communist military regime of President Park Chung-hee was ended with Park's assassination by

Kim Chaekyu, his right-hand man and the Director of the Korean Central Intelligence Agency. A second military coup soon followed, bringing General Chun Doo-hwan to political power in a period of rule that lasted from October 1979 until February 1988. It should not be surprising to note that the historical trajectories of these South Korean military regimes are more or less coeval with that of the Cold War itself. Tragically, however, although the Cold War between the US and the USSR officially ended with the collapse of the Communist regime in August 1991, on the Korean peninsula the Cold War battle-lines persist to this day. As a result, Myong-jun's vision of a unified political future, one to which many of the non-repatriated veterans of the Korean War as well as many progressive intellectuals of the 1960s and 1970s subscribed, lingers, somewhat cruelly, in the mind of the reader, when they turn to contemplate the icy realities of inter-Korean politics.

Notes

1. Two translations are available of *The Square*: Kevin O'Rourke's translation published in 1985 and Kim Seong-kon's in 2014. Since Choi revised his novel ten times following its initial publication, there are eleven editions: the first edition was published in 1960; this was then revised in 1961, 1968, 1973, 1976, 1989, 1994, 1996, 2001, 2008 and 2010 (Y.-G. Choi 2014: 356). Although O'Rourke does not specify the edition that he used for his translation, my conjecture is that it is the 1973 edition. My reasoning is based on the fact that O'Rourke's translation does not contain one particular scene commonly found in the earlier editions: the scene in which the two seagulls that follow the protagonist's sea voyage are transformed into images of his past lovers who chide him for leaving them. O'Rourke's translation also does not include a scene found in the 1976 and later editions: the scene where the protagonist hallucinates that certain pairs of eyes are watching over him. As for Kim's translation, it is difficult to pinpoint which edition the translator actually used. This is because Kim's translation contains a revision that belongs exclusively to the 2010 edition: the last revision in which the protagonist's torture of Tae-sik and his near rape of the latter's wife become merely dream episodes. Curiously enough, Kim, at the same time, relied on an earlier edition for the scene about the protagonist's encounter with the mummy at Mr Chung's house. In the earlier editions up to the 2001 edition, one of which Kim appears to have used, the protagonist sees a real mummy whereas in the 2008 and 2010 editions, he finds only an empty coffin. Whenever there were major discrepancies between the texts of O'Rourke and Kim, I compared both translations.
2. This sentence contains a mistranslation of the Korean word *poksu* (복수). As a homophone, this Korean word can mean many things, including both 'revenge' and 'a multiple number'. Contextually, the translation of this word as 'revenge' makes little sense, while Kim's translation of the word as 'companion' is better.

178   *The Korean War Novel*

3. In accordance with the Armistice Treaty, on 24 September 1953, a total of 22,640 non-repatriates, from both South and North, were delivered to the neutral zone at the thirty-eighth parallel. They remained there under the authorities of the Neutral Nations Repatriation Commission until 23 December 1953. During this period of four months, these POWs were subject to exhortatory speeches by the Communist and the UN Command and then had to make a final decision regarding repatriation. A total of eighty-eight non-repatriates, Chinese and Korean, finally decided to choose a neutral country, although they were not able to depart for India until 9 February 1954 (S.-W. Lee 2013; M. Kim 2019). Lee Sun-woo maintains that the number of Korean POWs who chose a neutral nation was seventy-seven; Monica Kim claims it was seventy-six. According to Lee, one Korean, a man named O Ilkuk (but misspelled as Il Kwo Woo), was misclassified as a Chinese POW. Among the eighty-eight POWs, there were only two ROKA soldiers, eleven Chinese Communist soldiers, while the remainder were KPA soldiers (S.-W. Lee 2013: 338).
4. Although he praises both India for its democracy and its Prime Minister Jawaharlal Nehru for his humanitarianism, Ju criticises the high-handedness of the local officials and the Indian government for pressuring the Korean POWs to choose between India and North Korea after Mexico backtracked on its promise to accept the POWs. At one point, he also takes issue with the caste-based discrimination practised in India, remarking that 'India despised the POWs worse than its lowest caste' (Ju 1993: 171, 264–6, 276).
5. See 'A "Neutralized" Korea' 1953; 'Future of Korea' 1953. In 1960, the proposal was again made by US Senator Mansfield, although it was flatly turned down by a South Korean high official ('Korean Rejects' 1960).
6. See 'Chungnibiran' 1957; 'Kongsanseryŏk' 1957.

Chapter 6

A Postcolonial War in Reverse

Born in Changchun, Manchuria, Hwang Sok-yong (1943–) came to Korea following national liberation from the Japanese and spent his childhood in Pyongyang. His family then fled to the South during the Korean War. He witnessed the 19 April 1960 Revolution, which saw the ousting of the Syngman Rhee government, and the 16 May 1961 coup d'état that brought General Park Chung-hee to power. When the South Korean government dispatched troops to assist the US in the Vietnam War, Hwang was one of those who volunteered to fight. Nowadays, Hwang is acclaimed as a major novelist and a progressive intellectual who has been forthright in his criticisms of such grave social issues as the exploitative nature of capitalism, the scourge of military dictatorship and the military standoff caused by the division of the Korean nation. As a democratic activist, Hwang participated in the Kwangju Uprising of 1980 against the crushing of democracy by the military regime of Chun Doo-hwan, and he has carved out a role for himself as a pro-unification activist who advocates non-governmental-level dialogue between the two Koreas. Hwang's work includes *Samp'oro kanŭn kil* (The Road to Sampo, 1973), a collection of short stories that focuses on the wretched conditions of the urban subproletariat; *Jang Gil-san* (1974–84, in Korean), an epic novel based on the tales of a well-known historical bandit and popular hero of the Chosŏn dynasty; *The Shadow of Arms* (1985, 1988 in Korean, 2014 in English), a critical novel dealing with the participation of South Korean soldiers in the Vietnam War; *The Old Garden* (2000 in Korean, 2009 in English) and *Princess Bari* (2007 in Korean, 2015 in English), two novels that deal with the North Korean diaspora at the time of the Korean War; and *At Dusk* (2015 in Korean, 2018 in English), a novel that was awarded the Émile Guimet Prize for Asian Literature in 2018 and that in 2019 was nominated for the Man Booker International Prize.

Mr Han's Chronicle (1972) and *The Guest* (2001 in Korean, 2005 in English) are numbered among the exemplary Korean novels of the

180   *The Korean War Novel*

'Literature of National Division'. In the form of individual, community and social incident, this series of major literary works seek to narrativise the run-up to the outbreak of conflict, the events of the Korean War itself and the range of social aftermaths, whether that be in South Korea, North Korea or the Korean diaspora. *Mr Han's Chronicle*, Hwang's first contribution to this genre, depicts the life of a doctor from the North Korean diaspora. Rejected by both North and South Koreas, Mr Han lives a dejected, self-enclosed life and finally dies a lonely death. *The Guest*, Hwang's second contribution, revisits the slaughter of 35,000 civilians in Shinch'ŏn, Hwanghae Province, North Korea, during the Korean War. Unlike *Mr Han's Chronicle*, *The Guest* ends with a vision of reconciliation, a unification of the two Koreas. Translated into eight languages, the novel is based on the author's unauthorised travel in 1989 to North Korea, during which he visited the American Imperialist Massacre Remembrance Museum in Shinch'ŏn, a site exploited by the North Korean regime as a fertile source of anti-American propaganda. Following this unlawful visit, Hwang took the decision to live as an exile. When he eventually returned in 1993, he was arrested and sentenced to seven years in prison under the terms of the South Korean National Security Law that forbids unauthorised visits to North Korea. After serving five years of his sentence, Hwang was granted a special amnesty by the former democratic activist and newly elected president, Kim Dae-jung.

Ryu Yosŏp, the protagonist of *The Guest*, is a Presbyterian minister living in Brooklyn, New York. In his early teenage years, which are the years of the Korean War, Yosŏp fled with his family from his small hometown of Ch'ansaemgol in Shinch'ŏn to South Korea, before subsequently emigrating to the United States. Five decades later, he decides to join the Homeland Visitors, the tours of North Korea organised for overseas Koreans, and revisits his hometown. During the visit, Yosŏp meets both his sister-in-law and the nephew whom his elder brother Yohan had to leave behind in the North. The ghost of Yohan, who dies three days before Yosŏp's departure for North Korea, then appears to his younger brother. Later, the ghost of Sunnam, a man who once worked in the Ryu family's orchard but was killed by Yohan during the rightist insurrection known as the '13 October Patriotic Anti-Communist Incident', also appears to Yosŏp. Sunnam expresses his wish to guide Yohan's roaming spirit to the next world. During his visit to North Korea, Yosŏp initially hides from the North Korean officials the fact that he has relatives in the North. This is because he is afraid that there will be trouble if the North Korean authorities discover that his brother led a rightist uprising and helped orchestrate the ensuing anti-communist massacre. However, having already found out about

Yosŏp and his family, the North Korean officials instead assist him in reuniting with his relatives. In the meantime, the ghosts of Yohan and Sunnam appear to Yosŏp together, sharing with the latter their different perspectives on the clashes between the Christian Nationalists and the Communists prior to the uprising. Later, when Yosŏp visits his maternal uncle An Sŏngman, who is also called 'Uncle Some', the ghost of Yohan is joined by the ghosts of all of the villagers whom Yohan and his rightist *ch'iandae* (security forces) members slaughtered in the wake of the uprising. At this meeting, both living and dead take turns in sharing their experience of the massacre. The story ends with Yosŏp burying a bone fragment taken from his brother's post-cremation remains on a mountainside close to his hometown.

The tragic stories of the ghosts are couched within the twelve-act structure of a *chinogwi* exorcism, a shamanistic ritual popular in Hwanghae Province, performed to appease the restless spirits of the wronged (S.-Y. Hwang [2001] 2005: 7). The ritual works by inviting the dead to tell their stories in order to vent their pent-up feelings of anger and resentment. In this way, they will be able to embark on their journey to the next world in peace. By marrying the act of storytelling to the ritual of shamanistic appeasement, the author intends both to console the resentful spirits of the dead and to transcend the traumatic history of internecine struggle.

Two rival modernities

In his author's note to *The Guest*, Hwang elucidates the significance of the title of his novel, relating it to a certain Western epidemic:

> When smallpox was first identified as a Western disease that needed to be warded off, the Korean people referred to it as *mama* or *sonnim*, the second of which translates to guest. With this in mind, I settled upon *The Guest* as a fitting title for the novel that explores the arrival and effects of Christianity and Marxism in a country where both were initially as foreign as smallpox . . . Because of Korea's identity as both a colony and a divided nation, both Christianity and Marxism were unable to achieve natural, spontaneous modernization; instead they were forced to reach modernity in accordance with conscious human will. In North Korea . . . the tenets of Christianity and Marxism were zealously adopted as facets of enlightenment.
>
> During the Korean War, the area of North Korea known as Hwanghae Province was the setting of a fifty-day nightmare during which Christians and Communists – two groups of Korean people whose lives were shaped by two different guests – committed a series of unspeakable atrocities against each other. (S.-Y. Hwang [2001] 2005: 7–8)

182   *The Korean War Novel*

Here, the author notes the way in which the ironic use of the Korean word for 'guest', initially a term denoting the arrival of smallpox, a disease which came from the West, as a threat to the Korean body was extended to embrace the subsequent invasion of the Korean mind by those two rival Western ideologies, Christianity and Marxism. From this point of view, Koreans from the northern half of the peninsula, those who had been excluded from the material and cultural development of the Chosŏn dynasty and who were thus more eager for change, imbibed these foreign toxins as part of their project of modern enlightenment in order to wipe out the prejudices and superstitions of an outworn social structure. But, just as smallpox causes devastating sickness in those who have had no previous exposure to it, so these powerful new Western ideologies caused a multitude of Koreans to fall sick too. In this way, Hwang points an accusing finger at the rivalry between the two extraneous modernising forces for the 'fifty-day nightmare' that decimated the population of Shinch'ŏn township.

Following the author's cue, a number of Korean critics have noted the culpability assigned within the novel to these two Western modernities for the Shinch'ŏn massacre. For example, one Korean critic contends that the novel 'writes back' to the ideologies of both Christianity and Marxism and raises the issue of how to appropriate Western culture in a secure manner (Go 2005: 288). A second critic, on a slightly different note, maintains that Korean Marxism, unlike that central European religion, had 'a material base of its own' (C. Kim 2001: 329). Most Korean critics have complimented Hwang for his courageous critique of the system of Korean division (*pundanch'eje*), given the fact that, in the volatile state of South Korean politics, anything deviating from the official ideology of outright anti-communist discourse causes an instant violent backlash from the hegemonic forces of the right. This seems clear enough from Hwang's voluntary exposure of himself to a five-year period of incarceration under the conservative, anti-communist regime. Asian American critics have also drawn attention to the subversiveness of Hwang's novel. For example, Youngju Ryu has maintained that *The Guest* performs a dual historical demystification: it both 'dismiss[es] North Korean history as simply untrue (by presenting a narrative of Shinch'on in which US troops are nowhere to be found) and undercuts South Korean history as grossly unjustified (by identifying the right-wing forces as specifically Christian rather than more benignly nationalist)' (2015: 641). Daniel Y. Kim has expanded on this latter point by calling attention to the class dimension to this incident while at the same time reading the ideological conflict as analogous to the racial conflict between Korean Americans and African Americans (2020: 258–61).

However, this chapter is predicated on the idea that *The Guest* is an incoherent work of fiction. Read with the author's note in mind, the story just does not add up. To put it differently, Hwang's view of his own novel as a dramatisation of the clash between two poorly assimilated modern Western ideologies is misleading. Above all, the author's own reading is tantamount to denying the North Koreans, whether they be Communist or Christian, any form of genuine political agency by its casting of two Western ideologies as the key players in the tragic incident. In her insightful essay, however, Jini Kim Watson maintains: '[d]espite Hwang's title, the novel is in fact less concerned with the content of imported Marxism and Christianity than with their incorporation into local spatial practices by the "host"' (2014: 77). Ironically enough, then, one must read against the author's proclaimed intention in order to grasp the full implications of the novel. This is because the narrative's complexity is not fully captured within the framework of two poorly assimilated and mutually antagonistic ideologies. In this regard, this chapter first examines the author's representational strategies concerning the right-wing insurgents by measuring the novel against both historiography and personal testimony. By focalising the main social division as that between the Christian youth led by Yohan and his Communist adversaries, Hwang portrays the Shinch'ŏn Uprising as a crusade against Communism. This is a narrative pattern that confirms the intention that Hwang sketches out in the author's note. Despite the author's decking out the historical incident as an anti-communist religious conflict, the novel nevertheless contains an unfolding of the older class conflict, as some critics have already pointed out (Watson 2014: 77; Y. Ryu 2015: 638; D. Y. Kim 2020: 261). This chapter then recentres *The Guest* at the level of class conflict by situating the 'religious' divisions in the context of the legacy of Japanese colonialism.

As testified in a number of farm tenancy disputes of the colonial era, the Japanese colonisers left the exploitative class structure of northern Korea in a much worse state than it had been during the Chosŏn dynasty (E.-J. Choi 2020; K.-T. Kim 2016). As discussed earlier, the Communists in the North settled these old class grievances at one stroke, for a time at least, by means of its sweeping programme of land reform in March 1946. Within this historical context, the Shinch'ŏn Uprising was merely another 'rollback' campaign against the new economic structure created by the programme of North Korean land reform, a campaign that capitalised on the much larger rollback campaign waged by the US against Soviet expansionism for more local purposes of its own. In this regard, the insurrection may be seen as another act in the much older class war drama, decked out in the new costumes of an anti-communist

184　*The Korean War Novel*

crusade. What chiefly distinguishes this age-old domestic conflict was the ability of the combatants to champion their interests in the language of Christian Nationalism and Communism, each of whom were in turn allied with the bipolarised camps of the Cold War.

When it is considered that many members of the landowning classes are revealed in the novel to be pro-Japanese collaborators, the rightist uprising may be seen as taking the form of a reverse postcolonial war, one that attempts to restore the class structure of colonial times by means of an anti-communist rollback campaign. In this light, Hwang's narrative displays the convoluted, multilayered nature of the Korean War: at once a civil war, a class war, a religious conflict and a Cold War. At the end of the novel, Hwang attempts to overcome the system of national division by means of a vision of reconciliation between the massacre's perpetrators and victims.

A crusade?

A few points of division emerge in the past historical studies of the Shinch'ŏn Uprising on the issue of the composition of the insurrectionist forces of the right. According to Monica Hahn, the main forces of the uprising consisted of two groups: the first were members of the nationalist Chosŏn Democratic Party; the second were local anti-communist students. For instance, Kim Pongsun, the leader of the uprising, was the chairperson of the Shinch'ŏn County branch of the Chosŏn Democratic Party; and Kim Hwakyŏng, who proposed the uprising to Kim Pongsun, was the former chairperson of the Chaeryŏng branch of the same political party. In Hahn's opinion, the greatest contribution to the insurgence came from the local upper-middle (the equivalent of high school) students who had gone into hiding because of the KPA's conscription campaign (2013: 109–11).

According to another source, the uprising was mainly the result of the actions of two forces: a patriotic student organisation called *Kuguktongjihoe* (League of Save Our Nation) and guerrillas from Mount Kuwŏl, who consisted of members of both the Chosŏn Democratic Party and *Kuguktongjihoe* (Cho 1957: 38–66, 78–80). As Ryu Tae-ha recounts, *Pan'gonghaksaenghoe* (the Anti-Communist Student League) was established in Shinch'ŏn on 1 June 1950. This organisation expanded its network by recruiting more members from the general public and, on 17 July, changed its name to *Kuguktongjihoe*. The rioters numbered 220 individuals, among whom were 150 teachers and students, several dozen youth, Christian ministers and churchgoers and local dignitaries

A Postcolonial War in Reverse   185

(T.-H. Ryu 2005: 192–3). Ryu's account is significant in locating the presence of Christians in the make-up of the insurgent forces; however, what is worth noting here is that this religious group comprised only a part of the total rebel forces. For example, as Kwak Pokhyŏn, a refugee from Shinch'ŏn, testifies, Kim Pongsun, the uprising's leader, was not a Christian; and other people joined the uprising irrespective of their religious convictions. Of the actual presence of Christians in the forces that carried out the uprising, Kwak states:

> Sure, there were Christians, Christian youths in particular. But people who participated did, no matter what their religion was. The leadership of the 13 October Uprising did not plan it for a religious cause in the first place. ('Ijenŭn' 2002; author's translation)

According to these historical studies and testimonies, a number of the students and Nationalist Party members who participated in the uprising were Christians, but Christians did not form an exclusive leadership nor were they heavily represented in the ranks of the insurrectionists.

In *The Guest*, in contrast, it is Christian youths that constitute both the majority of the insurrectionist leadership and the majority of its rank and file. According to the novel, the Christian youth plan the uprising under the vigilant guidance of members of the rightist youth corps sent by the South; and their forces are later reinforced by the Unification Corps, a group of guerrillas that have been hiding in Mount Kuwŏl (S.-Y. Hwang [2001] 2005: 185). In the novel, this group's contribution to the insurrection is almost entirely eclipsed. In Hwang's rewriting of the incident, both the majority of the local student body and the wider youth population, who, according to these historical studies, constituted the majority forces of the insurgency, become, to a man, a group of militant Christian combatants. In this fictional account, the leadership of the uprising consists of Yohan and a second youth group leader from the Sŏbu church in Chaeryŏng. These figures function as Christian substitutes for the historical figures of Kim Pongsun and Kim Hwakyŏng. Most importantly of all, the uprising in Shinch'ŏn in the novel is pointedly made possible through the mobilisation of the local Christian network, 'the presbytery organizations of the church [that were] still active' (S.-Y. Hwang [2001] 2005: 184) at the time. When they are told of the news of the UN forces advancing fast across the thirty-eighth parallel, these religious organisations issue a call to arms to 'all the Christian Youth who had gone into hiding' (S.-Y. Hwang [2001] 2005: 184).

By identifying the right-wing forces as mainly consisting of Christians, Hwang initially depicts the uprising as a war between the young members of the Church and the Communist regime. Not surprisingly,

186   *The Korean War Novel*

the novel notes that tensions between Communists and Christians are building up in the North, just before the uprising takes place. According to the narrator, Shinch'ŏn and the adjacent townships of Anak and Chaeryŏng bear witness to this growing tension. One of the earliest clashes depicted in the novel takes place in the context of a three-county joint worship held at Sŏbu church in Chaeryŏng in 1946 in order to celebrate the 1 March 1919 Independence Movement. The hostility of the Church toward the Communists emerges in an unmistakable manner in the speech made by the Presbyterian minister of Sŏbu Church. Calling for the congregation to build a Christian nation, the minister denounces Communists as 'heathen trash, ignorant atheists, . . . idiots who simply did anything the Soviet Union told them to do' (S.-Y. Hwang [2001] 2005: 112). This condemnation triggers an act of stone-throwing on the part of the Communists who surround the church, in the hope of finding an excuse to crush the separate Christian celebration of the independence movement. As anticipated, the church service leads to a violent clash between the two groups, resulting in mass arrests of the Christians by the Communist authorities. Hwang's fiction reports a second roundup of Christians following their boycott of the election – spitefully scheduled for the Sabbath – of the People's Committee representatives (S.-Y. Hwang [2001] 2005: 132). These fictional accounts accurately portray the predicament of the beleaguered Christians in the wider context of the North before the outbreak of the Korean War, although the author's attribution of the Shinch'ŏn Uprising mainly to Christian youths remains a point of dispute.

In his conversation with the ghost of Sunnam about the major pre-war conflicts in the Communist North, the ghost of Yohan ascribes all of the conflicts to the Christian youth-led uprisings:

> All these insurrections were the work of the Christian Youth. Of course, they were helped by young men from the South, members of the Anticommunist Youth Corps and the Korean Independence Party. If the Communists had Marx's *Das Kapital*, we had our Bibles. We'd become the Lord's crusaders; they were the minions of Satan. It was *a conflict that had begun long before, in the generation of our grandfathers*, when the people of Chosŏn got their taste of enlightenment. (S.-Y. Hwang [2001] 2005: 113–14; emphasis added)

In this speech, the Christian Nationalists are described as allied with the rightist youth corps, the youth vanguards sent north by the South Korean government. By choosing to see the conflicts through the eyes of Yohan, a zealous anti-communist Christian, Hwang is able to categorise the uprising and its subsequent massacres as the battle between 'the Lord's crusaders' and 'the minions of Satan', or to quote Yohan's metonymic phrase, between 'Bibles' and '*Das Kapital*'. What is note-worthy about Yohan's speech is that the crusade against Communism is seen as something that goes back at least two generations.

Nonetheless, although Yohan locates the origins of this crusade in the period of enlightenment during the era of late Chosŏn, Korean history does not testify to a war, Christian or not, waged against Communism during the period in question. This is hardly surprising since the ideol-ogy of communism was first introduced to Korea during the period of Japanese rule. Perhaps Yohan has in mind the period of Christian religious persecutions in Chosŏn? But this series of unfortunate inci-dents were over by the time the isolated dynasty first opened its door to the West in 1876. And unlike its sister faith of Catholicism, Protestant Christianity was first introduced in Chosŏn only after the country offi-cially ceased to repress foreign religions.

If the reader attempts to find in earlier Korean history a more accurate parallel for the conflict between the Christians and Communists, the peasants' revolutionary war of 1894–5 would be the obvious candidate. This was a war waged by the Korean peasantry against both the feudal-istic order of the Chosŏn dynasty and the foreign powers of the time. These revolutionary struggles, dubbed the '*Tonghak*' (Eastern Learning) Movement, were carried out as counter-measures against the spread of Western religion, then known as '*Sŏhak*' (Western Learning), a body of knowledge that was also associated with the technological and military power of encroaching Western powers. What is more, the Communist call to dismantle the feudal order in the name of a revolutionary eco-nomic equality corresponds, if it corresponds to anything at all, to the revolutionary acts taken by the peasants in burning the land registers and enfranchising the slave class (Sun 2018: 155–76). Equally, the rich North Korean Christian leaders and their middle-class followers bear an obvious resemblance to the wealthy landed aristocracy of the late Chŏsun dynasty, with its zealous protection of its inherited right to own-ership of the land.[1] Since the Korean peasant class took up arms against both Western religion and the landed ruling class, Yohan's invocation of this revolutionary war as a means of justifying the anti-communist war of the landed Christians is based on a gross misreading of the historical parallel.

There again, if Yohan's reference to '*the conflict . . . in the generation of our grandfathers*' is meant to signal the relations between Christianity and communism during the period of Japanese colonialism, this does not do justice to the attempted alliance between these two social forces. Since communism was introduced into Korea following the victory of the Bolsheviks in Russia in November 1917 and the formation of the

188 *The Korean War Novel*

Chinese Communist Party in October 1921, the relationship between Christians and communists was more complex and dynamic than later generations may tend to believe. As the historical studies on colonial-era Korean Christianity reveal, these two groups pursued a united front for a time, although the alliance started to fall apart from the late 1920s. The split in the alliance was caused in part by the tendency of the Christians to lean toward a conservative social outlook, attendant upon their desertion of the cause of Korean nationalism, and the tendency of the Communists to take up more radical positions. Even here, however, the attitudes of Korean Christians towards the forces of Communism were far from uniform, being dictated largely by their own political interests.[2] Given the range of relations between these two diverse ideological camps, Yohan's view appears to offer a retroactive projection of their much later fierce rivalry.

If Yohan's comment on the earlier historical struggles of the Korean Christians is chronologically inaccurate, it is also over-schematic in its division of the entire population of the North into two opposing camps, that of 'the Lord's crusaders' and that of 'the minions of Satan'. In particular, the use of the second term in referring to the non-Christian or pro-Communist population of the North raises the question of whether or not his understanding of postliberation Korea too readily transposes the complex politico-economic relations of the times into a religious framework of good and evil or, by extension, into the equally rigid binary logic of the Cold War. To cast this zealous Christian as one of the leaders of the rightist uprising is obviously intended to highlight the self-righteousness of the insurgents, who are ultimately exposed as being motivated by an extreme un-Christian materialism.

The religious framework by means of which Yohan tries to make sense of the uprising is made clear in the prayer he offers up at the very moment when he and his friends rise in arms:

> Our Father in Heaven, we have guarded our faith under the oppression of the Communists, the enemy of the Holy Ghost. Thou hast told us to wear the armor of God, to become strong so that we can fight against the scheming designs of the devil ... The only way we will win this war is to rely upon the power of God and to prepare ourselves with the weapons of God. The Crusaders of freedom are just around the corner, coming to liberate our brothers in faith, but the army of Satan continues to threaten us. Let Michael, the Archangel, come among us and grant us [the] wisdom and courage that was once bestowed upon Joshua and David. (S.-Y. Hwang [2001] 2005: 186–7)

The religious Manicheanism informing Yohan's prayer sees no middle ground between good Christians and evil Communists. Instead, the

KPA becomes coterminous with 'the enemy of the Holy Ghost', while the UN forces are transformed into the 'Crusaders of freedom'. The Communists, their families and those who were forced to join the Party's auxiliary associations are all lumped together under the single category of 'Satanic forces'. The complex politico-economic realities, realities whose origins lie in a period of history stretching back to a time well before the outbreak of the Korean War, are reduced to the simple binaries required by a dogmatic, belligerent Christianity in league with a murderous Cold War logic. The sociological outcome of such thinking is the civilian slaughter that ensues.

A similar form of reductionism is found in the work of those historians who attempted to understand the Korean War as exclusively a proxy war. As Cumings asserts (1981: xxi), what tends to disappear in the writing of those who see the Korean War as simply a proxy war (or international war in disguise) is its nature as a people's struggle to liquidate the legacy of Japanese colonialism. In much the same way, an alternative understanding of the Shinch'ŏn incident may begin with the consideration that one of the major factors triggering the reprisals of the right-wing Christians was a complex of economic grievances, although the religious and political persecutions of the religious group by the Communists certainly aggravated this too. When situated in this historical context, the author's professed view of the uprising as a conflict between an ill-assimilated foreign Christianity and an equally poorly enculturated Communism does not do justice to his book. Curiously enough, then, the novel may be seen to complement or rectify this authorial view by the way in which it demystifies the crusade as a sordid materialistic war between opposing classes.

A secular war behind the holy war

The history of North Korea during the transitional, postliberation period may not be the immediate background of *The Guest*; nevertheless, this history is crucial in understanding the older grievances couched within the religious rhetoric of the youthful Christian crusade. As Ko Young-Eun's study recounts, when the Soviet army moved into northern Korea, they could not ignore the local Nationalists. After all, these forces had established their own CPKI and had started performing the basic function of a new sovereign administration prior to occupation by the Soviets. In both Pyongyang and Hwanghae Province, many of these Nationalists were Christians. In this respect, the Nationalists felt a strong need to cooperate with the Communists in building a new

190   *The Korean War Novel*

nation. For this reason, at an early stage in the postliberation period, the Communists and the Nationalists formed a working coalition (Ko 2016: 878–80). The coalition soon fell apart, however, over the issue of the five-year international trusteeship of Korea, an outcome of the Moscow conference of the United States, United Kingdom and Soviet Union in December 1945.[3]

A second major incident that further antagonised the two camps was the commemoration of the 1 March 1919 Independence Movement. While the newly formed Provisional People's Committee, chaired by Kim Il-sung, wanted to celebrate this event as a public ceremony for all the citizens of Pyongyang, the Church leaders wanted to hold a separate Christian ceremony. This was because, they rightfully contended, many of the leaders of the movement were Christians. As a consequence, the security forces arrested the leaders of the Church and brutally attacked those Church members who had resisted by arranging to hold a separate ceremony. These persecutions generated a chain reaction of revenge and recrimination among members of the two groups. As recounted in *The Guest*, Christian youth, in league with secret agents of the Korean Youth Corps from the South, chose to retaliate violently against the Communists, by throwing grenades during the Communist-organised 1 March 1919 Independence Movement ceremony. They also hurled bombs into the Soviet military commander's home and the home of the Reverend Kang Yanguk, an attack which resulted in the death of the minister's oldest son (S.-Y. Hwang [2001] 2005: 113). The minister was targeted because, as the newly elected Secretary General of the Provisional People's Committee, Kang was seen as a Communist sympathiser. Again and again, the two antagonistic forces clashed with each other over the scheduling of the elections of the representatives of the People's Committee. Each of these important clashes between the two camps is narrated in Hwang's novel; they form the matrix for the subsequent Shinch'ŏn Uprising.

Of all the issues that gave birth to the uprising, the single most important one was that of land reform. The passage of the land reform bill, which was announced in a surprise move by the Provisional People's Committee in March 1946, confiscated all of the land owned by both the Japanese colonialists and those Koreans considered to be national traitors; land was also taken from landowners who possessed more than 15,000p'yŏng or 49,500m². This move not only dealt a severe blow to the class of landowning Nationalists but served decisively to transform the political structure of northern Korea. If land reform snatched from the northern Nationalists their economic livelihood, it rallied a large number of small and tenant farmers to the Communist cause as a result of this collective gift of free confiscated land.[4] With the consolidation of Communist rule, the Christian Church suffered a large drop in membership.[5] In Hwang's novel, Yohan expresses the consternation that was almost certainly shared by the vast majority of the landowning Christian Nationalists when he recalls that the news of the impending land reform had been 'something we could never have imagined, something completely unheard of' (S.-Y. Hwang [2001] 2005: 114).

The fact that the middle- and upper-class Christian Nationalists had to give up their wealth and political privileges under the Communist regime invites the interpretation that the 'holy war' waged by Yohan and his fellow Christian youth against 'Satanic forces' was simultaneously a politico-economic one. The secular roots of this supposedly religious conflict are detectable in the scenes where the right-wing forces, having taken over the local county, start to arrest every officer from the township's Communist organisations and their auxiliary associations on whom they can lay their hands. In one of these scenes, Yohan and his men arrest Pak Illang, the chairperson of the local branch of the Communist Party. Yohan vents his pent-up rage at Illang because he knows that it is Illang who has been responsible for confiscating the land formerly belonging to Yohan's family. Yohan takes his revenge by knocking Illang unconscious with a pickax, and when he regains consciousness, Yohan angrily shouts at him – and divulges his ulterior motive for helping to launch the religious war: 'You son of a bitch, you took our land – thought you'd be Party chairman for a thousand, ten thousand years, didn't you?' (S.-Y. Hwang [2001] 2005: 195). In the end, for Yohan, the crusade was nothing more than an elaborate façade for the more immediate task of retaking the land that had been confiscated from his family. A second member of the security forces, Pongsu, is motivated by much the same set of reasons. In his case, his family has been forced to give up both their land and their mill to former employees. Having arrested the two men who received these former possessions, Pongsu strips them naked and starts to beat them. Pongsu concludes his revenge on the two ingrates by pouring gasoline all over their naked bodies and throwing a lit match on them (S.-Y. Hwang [2001] 2005: 202). For him too, the holy war is a pretext for reclaiming his stolen bourgeois rights and privileges.

Strictly speaking, the origin of the class conflict behind the religious war stretches back to a time well before the Communist-inspired land reform of March 1946. Although overshadowed by the issue of Communist anti-Christian persecutions and subsequent Christian reprisals, the postcolonial dimensions of the land dispute are detectible in one of the supernatural scenes in the novel. In this scene, the ghosts

192   *The Korean War Novel*

of the aggressor and his victims converse with one another in front of Yosŏp and Uncle Some. When Yohan accuses the Communists of stealing his family's land, Sunnam responds by suggesting that the issue dates back to a time long before the generation of Yohan and Pongsu:

> To tell the plain truth, your father, Presbyter Ryu Indŏk, and your grandfather, Reverend Ryu Samsŏng – they came into their land by working as agents for the Japanese Oriental Development Company, managing the contracts of tenant farmers. Practically everyone who attended Kwangmyŏng Church, in fact, lived quite comfortably, and most of them had at least a plot of land to their name, small or large. As for the churchgoers who lived in town, they were all restaurant owners, pharmacy owners, schoolteachers, millers – all pretty loaded, really. And the members of the so-called Committee for the Preparation of Korean Independence, they were the same kind of people. The only thing different about them was that they called themselves the Nationalist Camp. Anyway, we stood firm. Land reform had to be implemented using blind confiscation and blind distribution. That's when the Nationalist Camp flared up in a rage and refused to compromise. They said the very notion of abolishing the landownership system was unpatriotic . . . Show me a Christian leader who didn't come from a family of landowners. (S.-Y. Hwang [2001] 2005: 115–16)

In this passage, Sunnam brings a serious charge against the Ryu family: they belonged to the collaborator class that prospered in exchange for their service to a Japanese land development company, one which was notorious for plundering the land of small Korean farmers and exploiting them as underpaid tenant farmers. What is more, he highlights the fact that many pro-Japanese collaborators, who were able to amass wealth in return for their traitorous acts, transmogrified into right-wing Nationalists after the national liberation from the Japanese. This trajectory is one that can be observed in the cases of both the families of Yohan and Pongsu. What is more, the case of the Protestant minister, Reverend Ryu, was far from being an isolated one. As the historian Park Chung-shin asserts, 'In the last two decades of Japanese colonial rule in Korea, the Protestant church community did not show any interest in nationalist politics and social reform. Instead, many prominent Christians . . . became active collaborators with the Japanese' (2003: 156; see also S.-T. Kim 2006). In effect, the histories of these families illustrate the convergence of four different group categories: Christian, Nationalist, Agricultural and Manufacturing Capitalist and Pro-Japanese Collaborator. Placed within this larger historical context, the confiscation of land from people such as the Ryu family may seem more like the righteous liquidation of one of the central legacies of Japanese colonialism.

A Postcolonial War in Reverse   193

According to Sunnam, the agents of Korean farm tenancy management were as vicious as the Japanese colonisers in exploiting their compatriot tenants. In an earlier appearance to Yosŏp, the ghost of Sunnam testifies why, as a twenty-year-old, he had had to sell his labour in the Ryu family's orchard:

> You know what an [tenancy management] agent does? He raises the taxes that tenants have to pay and he makes them pay for his own tax, and if the tenants don't obey, he just terminates the contract and transfers their tenant rights to another farmer. The Oriental Development Company and the Financial Union, not to mention the landowners – they liked the go-getters, you know. They'd trade their best agents with each other, so after being transferred to a different area, these new agents could simply refuse to acknowledge the tenants' claims to taxes they paid the previous year. . . . Our family had to deal with it all – depending on the season, we would take them the bass, catfish or carp we caught in our nets, pheasants or a roe deer we'd been able to trap . . . None of it mattered, though. If the harvest was under quota because of cold weather or a typhoon, our tenant contracts would be taken away on the spot. Some of the villagers just filled their stomachs one last time and fled to Manchuria in the dead of night. You can't blame them, really. The price of rice was about as good as the price of shit, and after you paid off the expense of your irrigation system and fertilizer, what with the fees for Financial Union, you could have sold every last thing you owned and you'd still be in debt. (S.-Y. Hwang [2001] 2005: 73–4)

In this passage, it is strongly suggested that even while both the Japanese land development company and the Financial Union lived off the backs of the poor Korean tenant farmers, the contract managers, who were ethnic Koreans, also tried to wrest, in every conceivable way, control over whatever was left over. They forced the tenant farmers to come up with the price of their own farm rent and received all manner of small gifts in the process, yet still threatened to terminate the tenancy contracts for ever more money. From this perspective, it seems that the tenant farmers existed mostly to fill the pockets of the landowners and the loan-sharks. As Cumings suggests: '[m]ost peasants had to secure loans at some point in the agricultural cycle to enable them to survive. A stratum of moneylenders and other intermediaries, seeking profit from such misery, charged 60 to 70 percent interest annually on loans' (1981: 44).

This inequitable situation was an integral part of the legacy that the Japanese colonisers bequeathed to a liberated Korea, and the area of Shinch'ŏn was no exception to this predatory economic structure. It was also because of the rapacious Korean management agents that Sunnam's family, like their neighbours, had to move to a dugout in the mountains, eking out a meagre existence by feeding on a mixture of roots, wild

194   *The Korean War Novel*

greens, berries and tree bark. Seen from the perspective of members of the subproletariat like Sunnam, land reform served as a form of delayed national justice, even if it ended up being implemented by the Communists. In the eyes of Sunnam, it does not much matter by whom the colonial injustice was rectified.

The reason Sunnam left Ch'ansaemgol was that he could no longer bear the tyranny of the local landlords. When the tenant farmers in Ch'ansaemgol form a Farmer's Mutual Aid Association to help one another financially, the landlords' union, finding that the mutual aid threatens its vested interests, intimidates them into disbanding it. Driven out by this tyranny, Sunnam moves to the neighbouring town of Ŭnnyul. But even here, Sunnam witnesses members of the local Farmers' Association beaten and maimed by the landlords as a punishment for participating in the self-help organisation, so he decides to move again – this time, to a mining town. From Sunnam's point of view, whether they cloak themselves in the banners of Nationalism, Christianity or some combination of the two, the large landowners function as nothing more than a class of vampires feeding on the blood and tears of the impoverished tenants.

Viewed within the context of these postcolonial class struggles, the Korean War is made to assume a radically different form from its better-known and more conventional interpretations. Nonetheless, this aspect of the war was actually revealed in an announcement made by President Rhee on the very day that Pyongyang was captured by the forces of the UN and the Korean Army. Speaking on behalf of the northern landlord class, Rhee declared that he would annul the land reform carried out by the Communists. In order to escape persecution at the hands of the Communists for their pro-Japanese positions, many of these men had had to flee to South Korea after national liberation. From the class perspective of the landowners, the Korean War was waged in order for them to recover their semi-feudal privileges, privileges that the North Korean land reform had taken away. For the landed class, the significance of the war is articulated by Cumings in the following sarcastic terms:

> Nothing better expressed the twilight power and the ineffably recalcitrant backwardness of Korean landlords, and the basic character of the class conflict in Korea, than their obstinate determination to get back what they took to be their birthright, their holdings in both South and North, even in the midst of a devastating war being fought for them by the world's premier power. To them, this is what the war was about. (1990: 760)

Viewed in this context, the Shinch'ŏn Uprising was just another incident during which the old grievances between the two classes fiercely pursued

A Postcolonial War in Reverse   **195**

redress. In this light, I argue that the (post)colonial conflicts that existed between the pro-Japanese landowning class and the tenant farmers constitute a hidden, and yet fundamentally crucial, dimension to the crusade of the right-wing Christians.

A class bias against the 'ugly pots'

Was Christianity in colonial Shinch'ŏn a religion for everyone? Although most Korean Christians took part in Japanese Shinto shrine worship during the late colonial period, which represented a sign of their submission to colonial rule, it is still true that many of the patriotic independence fighters were Christians. According to Sunnam's testimony, however, Christianity in colonial Shinch'ŏn was mostly for one class only, the class of 'haves'. It was 'a place someone like me wouldn't dare go near, not once' (S.-Y. Hwang [2001] 2005: 76). The church in Ch'ansaemgol, frequented by the landowning class, did not go so far as to exclude the tenant farmers from participating in Sunday worship – so long, that is, as they met certain qualifications of social decorum. They needed to raise a family and maintain a social status above that of being mere hired hands. For all its professed Christian concern, however, members of the lowly servant class were categorically denied membership in the church. By way of contrast, it was the Communists who warmly embraced those excluded from the bourgeoisie-led community and its religious worship. Sunnam, for one, first receives the teachings of Communism while working as a miner in another county in Hwanghae Province. The new ideology promised an alternative society for the dispossessed, the displaced farmers and labourers who, like Sunnam, had had to leave their hometowns in sorrow or in anger because of the unconscionable actions of the tenancy management agents, predatory landlords and loan-sharks.

In Hwang's novel, it is noteworthy that when the tables are turned under Communist rule, the Christian Nationalists significantly dismiss the opportunity to work with their tenants and servants whose community status has suddenly risen to match that of their masters. When the Provincial People's Committee is formed in Shinch'ŏn, the right-wing Christians look down on the left-wing committee members. To quote from Yohan's scorching remarks on the rise in social status of 'the lowly scum':

When we got back home, the Provincial People's Committee had been already founded – the state of the town was just ridiculous. Everyone and

196   *The Korean War Novel*

his grandmother, all the servants and good-for-nothings and vagabonds, the ones who felt they'd been treated badly in their own towns and villages, they were all sticking together. Naturally we cut ties with this so-called People's Committee and formed our own groups, centered around the church. (S.-Y. Hwang [2001] 2005: 110)

Here, when Yohan talks about getting 'back home', he is referring to a trip to Shinŭiju (Sinŭiju). He has gone there along with the other Christian youth to join what is probably the first anti-Communist student uprising of 23 November 1945, which took place in North P'yŏgan during the Soviet occupation. Following the recommendation of the Soviet military command, the seats of the People's Committees were typically divided between the Communists and local Nationalists (S. Kim 2020: 117–18). However, according to Yohan, because the right-wing members regarded the left-wing members of the People's Committee as underserving social outcasts, they 'formed [their] own groups'. In other words, the Nationalists in Shinch'ŏn not only sabotaged the possibility of a working coalition with the Communists but brought about their own political isolation not just from the Communists but also from the wider local population by forming their own groups 'centered around the church.' This proves to be a great political loss for the Shinch'ŏn Nationalists.

Yohan's dim view of the merits of the Communist self-governing organisations actually stands in stark contrast with the account offered by Sunnam. According to the detailed report of the latter, nothing much has changed in the wake of national liberation. Under Soviet sponsorship, the representatives of all community organisations in Hwanghae Province have gathered to elect the members of the self-governing organisations. The initial results, however, have not matched the Soviet recommendation of an equal distribution of seats for the two camps. According to Sunnam's recollection, a Christian presbyter has been appointed as chairperson of the Hwanghae Province People's Political Committee; and '[e]xcept for a few Leftists, all the members were either landowners and other rich folk with lots of influence' (S.-Y. Hwang [2001] 2005: 114). That is, even after national liberation, the members of the collaborator class, who could have been expected to be punished for their pro-Japanese activities, are still the dominant social and political force. To quote Sunnam again, 'the bastards who'd lived so well through the occupation, fawning all over the Japs – they were still the same ones who were getting the higher positions, even after liberation and still ordered us to do this and that' (S.-Y. Hwang [2001] 2005: 115). Sunnam's appraisal of the political situation in Shinch'ŏn reflects the local history. According to Monica Hahn, both the first chairperson

A Postcolonial War in Reverse   197

and vice-chairperson of the County Committee, as well as the chief of the security forces, were Christian Nationalists (2019: 161). In Hwang's novel, the two major cases of pro-Japanese collaborators who become right-wing Nationalists are the Ryu and the Pongsu families. The rise of the Ryu family to landlord status is principally due to the employment of Yohan's father and grandfather as farm tenancy management agents for a Japanese land development company. During the period of Japanese colonial rule, Pongsu's father also amassed great wealth by running a milling factory, and Pongsu ran a large general store in Pyongyang. After liberation, both Yohan and Pongsu join the Chosŏn Democratic Party and become key members of the Nationalist organisation.

In Sunnam's opinion, it is the actions of these bourgeois Nationalists that have driven the workers and the poor farmers to an embrace of Communism in northern Korea. Using an extended metaphor, Sunnam describes the harsh treatment that the poor became accustomed to during the long years of Japanese rule:

> [I]f you went to the marketplace and entered a pottery shop, you'd probably have seen a malformed pot or two. The irregularities happen after the lump of clay has been formed into a pot, probably from some mistake in the drying process. Anyway, in the end, what you've got was a defective pot. These pots, they were never thrown away – they just got sold for half the price. The nicely shaped, well-made pots cost several times more. Really rich folk would even buy ceramics that had colored glazes and elaborate designs. The defective pots were for the poor. Placed in a sunny spot in a three-room, straw-thatched hut, they would be used to keep soy sauce or kimchi, food you saved to eat during the long winter days. You know, even when a poor family somehow moved on up in the world, they always held on to those ugly pots, passing them down as family heirlooms.
>
> You see, the poor people and needy farmers of Chosŏn – they were the ugly pots, bashed in by the Japanese. To hold them up, to display them as something precious – that's been the position of our class. You people, you people just want to smash them to bits and be rid of them. (S.-Y. Hwang [2001] 2005: 118–19)

Here, Sunnam contrasts both the Japanese rulers and the Korean bourgeoisie with the Communists in their attitude towards 'the poor people and needy farmers'. While both the Japanese colonisers and the Korean landlords treat the poor like 'defective pots' to break up and throw out, the Communists 'hold them up . . . as something precious'. As a matter of fact, the lives of the poor farmers were much harsher during the colonial period than in earlier times. As Cumings maintains, the tenant farming system during the Chosun era was at least a stable one based on a recognition of unequal but mutual obligations between landlord

198 *The Korean War Novel*

and tenant. During the colonial era, when this feudal system was transformed into a new system based on legal contracts, it became much more precarious for the tenants. Under this new system, the greedy landlords, both Japanese and Korean, began to squeeze the tenants in a nightmarish way by constant threats to replace them in return for higher rents (Cumings 1981: 44). In Sunnam's view, in the era of national liberation, the bourgeois Nationalists proved to be no different from the Japanese colonisers they replaced.

Sunnam's portrayal of the landowning class as intent upon exterminating the poor farmer class is a reference to the murderous practices of the unbridled laissez-faire economy under the Japanese rule, and yet it also anticipates the spirit of murderous vengefulness that possessed the Christian Nationalists at the time of the Shinch'ŏn massacre. However, one important point that is omitted from Sunnam's account concerning the clashes between the right-wing forces and the Communists in Shinch'ŏn is that the rightist uprising and subsequent carnage are triggered by the pre-emptive arrests and executions of the right-wing figures by the retreating Communists all over Hwanghae Province. It also needs to be noted that Sunnam's view of Communists as treasuring the 'ugly pots' is only truly applicable to the first few years of Communist rule. A more balanced assessment of what was really going on can be made only after we consider the subsequent history of land reform in North Korea. By August 1958, by means of an extensive programme of collectivisation, the North Korean leadership had taken almost all the land it had previously distributed back from the farmers (C.-S. Lee 1963: 76).

If the reader searches for the most dented, ugliest pot in *The Guest*, they will probably settle on the figure of Illang. Illang, who also went by the name of Ichiro, was once a social nobody. No one in Ch'ansaemgol appears to remember when he first came into the village; no one knows his exact age. In the past, Illang was a village servant. A range of communal tasks, both light and heavy, was his to perform, from helping with the village farming to mending broken stepping stones to keeping the watermill in working order to maintaining the community compost ground. At first, he had lived in a dugout; later, he was allowed to stay in a village *sarang*, or community lounge. No one spoke using the forms of polite language to him since he was obviously from the lowest rung of the community. Sometime after liberation, however, Ichiro returns to the community: only now he says that his name is Comrade Pak Illang. Accompanied by other members of the Democratic Youth League, Illang walks into the Ryu family's house and holds out the land confiscation notice before them. Thinking that this lowly figure must be illiterate, Yohan's father, pretending to have bad eyesight, requests that Illang read out the notice for him. However, his plan to humiliate this self-important former village servant is completely shattered when the latter begins to read the document, in a slow but articulate voice. Enraged, Yohan's father snatches the piece of paper from him and tears it to pieces. This sudden temper tantrum results from the immediate prospect of losing his land as well as his disappointment at failing to disgrace this once lowly fellow in front of his men. At the same time, his loss of self-control may be ascribed to his unsettling realisation of the fact that literacy, which has long undergirded his ascendant social status, is no longer the property of the landowning class alone. The episode ends with Illang walking away with the family's land title after he has punched Yohan's father in his face and thrust the mother, who has attempted to intervene, to the floor. Yohan's father is ignorant of the fact that Illang has been zealously learning to read and write by attending an educational program run by Communists at the county community centre for the last few months. By means of this episode, the author reveals not only the impact that land reform has made on the large landowning class in the North but also some of the reasons why the proposed coalition between the Communists and the Nationalists in Shinch'ŏn collapsed. Again, what has caused the Christian Nationalists to refuse to work with the Communists as colleagues in civic affairs? Unmistakably, Hwang's answer is the social elitism of the Christian Nationalists – that is to say, this group's class bias.

Simultaneously, Hwang raises the issue of what liberation means to people like Illang, this former member of the subaltern or subproletarian class. Speaking of Illang's transformation after national liberation, Sunnam suggests:

> Ichiro, the same Ichiro you all thought was a brainless half-wit, the same Ichiro you talked down to – just think about it for a second – that same Ichiro learned to read and write. He learned to write his own name. Pak Illang. If that's not what the liberation was all about, I don't know what is. Comrade Pak Illang, who used to carry firewood and work like a cow while you people ate white rice, slept under warm blankets, learned at schools, sat in churches, read Bibles, prayed and sang hymns – well, he learned too, and he could read and write words like *land reform*. (S.-Y. Hwang [2001] 2005: 128; emphasis in the original)

During the colonial era, Sunnam attests, Illang occupied an abject status in the small rural community of Ch'ansaemgol. He was not only a social nobody to whom even small children 'talked down' but he was also considered 'a brainless half-wit'. It is national liberation that has given a sense of human dignity to this formerly despised community servant.

200   *The Korean War Novel*

However, Sunnam's statement is not entirely accurate: it is not the fact of national liberation that gave Ichiro his humanity back. Arriving with the Soviet occupying forces, the Communists are the ones who have helped him achieve self-respect. They have done this by helping him to become literate and by offering him a new type of communal work, drastically different from the communal work he had undertaken in the past. They have done this, above all, by offering, at least for a time, what Benedict Anderson would call a 'deep, horizontal relationship' (1983: 7) to his newly liberated nation.

When the rightist uprising, engineered by the Korean Youth Corps and encouraged by the northern advance of the UN forces, turns Communist-run Shinch'ŏn upside down, the members of Illang's immediate family are among the first to be executed by Yohan and his rightist chums. While his young wife and children are beaten to death, Illang is dragged along to the county hall attached by a wire running through his nose. Here, he is thrown into an air raid shelter, along with hundreds of other Communists and their families. Before they all are incinerated, Illang reflects on his past life, not in grief, nor with regret, but rather with contentment:

> [M]y whole life I've had nothing, no name, no nothing; I've worked my fingers to the bone without ever getting a chance to stretch my back – but at least I've had these past few years. They make it all worthwhile. (S.-Y. Hwang [2001] 2005: 204)

The time during which Illang walked with his head held high amounted to only five years of his life. Nonetheless, he finds, in these last few years, a worthiness that redeems his past entirely.

Just as the rightist security forces are about to pour gasoline in through the airshaft of the underground shelter in order to blow the captives up, Illang ruminates again:

> I never hated anyone, not once in my entire life. For a bowl of rice – maybe two bowls on a lucky day – I worked hard, and I kept working hard so that no one would have a reason to complain. And still, still I had to watch as my own family was killed right before my eyes. That was when I understood. If your heart isn't in the right place, you're no different from the beasts in the forest. (S.-Y. Hwang [2001] 2005: 204–5)

Here, the novelist highlights the madness of the rightist violence by laying bare the gruesome details of the way in which people like the humble, good-hearted Illang were slaughtered. At the same time, the author sends a poignant message to the elitist Nationalists through the mouth of this despised ex-community servant, the message that

A Postcolonial War in Reverse   **201**

one whose 'heart isn't in the right place' is really no different from wild beasts. Given the fact that the Nationalist bourgeoisie also constituted the class of learned Korean men, Illang's last-minute reflection is intended to drive home a further point: true enlightenment does not come from one's learning but rather from one's heart.

The truth about the massacre

According to Uncle Some's memory, it was on 17 October 1950 that the US Army moved into Shinch'ŏn. Although they stayed for two hours, they soon moved north and were never seen again until the general retreat the following winter. During the interim period of fifty-two days, a series of mass murders and reprisals took place in Shinch'ŏn. By Uncle Some's count, '[o]ver thirty-five thousand were killed, they say, and for all I know that may be true . . . One fourth of the county's entire population was killed' (S.-Y. Hwang [2001] 2005: 206). Uncle Some's recollection about the number of casualties matches the claims made by the North Korean state. The North Koreans insist that in the wake of the uprising, 35,383 people, or one-fourth of the entire population of the township, were killed in the civilian carnage (Hahn 2013: 103). In this way, Hwang endorses the North's claim about the extent of the massacre but, curiously enough, he challenges the North's position on the identity of the perpetrators.

According to the North, a US Army Lieutenant named Harrison, at that time the acting commander of the American soldiers stationed in Shinch'ŏn, ordered the civilian slaughter. In Hwang's novel, this allegation is repeated by a female tour guide at Shinch'ŏn Museum, a site that Yosŏp is encouraged to visit as part of his 'education' by the North Korean authorities. Referring to the Shinch'ŏn massacre, his tour guide claims: 'On October 18, the day that followed the beginning of their occupation, the fiendish American imperialist murderers enacted the mass slaughter that they had been planning for so long' (S.-Y. Hwang [2001] 2005: 93). The tour guide's account, which reflects the North's anti-American propaganda, is contradicted by the novel's anonymous narrator. The narrator records the movement of the US Army in this way: 'The Americans stay in the town of Sinch'ŏn for two hours. . . . They do not return until they retreat again the following winter' (S.-Y. Hwang [2001] 2005: 203). The contrapuntal presentation of these two opposing views on the same historical event is supposedly intended to debunk the North Korean account in order to earn the novel its credentials for keeping a wary distance from the propaganda mills of

202   *The Korean War Novel*

both South and North. That is, the novel attempts to tread a fine line between the South's celebration of the events in Shinch'ŏn as a heroic undertaking on the part of the Nationalists and the North's condemnation of these events as an outrageous war crime on the part of the American imperialists. Nonetheless, the question must be asked: Is the narrator's view of these historical events correct? Is the view of Hwang, as the novel's author, correct?

In the novel, Hwang's portrayal of the US Army supports the so-called 'two-hour-stay theory' held by most South Korean war historians and the Ministry of Korean Military Defense (T.-H. Ryu 2005: 208; KIMH 1997: 800–2). This is the view that, after a stay of just two hours in Shinch'ŏn, the US Army continued its northern-bound march. In an interview, Hwang repeats the historical view held by the South Korean government and the majority of scholars on the Shinch'ŏn incident:

> According to the war history, both the US and the ROK Army continued their non-stop march towards Pyongyang, Ch'ŏngch'ŏn River and Amnok River after the US Force's landing at Inchon. Although many civilians were indeed slaughtered by these armies on their route, the US Army did not stop in Shinch'ŏn. I wondered if the US Army Lieutenant Harrison, whose rank indicates his being a platoon commander, had the kind of authority to perpetrate such mass murder. While I was harbouring the idea that I would sometime write a fiction about the Shinch'ŏn incident, I had a chance to hear a detailed testimony about it from Reverend Ryu with whom I became acquainted in the US. When the incident occurred, he was a middle school student living in Shinch'ŏn, and his elder brother was one of the perpetrators. As I came close to the truth of the incident, putting testimonies together from other witnesses, I thought that I wanted to write a story that is new in stylistics and can resolve the Cold War at one stroke. (Pak and Pak 2001: 163–4; author's translation)

In short, the 'truth' of the events that Hwang came to favour was that the Shinch'ŏn massacre was carried out by rightist Korean Christians, not by the soldiers of the US Army. The author's conclusion is supported by both South Korean war history and the testimony of the survivors. All evidence points to the conclusion that it would have been impossible for the US Army to have slaughtered 35,000 people within the space of two hours.

However, this view does not go uncontested. Among those who questioned it is the Commission of International Association of Democratic Lawyers.[6] After an on-site investigation and testimonial hearing, this left-leaning international collective of legal professionals reached the conclusion that '35,383 civilians (19,149 men and 16,234 women) were murdered in the district of Sinchon during the American occupation, which lasted from October 17 till December 7, 1950, that is, for less than two months' (1952: 13). This report points to the US soldiers under the command of Harrison as responsible for the massacre. On a related note, the historical view that Hwang advances in his novel is questioned by none other than his own primary source, Reverend Yu T'aeyŏng. Reverend Yu is the real-life individual on whom Hwang's protagonist, Ryu Yosŏp, is modelled. Every major event of Reverend Yu's early life, from his visit to the North for a reunion with his sister-in-law and nephew to his brother's slaughter of Communist villagers and killing of the two stray female KPA soldiers whom Yu had secretly helped, is reflected in Hwang's novel. According to Yu, the autobiographical account that inspired Hwang's novel refers only to what happened in Yu's small village of Pujong-ri, rather than within the larger township of Shinch'ŏn. What is more, he claims to have no knowledge about the larger issue of who was responsible for the massacre (Kang 2001: 52). In this sense, Hwang has taken the story of what took place in a small village and extrapolated these events to the larger canvas of the township as a whole.

One consequence of the publication of *The Guest* was to trigger a thorough investigation of exactly what happened. The producers of a social investigation program at Munhwa Broadcasting Corporation, one of the major Korean TV stations, conducted extensive new research into the massacre. The TV program gathered testimonials from a number of survivors and visited the US National Archives to investigate the US Army war logs in an effort to ferret out the identity of those persons ultimately responsible for the slaughter. Aired on 21 April 2002, the TV programme confirmed the South's historical view that the mass killings were perpetrated by civilians, bringing into question the claims of the North about these events. Nonetheless, at the same time, the programme unearthed the fact that although there was no evidence of the US Army's direct involvement in the prolonged slaughter, the US Command did continue to receive reports about what was happening from its civil affairs officer who was still stationed in the township. What is more, although a US Army unit did leave the area on 17 October after a brief stay, a number of different units continued to be stationed near the town for a few days afterwards in order to secure the wider area ('Ijenŭn' 2002: 209–11, 218, 227–31). Thus, the two-hour-stay theory tends to account for only the first US military unit that passed through the town. The US Command appears to have been cognisant of what was taking place. Of course, this verdict is based on a form of hindsight to which Hwang did not have access while he was preparing to write the novel. What the author wanted to do, in the act of writing his novel, was 'to resolve the Cold War at one stroke.'

204 *The Korean War Novel*

Towards overcoming the entrenched Cold War

In spite of his somewhat obfuscatory critical commentary, Hwang's focus in *The Guest* is on understanding the Korean War as a civil conflict. Though decked out in the robes of a religious war against Communism, the Shinch'ŏn Uprising was fundamentally a class war – one which erupted in horrendous mass slaughter through an escalating series of enraged acts of revenge and counter-revenge. In his description of the carnage, the author lays bare the fact that the crusaders actually performed what they have previously condemned as the work of the devil. A good example of this is Yohan's act of revenge against Illang and the other members of his family. At dawn, Yohan, accompanied by members of the security forces, storms into Illang's house. Here, the first thing Illang sees, as he is violently awoken by a gun poked at him, is the face of Yohan. Illang recalls that seeing Yohan's face made him feel a shiver down his spine because 'it just didn't look . . . human. His eyes had a weird glimmer and the cold-blooded smile on his face made all my hairs stand straight up' (S.-Y. Hwang [2001] 2005: 194). Unfortunately, Illang's impression of Yohan's fiendish visage turns out to be accurate: at the bidding of Yohan, the crusaders drag the family out into the courtyard. One of Yohan's men picks up Illang's panicked, tearful daughter and slams her down on the ground; another strikes his wife so hard that he shatters her skull, even as she is attempting to go to the aid of her crying daughter; another kicks Illang's newborn child into the air like a soccer ball. The devilry of these events is fully confirmed when Yohan presses his revolver against Illang's head and threatens to shoot him. At this moment, the victim finds the firing pin of the gun 'wide open like the teeth of a snake' (S.-Y. Hwang [2001] 2005: 195). By employing the simile of the snake, the author associates the chief of the crusaders with the Biblical figure of Satan.

In the end, Yohan achieves a form of awakening from his self-delusion. Unfortunately, this new-found awareness arrives too late. When the UN army is pushed back by the Chinese People's Volunteer Army, the Christian Nationalists in Shinch'ŏn, worried about a counter-uprising, begin hastily executing not only those Communists that have been previously arrested but even those people whom they feel have even the slightest connections to Communism. In this pandemonium, Sangho, one of the other leaders of the uprising, goes to Yohan's eldest sister's house in order to kill her husband, who is a member of the Communist Party. Yohan's brother-in-law had felt an obligation to join the Party since he believed it was the only way for him and his family to survive

Communist rule. When he cannot find Yohan's brother-in-law, Sangho takes the decision to kill the brother-in-law's wife instead. When he learns of the death of his sister, Yohan is forced to confront an agonising conclusion about the nature of the struggle he is truly engaged in: '[i]t suddenly occurred to me that the whole notion of this side and that side, of us and them – it was all over. It was no longer the Lord's Crusade. We were no longer fighting to overthrow Satan' (S.-Y. Hwang [2001] 2005: 222). Unfortunately, this awakening does not serve to redeem Yohan for the forces of good but causes him to embrace an even blinder form of devil worship instead. In order to get even with Sangho, Yohan goes to the house of Sangho's fiancée, Myŏngsŏn, and kills both Myŏngsŏn's mother and her younger sisters. He later discovers that Sangho, on his way to the South, has murdered Yohan's other sister and all the members of her immediate family. When Yohan departs from his hometown at the end, he vows never to return: '[t]he place was doomed to become a hell on earth' (S.-Y. Hwang [2001] 2005: 224). What he appears never to realise is the role that he and his fellow Christians have been playing by carrying their own versions of Hell inside them all along.

It is Yohan's maternal uncle, Uncle Some, who serves as a foil against the devilish deeds of the Christian Nationalists. Unlike the Ryu family and the other Christians, Uncle Some stays behind. Under the Communist regime, he not only practises his religion faithfully but also receives state recognition as a model Communist. But he does not achieve this respect without suffering. On one occasion, for example, he experiences trouble from the North Korean authorities over his observation of the Sabbath. During one of the regular labour campaigns, Uncle Some is sent to a factory some distance from his hometown in order to assist with factory production for several weeks. When he requests permission to attend a Sunday church service from the superintendent of the factory, the latter scoffs at his cheekiness. In consequence, Uncle Some simply disappears in order to attend Sunday worship. When he finds out, the superintendent chastises Uncle Some for his disobedience. At this time, Uncle Some calmly reminds his superior official of his constitutional right to religious activities and offers to work some extra days to compensate. Naturally enough, this gesture of compromise is categorically rejected with the threat of legal charges against him in case of another disappearance. Undeterred, however, Uncle Some departs once again for church service the following Sunday. The second time he returns to face a much more severe reprimand. However, this incident concludes with Uncle Some winning the stubborn superintendent to his side. Looking deeper into this strange case of defiance, the superintendent realises that this man, whom he formerly dismissed as human 'garbage' addicted to

206 *The Korean War Novel*

religion, is, in fact, 'a man of integrity'. Uncle Some is someone who not only discharges his duties diligently but a man who also looks after his needy mates. Impressed by his noble behaviour, the superintendent grants Uncle Some permission to attend Sunday worship on the following Sunday (S.-Y. Hwang [2001] 2005: 166–8).

With his undaunted commitment to Christianity and his magnanimous attention to taking care of others, Uncle Some is presented as a saintly figure. This truly good person is speaking for the novelist when he refuses to distinguish the innocent from the guilty when assessing blame for the Shinch'ŏn massacre. When Yŏsup suggests to Uncle Some that both of them are innocent of mass murder, the usually calm and gentle person yells at him furiously: '[s]how me one soul who wasn't to blame!' (S.-Y. Hwang [2001] 2005: 162). This self-accusatory speech highlights the kind of person Uncle Some is by bringing into relief his communal or communitarian spirit towards the suffering of others. Implied in Uncle Some's reproach of his nephew is the belief that when injustices take place, everyone in the community is guilty, including the bystanders. In this paragon of communal responsibility, a virtue advocated by political theorists like Alasdair McIntyre and Michael J. Sandel,[7] Hwang offers his vision for a solution to a divided Korea:

> Back then I think, both sides were just very young. They needed to grow up enough to realize that things get quite complicated in the business of living, that a lot of things require mutual understanding and compromise. I mean, when you get right down to it, all business for us men on earth is based on material things – so we've just got to work hard and share the fruits of our labors with one another. Only when that is done righteously can we render our faith honorably to God. Within a generation of adopting a school of thought in the name of New Learning, be it Christianity or socialism, we all became such ardent followers that we forgot the way of life we'd led for so long. (S.-Y. Hwang [2001] 2005: 163)

Uncle Some's view is that the hasty adoption of Western ideology made a majority of Koreans forget 'the way of life we'd led for long.' This view echoes that of the author who sees the massacre as deriving from the poor assimilation of the two contrasting modernities. '[T]he way of life' that Uncle Some points out as a casualty of the uncritical subscription to foreign ideologies is a reference to humanism of 'mutual understanding and compromise'. Uncle Some goes on to chastise the materialistic Christians for their betrayal of the teachings of Christ. The churchgoer who does not share their wealth with the less fortunate cannot 'render faith honorably to God.' In other words, a true Christian would not oppose the idea of sharing the land with others so vehemently. Uncle

Some justifies this criticism by referring to Christ's practices of feeding the needy: '[a]nyway, the fact that the poor were being given land to live on so they wouldn't have to go hungry – that was a wonderful thing no matter what, especially when you think of the deeds of Jesus Christ' (S.-Y. Hwang [2001] 2005: 163). In this light, land reform is understood as an act faithful to the Christian spirit.

Uncle Some's philosophy that Communism and Christianity are not fundamentally different in their missions of working on behalf of the poor echoes the Marxist view of early Christianity. According to Frederich Engels, for instance, Christianity, in its earliest form, was also a social movement of the poor. As he states, what is often forgotten is that Christianity emerged as 'the religion of slaves and emancipated slaves, of poor people deprived of all rights, of people subjugated or dispersed by Rome.' In this regard, one might say '"socialism" did in fact . . . exist and even became dominant – in Christianity' (Engels 2008: 316–17).

In the character of Uncle Some, the novelist has attempted to reconcile the conflicting claims of the two ideologies, but he has gone further by demonstrating a communitarian spirit emboldened with a strong sense of mea culpa, a guiding virtue advocated by the author as a prerequisite for the goal of reconciliation between the two Koreas over the tragedy of the internecine war. Through the exemplary character of Uncle Some, Hwang appears to be offering a vision of the de-escalation of the Cold War in the form of an emergent harmonious inter-Korean relationship. In portraying the massacre as the responsibility of the local Christian leaders, thereby leaving out each of the other major players, Hwang was perhaps following the example of the past propaganda of the South Korean military dictatorships, only in reverse.

Hwang's criticism of the rightist anti-Communist Christians in the Shinch'ŏn incident of 1950 takes on special significance when it is placed in the historical context of the role played by the Protestant Church in both Korean and inter-Korean politics of the post-war South. If the Protestant Church in Korea, willingly or unwillingly, served the Japanese coloniser during the late colonial era, it also served the anti-communist dictatorships in the South during the postliberation era. As many theological studies have pointed out, those Christian refugees and immigrants who fled the Communist North have helped ensure that a spontaneous anti-communism is present in every sector of South Korean society, including its politics, its police force and army, its educational system and its religious practices (H. K. Lee 2020: 114; Kim and Kim 2018: 410–14). While in the postliberation era the Protestant Church has contributed to the nation-building project of the South, many

208 *The Korean War Novel*

right-wing Christian leaders and laymen have also encouraged the emergence of strongly polarised ideological rivalry between the South and the North. In this respect, Daniel Y. Kim maintains that 'Hwang's novel calls on readers in South Korea to recognize in evangelical refugees like Yohan the origins of the fusion of vehement anti-communism and Christianity that had served as the ideological engine that enabled a series of autocratic regimes and military dictatorships' (2020: 254). As a matter of fact, in an interview discussing his novel, Hwang suggested:

> I only wanted to take issue with the North Korean perpetrators of the interne-cine slaughters entrenching anti-communist pro-Americanism in South Korean society in which they took shelter. These established, anti-communist people are the enemy I would like to put a fight against since the South should change for the unification of the two Koreas. (Kang 2001: 52; author's translation)

In this speech, the author holds the northern right-wing Christians responsible not only for the civil massacre but also for transforming South Korea into their own Cold War battlefield, thus creating a major stumbling block to South Korea's attempted peace initiative towards the North. In this respect, in *The Guest*, the targeting of right-wing Christians carries a charge whose implications resonate well beyond the historical context of the Shinch'ŏn incident: it has relevance to the Cold War that is still being waged within the South today.

If his portrayal of Uncle Some illustrates the spirit of mutual tolerance and responsibility which he believes the two Koreas should maintain to achieve peaceful coexistence, Hwang seems to suggest that this spirit needs first to be one that is adopted by the pro-American, anti-communist Christians of the South. In this regard, the adoption of this critical spirit would constitute the first step in attempting to overcome the politics of division within South Korea itself. Indeed, it is surely no coincidence that Hwang's criticism of right-wing Christianity reverber-ates in a commentary by I Manyŏl, a South Korean church historian, on the role of Korean Protestantism in the inter-Korean politics of the past seventy years:

> The Korean Christian Church, persecuted by Communists, played a van-guard in the ideological rivalry in the postliberation era. Does it not still incite hatred against the North at the frontline of the ideological war? It is about time Korean Christianity turned its gun away from the northern brethren. It should lead the South–North relationship from rivalry to reconciliation and peace. (M. I 2016: 25; author's translation)

As the historian attests, the establishment politicians of rightist anti-communist Christianity who have resisted anything but a violent uni-

Figure 6.1 A crowd of 20,000 South Koreans at a rally on 11 July 1951, listening to speeches calling for the rejection of the armistice on the grounds that it lacked provisions for unifying the two Koreas. (Source: National Archives photo no. 111-SC-372325)

fication of the North by the military forces of the South are partially responsible for the entrenched division of Korea today.

Christians' excessive zeal for military reunification dates back to the summer of 1951 when the US wanted to bring the harrowing three-year period of bloodshed to an end by signing an armistice agreement with China and the Soviet Union. Over the years, however, South Koreans have been divided over this issue. For example, Figure 6.1 illustrates one of these earliest protests against the proposed armistice. As a means of improving his low popularity rate among the South Korean population, President Rhee endeavoured to exploit this issue. Just as it did in the pre-war years, the radical demand for military reunification served the cause of the unpopular national leader. In the spring of 1953, massive public rallies sprang up to protest the peace proposals. While politicians such as Chang Myŏn, Cho Pyŏngok and Kim Hwalran supported the cause of peace, the National Assembly came out in support of military reunification, with the Korean National Christian Council, led at that

210   *The Korean War Novel*

time by right-wing Christians of northern origins such as Reverend Han Kyŏngchik, at the forefront of the armistice protests (C. Yun 2013: 20–3; E. S. Lee 2018: 239–42; B.-K. Park 2019: 13–18). The latest intervention in South Korean politics by these ultra-right-wing, anti-communist Christians took the form of the reactionary political activism of the so-called '*T'aegŭkki* protests'. The significance of this political activism will be addressed in the conclusion of this book.

Notes

1. Although they were eventually vanquished by the allied forces of the Korean government and the Japanese army, the peasant revolutionaries did implement their social vision of egalitarianism in the areas that they managed to occupy. Indeed, Shin Yong-Ha maintains that 'the peasant rule . . . implemented the revolutionary self-rule by peasant aiming to abolish the whole system of the feudalistic *ancien régime* and to establish a new regime of peasants' (1989: 30).

2. In practice, Christian attitudes ranged from open hostility on the part of the more conservative forces, to the advocacy of Christian Socialism by the moderate centre forces, to the attempt of the progressive forces to integrate socialism and radical nationalism (Y. Choi 2018: 329). For instance, An Ch'angho (1878–1938) and Son Chŏng'to (1882–1931), both of whom were Christian Nationalist leaders who played key roles in the Provisional Government in Shanghai, searched for a way to work with the Communists in the name of national independence. An's *taekongcjuŭi* called for concerted efforts among different ideological groups for the greater cause of national liberation (J. Pak 2006: 120–2), while Son and the progressive leaders of the Young Men's Christian Organisation built their national independence movement along the line of Christian Socialism (T. I 2008: 109–10).

    Attempts at a coalition with the Korean nationalist and religious groups were also made on the part of Korean socialists. As a matter of fact, they formed an alliance with the Korean nationalists, creating the organisation *Shin'ganhoe* (1927–31), a nationwide united front for national independence. In 1926, the Korean socialists staged the 10 June Anti-Japanese Protest in collaboration with *Ch'ŏndogyo*, the members of an indigenous Korean religion based on the late nineteenth-century *Tonghak* Movement. During the colonial era in Korea, among all the liberation organisations, the socialist forces were known for waging the most militant struggle for national independence (Suh 1998: 357).

3. Despite the insistent pleas of the Communists, the Christian Nationalists refused to withdraw their opposition to the trusteeship plan. Once the security forces were under their control, the Communists then began to persecute and expel the Nationalist leaders from the Party the Nationalists themselves had originally created (S. Kim 2020: 105–28; Kim and Kim 2018: 405–6).

4. After the land reform, as Hahn records, the number of Communist Party members in Shinch'ŏn increased dramatically: most farmers eagerly volun-

teered for service in the Peasant Committees, with some of them becoming the new executive officers for these Communist organisations. As a consequence, the Peasant Committees fell under the complete control of the Communists (Hahn 2013: 110).

5. For example, in April 1946, the number of churchgoers in Shinch'ŏn fell to just 1,000 worshippers; in 1925, it reached a high of 3,280 (Hahn 2019: 164).

6. Following the Berlin Conference in September 1951, the Council of the International Association of Democratic Lawyers, which was first headquartered in Paris and later in Brussels, Belgium, set up a Commission to investigate North Korea's allegations about the US Army's violations of international law during the Korean War. The Commission, which, headed by Heinrich Brandweiner, Professor of International Law (Austria), consisted of five lawyers, one judge (from Italy, UK, France, Belgium, Brazil and Poland) and one personage from China, visited North Korea from 3 March to 19 March 1952 and conducted an on-site investigation. It is worth noting here that this organisation was well known for its leftist, anti-American leanings at the time.

7. According to McIntyre, a self inherits 'rightful expectations and obligations' from the communities it belongs to and thus its moral identity has to be found in and through its membership in them, although this does not mean that it has to necessarily accept the moral limitations of those particular communities (1984: 142–3). Viewed from this perspective, one is accountable for others and vice versa. In his criticism of the liberal notion, espoused by John Rawls, of an independent self, Sandel makes a similar argument (Sandel 1984: 159–76).

Conclusion:
Living the Cold War Legacy

Historical alterations in the portraits of war

In contrast to the conservative Korean belief in the US as a benefactor nation that has protected South Korea from the threat of the bellicose Communist regime of the North, many Asian American writers subscribe to the view of the US as an empire whose military enterprises in Southeast Asia have ended up either establishing or assisting a network of authoritarian right-wing regimes – what Christine Hong calls 'an anti-communist necropolitical order' (2020: 3). From this perspective, although it may have begun as a civil conflict, the Korean War was cleverly exploited by the US in order to initiate the military origins of the Cold War. As a result, not only the push for Communist expansion but also the decolonising aspirations of the Korean people in the post-colonial era were contained by the US military intervention. Jodi Kim, one of its earliest proponents in literary circles, explains it in these terms:

> Leading up to the formation of this parallel or 'double bipolarity,' one within Korea itself and the other between the superpowers, there were radical Korean nationalists and communists who were both anti-Soviet and anti-American, and before U.S. intervention in 1950, Koreans themselves were more welcoming of armed efforts at reunification than either superpower. Seen in such a light, in [*sic*] can be said that the Korean civil conflict, which then erupted into and was superseded by America's Korean War as a 'proxy' or 'hot war' in the bipolarizing Cold War between the superpowers, was also a project of decolonization. (2010: 147)

Drawing on the arguments of Giovanni Arrighi and Thomas J. McCormick, Kim explores the economic dimensions to the launching of the Cold War. According to Arrighi, the world economy in the aftermath of World War 2 suffered from a structural impasse: it was the Cold

War that enabled the US to bail itself out of it. That is to say, while the instigated fear of World War 3 helped to implement a form of military Keynesianism, the Korean War signalled the earliest opportunity to continue to justify the US government's massive military expenditure. For his part, McCormick argues that the Korean War enabled the US to shift the political, military and economic hegemony from Europe to itself (J. Kim 2010: 25–6). What this national tragedy for the Korean people meant to the US administration can be gauged by Secretary of State Dean Acheson's statement that the opening weeks of the war represented the greatest four weeks in American history (qtd in J. Kim 2010: 26).

Most Asian American critics tend to premise their criticism of the Korean War novel on similar lines of argument. For instance, critics like William Nessly and Steven Belletto see *The Martyred* as a novel which seeks to recover the superseded civil war (Nessly 2018: 57) or as one that attempts to interrogate the framework of the Cold War (Belletto 2015: 63). Both Daniel Y. Kim and Josephine Nock-Hee Park interpret Susan Choi's *The Foreign Student* as performing a postcolonial historiography that challenges the protagonist's understanding of the Korean War as a war of containment (D. Y. Kim 2006: 553–7; D. Y. Kim 2020: 184; J. N.-H. Park 2016: 94). In a similar light, Jodi Kim argues that Susan Choi's novel critically demonstrates 'how the Korean War gets "translated" through the dominant Manichean schema of the Cold War rivalry', proposing a third way in the protagonist's political non-alignment (2010: 156, 158).

My project differentiates itself from these critiques in that it focuses on odd imbalance or blindness, willed or haphazard, in Richard E. Kim's and Choi's reputedly revisionist portrayals of the Korean War as a civil conflict. This book contends that *The Martyred* occludes those realities of the Korean War that proved unsavoury to its American and South Korean readership, such as the US Air Force's massive air strikes and the civilian slaughters perpetrated in the recaptured North by ROKA and the rightist youth associations. By centring his narrative on the Communists' religious persecution and its aftermath, Kim limits the internecine brutalities of the civil conflict to the citizenry and the Communist police force north of the thirty-eighth parallel. In other words, a conflict between North Korean Communists and Christians is substituted for the ROK and US brutalities in the recaptured North. Later in the novel, the aggressive Pyongyang Christians who do not only not hesitate to antagonise but also attempt to murder their own leaders are seen to repent and regroup in the common cause of anti-Communism. The narrative's exclusive focus on the prodigal Pyongyang

214   *The Korean War Novel*

Christians and the self-sacrifices of certain South Korean army officers forecloses the embarrassing issue of ROK and US atrocities in this war. In this light, as Christine Hong argues, this novel 'propagates a fiction that sidesteps questions of U.S. and South Korean accountability, if not war criminality, vis-à-vis North Korea' (2012: 156–7). Although Richard E. Kim at times reveals the expedient propagandist work of the South Korean military intelligence corps, it is uncertain if this occasional criticism of the characters' counter-intelligence operation can be automatically construed as the author's taking distance from his own novel's use of the tactics of omission and displacement to mitigate the savage reality of the rollback operations.

The Foreign Student appears to rectify such imbalance by placing on display the violent conscription of civilians, the ROKA's brutal treatment of those suspected of Communist sympathy and the US Air Force's devastating air strikes in the North. Susan Choi even allows the Communist perspective on the Korean War within her text by giving a voice to the Communist Jaesong Kim and his sympathiser Miki. According to Miki, the US is responsible for the division of the Korean peninsula in the first place; and people like Jaesong, although persecuted in the South as insurrectionists, are only struggling to reunite it. A second crucial element that differentiates *The Foreign Student* from *The Martyred* is the presence of this working-class voice, however marginalised it is, which attests to the class struggle dimension to the war. This attempt at challenging the much-glorified narrative of the US military intervention is, however, compromised by the author's choice of the Manichean lens of the Cold War in portraying the decolonising struggles of South Koreans during the pre-war years.

A similar self-contradiction is found in Ha Jin's anti–Cold War project. Initially, the author's scathing portrait of the US-run POW camps in South Korea successfully gives the lie to the official narratives, exposing the brutalities of the US prison guards and their 'captive allies', the pro-Kuomintang Chinese inmates, against the Communist inmates. Yet, such demythologisation in the end backhandedly endorses liberal capitalism, the ideological foundation of one of the two global contenders for world hegemony, in the process of accusing the Communist inmates' leadership of hypocrisy. Above all, the self-centred, psychologising manner in which the protagonist analyses the motivations of the Communist leadership mars the objectivity of his own criticism. This serves to compromise the political neutrality with which the author credits his anti–Cold War project.

The 'counter-intelligence' strategy of omission and fictionalisation is also employed in *Silver Stallion*. In this novel, all direct clashes between the two Koreas are, oddly, absent. Instead, the author brings into relief the status of the US Army as unwelcome outsiders by exaggerating the friendliness of the KPA. That is to say, he portrays the lives of local people unaffected by the arrival of the KPA while emphasising the excessiveness of the US air campaign and the war crimes of the US military against the women of the village. The absurdity of the involvement of the foreign armies, whether backed by the UN or by the People's Republic of China, in a civil strife is further insinuated in the conversation among the five boys of Kumsan village. In their ignorance, the young boys wonder why they have to be liberated by foreign soldiers. However, in this text, the significance of the US military intervention is far from being one-dimensional. Considered in relation to the life of the protagonist Ollye, one of the victims of US military rape, the US Army is figured in ambiguous terms as a source of both liberation and affliction. That is to say, if the entry of American soldiers into the peaceful community ravages the lives of their rape survivors and disrupts the traditional structures of the village, a newly emerged small market economy dependent on a US military camp trains the submissive, uneducated Ollye to challenge the old gender shackles and grow into a despised, yet shrewd and independent, modern subject, presaging the tortuous path of 'dependent capitalist development' (T. J. Yoo 2020) taken by post-Korean War South Korea.

In Korean American Studies, the criticism of the Cold War tends to target the overseas military intervention of the US while blanking out Soviet expansionism. In this regard, *The Square* merits critical attention. Employing the protagonist as his mouthpiece, Choi In-hun explicitly articulates his disapproval of both Korean regimes and their superpower patrons. If the protagonist indicts the regime of the 'democratic' South for its corruption and tyranny, he also summons to trial its northern counterpart, the DPRK, under the same charges. In his view, postcolonial nation-building in the South has miscarried as a result of the Rhee government's uncritical mimicry of the ideology of the US-led Cold War. But the northern regime does not fare any better. The revolution that was responsible for the birth of the Communist regime in the North was, according to the author, not carried out by the people but imposed on them by the expansionist-oriented Soviets. It is the northern leader, and not the North Korean people, that has benefitted from the revolution. In this way, both the rival superpowers and the twin Korean political forces aligned with them are held accountable for the division of the peninsula. Instead of delving into the causes of the war, the author, however, limits himself to describing civilian suffering at the hands of the US military. For instance, the author exposes the issue of US war

216 The Korean War Novel

crimes against women in the figure of a North Korean POW who tells his fellow inmates about a Korean girl who was found with a bough stuck between her thighs, raped and killed by American combatants. Significantly, it is the US air strikes that kill the protagonist's lover, a woman who has served as a military nurse in the war. In sharp contrast, in the older editions of the novel, the KPA's civilian brutalities take the minor form of the protagonist's sexual harassment of his ex-girlfriend. In the final published edition, this episode is even further modified as it becomes merely a bad dream. In this way, the accountability of the KPA for war crimes is entirely erased from the final portrait of war. In the end, the Korean people's wish to break from the ideological chains of the Cold War is expressed in the protagonist's decision to seek refuge in a neutral third country during the POW repatriation interview.

The Guest revolves around the Shinch'ŏn Uprising that took place in Shinch'ŏn, Hwanghae Province, North Korea, during the Korean War. In this novel, the event that has been celebrated in the South as a rightist uprising is revealed to be a series of mass murders perpetrated among Communists and Nationalist Christians. Through the backstories of the characters, Hwang brings into focus what the arrival of Communism meant to the impoverished crop-sharing tenant class who formed the majority of the population in the North. In the latter's view, the rule of this foreign ideology promised both to purge the Japanese colonial legacy and to restore a long-denied economic justice. Viewed in this light, the uprising is interpreted as a reverse postcolonial war that is meant to bring back the deprived feudal privileges of the landlord class. By decking out this incident as a conflict exclusively between Communists and bourgeois Christians, the author departs from widely accepted historical facts of the incident. This historical reimagining allows the author to expose the hypocrisy and bellicosity of the northern far-right Christians. This has far-reaching ramifications that resonate with the role of the same group in the post-war nation-building of South Korea. According to the author, these militant Christians helped transform the South into an entrenched anti-communist state, the battlefield of their Cold War. Hwang's final message highlights the imperative need for reconciliation between the two Koreas as a preliminary step towards peaceful reunification.

Communist heroes in South Korean partisan literature

The Guest is the only one among the works discussed in this book that provides a sympathetic life-sized portrait of Communist characters

Conclusion **217**

such as Illang and Sunnam. Although Jaesong and Miki in *The Foreign Student* and Myong-jun in *The Square* profess Communist sympathies, Susan Choi's two characters are too marginal to earn the reader's full sympathy while Choi In-hun's protagonist turns his back on his earlier ideological beliefs. Fully-fledged portrayals of Communists were attempted in the *ppalch'isan* or leftist partisan fiction published in South Korea during the anti-communist military rule, although the latter's emergence had to wait till the end of Chun's iron-fisted rule (1981–7) to truly blossom. The Korean term *ppalch'isan* refers to Communist subversives in the South who waged guerrilla warfare first against the US military rule and later against the Rhee government. The partisans made their homes in such rugged areas as Mount Chiri and the Taebaek and Sobaek Mountains in order to evade the police even before communism was made illegal in 1947. Members of the reconstructed Communist Party of Korea (September 1945–November 1946) and its sequel, Namno Party (Communist Labour Party in the South, November 1946–June 1949), initially formed a majority of this resistance group. These insurrectionists suffered heavy losses due to the combined military operations of the ROKA and the police force before the outbreak of the Korean War, but they temporarily regrouped to fight again when the stranded soldiers of the defeated KPA joined them during the Korean War.

One of the earliest Korean epic novels to feature Communist guerrillas is *Chirisan* (Mount Chiri, 1981, 1985) by Lee Byeong-ju (1921–92). It was followed by a number of other guerrilla novels, including *T'aebaeksanmaek* (Taebaek Mountains, 1983–9) by Jo Jeong-rae (1943–), *Nambugun* (Southern Partisan Army, 1988) by I T'ae (1922–97), and *Ppalchi'sanŭi ttal* (Partisans' Daughter, 1990) and *Abŏjiŭi haebangilchi* (Journals of My Father's Liberation, 2022) by Chŏng Chia (1965–).

Chirisan was first serialised in the literary magazine *Sedae* (Generation) from September 1972 to August 1977 and published as an eight-volume series in 1981 and again in 1985 in an expanded edition. Ranging over the years from the 1930s to 1956, Lee's novel charts the political trajectory of the protagonist from his time as an anti-Japanese student through his membership in an idyllic small anti-Japanese community to his time as a Communist who ends up getting expelled from the Namno Party for dissenting from the Party's changed policy over the foreign trusteeship of Korea, to his final incarnation as a renegade communist who chooses to die as a partisan. This novel has an ambiguous reputation among South Korean critics: some denounce it as pro-communist while others hail it as anti-communist. The former group is displeased with the author's

218   *The Korean War Novel*

humanising portrayal of Communist partisans, whereas the latter feel reassured by the protagonist's criticisms of the leaders of the Namno Party for dogmatism, opportunism, sycophancy towards the Soviets and betrayal of their comrades.

The pro-Communist reputation of this novel is not unrelated to the author's own political background. During the Communist occupation, Lee was appointed to the directorship of the Communist Party's auxiliary, cultural and literary associations. When the tide of the war changed, the author was arrested by the police for pro-Communist collaboration but was subsequently released. Immediately after the 16 May military coup in 1961, Lee was prosecuted and sentenced to ten years in prison for violating the National Security Law. He was released after serving two years and seven months in prison. At the trial, the prosecutor focused his attention on two pieces of the author's writing: a newspaper editorial from 1 January 1961 that called for a national effort for reunification, raising the idea of Korea as a neutral state, and a magazine article from December 1960 that criticised the governing elite for pursuing its own interests. These articles, which some might regard as patriotic, were accepted by the court as evidence of endangering national security. In order to ward off the stigma of being a pro-Communist collaborator, the author publicly declared that since the end of the war he had been anti-communist after his own fashion. The reason Lee's partisan novel could be published during Park Chung-hee's military regime despite the author's suspicious political background is that the fiction is centred on the topic of the Communist protagonist's disillusionment with the Communist Party. In other words, if it portrays accurately how in the wake of national liberation, this radical ideology appealed to Korean intellectuals who grew up admiring the revolutionaries during the anti-colonial period, the novel at the same time sabotages its pro-communist stance by pointing out the folly of blindly embracing the ideology: '[i]f a person who is not a communist at the age of twenty is a fool, one who is still a communist at the age of thirty is also a fool' (B.-J. Lee [1981, 1985] 2006: 2: 315; author's translation).

Such didacticism also informs *Yŏngungshidae* (The Age of Heroes, 1984), a defection novel by Yi Munyeol (1948–). The hero of Yi's novel, like the protagonist in *Chirisan*, is exposed to communism while studying in Japan during the period of colonial rule. He later becomes a member of the Communist Party, fights for the reunification of Korea, participates in the Korean War as a political officer of the KPA and then follows the retreating KPA to the North. Witnessing at close range the ugly realities of the Communist Party – its corruption, opportunism, nepotism, the open struggle for power and the purge of the members of the Namno Party – the protagonist begins to question the wisdom of the ideological choices he has made, which have even involved risking the safety of his own family. His disillusionment with communism becomes more real after he returns from a visit to a rural community. He now recognises that freedom is a synonym for obedience and that equality is possible only in the coarse, poverty-stricken world of communism. He ends up coming to loathe radical ideals as well as himself for having been duped by them.

Yi modelled the protagonist on his own father, an intellectual who became infatuated with communism while studying in Japan during the colonial era, worked as a member of the Namno Party before the Korean War and eventually defected to the North, leaving his own family behind in the South. Because of his father's political choices, Yi and his family found themselves targeted by a form of guilt-by-association persecution during the time of the military regimes. The author's criticism of revolutionary ideals as a form of intellectual vanity attracted the attention of left-leaning progressives who were mounting resistance to the military regime of Chun Doo-hwan. Among progressive literary critics, Yi became known as a reactionary 'warrior fighting the democratic movement of the time' (Joung 2014: 11) or 'an unknowing staunch champion of the system' 'devoted to waging a nihilistic anti-ideological war' (M.-I. Kim [1990] 1991: 189, 191). In turn, Yi denounced the progressives and their people power movement, suggesting that they were motivated by a set of false beliefs and a sick sense of psychology. Their underlying motivations, for his way of thinking, included sadomasochism, a marked sense of social vanity and a reflex set of attitudes that caused them to respond to the word 'reunification' with a pounding heart and associate the word 'capitalist' with 'exploitation', 'chaebol' with 'thief' and 'military regime' with 'corruption and dictatorship' (Yi 1992: 27–41).

In 1988, I T'ae published *Nambugun*, a memoir based on his own past guerrilla activities. The memoir was based on a manuscript he had finished writing ten years before but which he had put aside during the reign of the military regimes. This piece of non-fiction, noted for its touching humanisation of the much-vilified Red, became instantly popular, selling as many as 500,000 copies in the first year.

To date, however, the most popular partisan work has been Jo Jeong-rae's ten-volume novel, *T'aebaeksanmaek*. As of 2018, more than 8.5 million copies of this epic novel have been sold. Unlike other examples of partisan or defection fiction, this novel, set in the politically turbulent period between 1948 and 1953, describes in detail why certain ordinary people chose to become Communists. Unlike the protagonists of *Chirisan* and *Yŏngungshidae*, the peasant characters in this novel become partisans not because of their exposure to a revolutionary ideology that teaches people to rise in arms against injustice but rather because of a lack of alternatives. In the old days, when they had tilled the land, they had suffered from the insatiable greed of the landlords on whose land they worked and had had to endure the rent-gouging of the farm tenancy managers. When even the rights to tenancy, the only means for eking out a meagre existence, were taken away and given to others in an effort to exact more rent money, they had no way left to feed their families. Out of despair, they executed their landlords and left to join the partisans in the mountains. One of the partisan characters speaks on behalf of this group of people when he states: '[a]lthough uneducated, numerous people who have had to endure endless pain from the contradictions in the basic conditions of life understand why they have to suffer; they know that such wrongs have to be rectified; and they have decided that such change must be wrought by all means' (Jo [1983–9] 2002: 5: 85; author's translation). This fiction reveals the class conflict that underlies the outbreak of the Korean War, something also noted by Hwang Sok-yong in *The Guest*.

According to Jo, *T'aebaeksanmaek* was written in an attempt at 'overcoming the division system' by means of 'restoring the history of the lower-class people's uprisings which have been buried and distorted by the anti-Communism' of the South (Jo 1995: 106). Only by restoring this forgotten history can an effective assessment be made of what went wrong and who was responsible for it. In this way, one can attempt to eliminate the obstacles on the path to reunification. According to Jo, '[t]he US Military Government, partnered with the pro-Japanese collaborators and national traitors, engineered the birth of an anti-nationalist regime and since then, the external factors of the territorial division of Korea have interlocked with the internal factors of the nation's division to which they gave birth' (Jo 1995: 104–5; author's translation). Faithful to this historical view, Jo idealises the partisans and their revolutionary efforts while erasing the negative aspects of the story: the guerrillas' forcible recruitment of civilians and their murder of uncooperative others, not to mention their slaughter of those whom they regarded as 'reactionaries'. In 1994, multiple South Korean anti-communist organisations pressed charges against the author for violating the National Security Law forbidding praise of an enemy organisation, and it was not until 2005 that the author was cleared of those charges.

What is more, Jo was not the only writer who had trouble with the South Korean authorities for publishing a book about the partisan struggle. After she published *Ppalchi'sanŭi ttal*, a memoir based on the

Conclusion   **221**

lives of her ex-partisan parents, Jeong Ji-a had to go into hiding for a number of years. The novel was banned from sale, and the publisher was imprisoned for violating the National Security Law. These successful attempts at prosecuting writers for their narrativisation of certain past Communist activities serve as a clear indication that even today South Korean writers are not free to write what they like about the regional Cold War that supposedly ended many decades ago. In some ways, the Cold War's hold on them in the twenty-first century has become even more intense. During the reign of former pro-democracy activist Presidents Roh Moo-hyun and Moon Jae-in, attempts were made to liquidate the decades-long Cold War legacy of the earlier regimes. However, these efforts led to the rallying of conservative citizens and eventually gave birth to a polarised mass politics.

South Korean politics haunted by the Korean War

On 14 June 2019, during an official state visit to Sweden, the nineteenth president of South Korea, Moon Jae-in, delivered a speech to the Swedish Parliament in which he held out the offer of a peace proposal to North Korea. During the course of what has become known as the Stockholm Speech, President Moon spoke of the casualties of the Korean War while emphasising the peace-loving nature of the Korean people: '[o]ver its long history of 5,000 years, Korea has never invaded other countries. In our sad history, we have only aimed firearms at ourselves' ('Full Text' 2019). Conservatives in South Korea were quick to attack this view of the Korean War as a set of internecine struggles ('we have only aimed firearms at ourselves'). According to the conservative point of view, the president's speech 'distorted the historical fact of North Korea's surprise attack and made both North and South Korea appear responsible for 6.25 [the Korean War]' ('Kimwŏnbong' 2019). In truth, this was not the first time that a speech by President Moon dealing with South–North relations or the Korean War has provoked a storm of protest from South Korean conservatives. In September 2017, Moon's speech at the seventy-second session of the UN General Assembly also caused controversy in South Korea because of his stance on the nature of the Korean War: '[t]his civil war, which evolved into an international war, devastated the lives of countless people' ('Address' 2018). According to his critics, Moon's reference to the Korean War as a 'civil war' turns what was in point of fact a war of aggression into a civil war. In his blog and magazine editorials, one leading journalist among the South Korean ultra-rightists suggested adding Moon to his list of the 'Big Three' who

222   *The Korean War Novel*

regard the Korean War as a civil war. To date, the list comprises the names of Joseph Stalin, Mao Tse-tung and Kim Il-sung. Conservative newspapers and bloggers were quick to echo the journalist's condemnation of the president as a pro-Communist ('6.25-lŭl' 2017).

To South Korean conservatives, the president's remarks confirmed the suspicion that he maintains leftist leanings, stoked by his past leadership in the college students' pro-democratic protests against Park Chung-hee's military regime, which were brushed off at the time by the regime as acts instigated by 'Commies'. One of the major ironies of Moon's supposedly pro–North Korean politics, of course, is that it failed to elicit sympathy in North Korea either. For example, in an article entitled 'Much Worried about [Moon's] Lack of a Sense of Reality and Judgement', *Meari*, the North Korean website, criticised Moon's inter-Korean peace initiative. What upset the North Korean leadership about Moon's Stockholm Speech was the sanguine views of the South Korean president that '[i]f North Korea takes the path of dialogue, no one would threaten [the] political system or safety of North Korea. North Korea must believe that every problem will be solved by dialogue and trust its dialogue partners' ('Full Text' 2019). According to the North Koreans, the conditional clause in Moon's appeal for dialogue and trust serves to place the blame for the current inter-Korean confrontation on the North. By intimating that 'inter-Korean dialogue and, furthermore, the peace process of the Korean peninsula have been baulked by North Korea', the overture serves to alienate its potential partners. In the end, the article dismisses Moon's peace proposal as based on 'an absurd, truth-falsifying claim' ('Puk sŏnjŏnmaech'e' 2019).

In the minds of South Korean conservatives, President Moon has a knack for making South Korea's staunch ally, the United States, uncomfortable too. In his address of 26 September 2018 at the UN General Assembly, for example, Moon emphasised North Korea's willingness to enter on the path of denuclearisation, and he called for a loosening of sanctions against the nation that George W. Bush once suggested was, alongside Iraq and Iran, an integral part of 'the Axis of Evil'. This call for an easing of North Korea sanctions as part of a peace- and trust-building process, however, appears to place the US in an awkward situation. This is because, in the eyes of the US State Department, North Korea has not yet taken any substantial steps toward denuclearisation; it has therefore not earned the right to an easing of sanctions. As a consequence, Moon's speech earned him the derogatory epithet of 'Kim Jong Un's top spokesman at UN' (Y. Lee 2018) from members of the international press.

President Moon was actually following the earlier views of the late Roh Moo-hyun, his political comrade and the sixteenth president of

Conclusion   **223**

South Korea (2003–7), in referring to the Korean War as a civil war. During his 2006 state visit to Cambodia, for example, President Roh made a similar remark during a meeting with some local Koreans: '[i]n the old days we had difficult times going through colonisation and a civil war.' When this view was publicised in the domestic press, conservative politicians and certain journalists in the mass media sought to raise the issue of the president's ideological orientation. They drew attention to the fact that only 'North Korea and leftist scholars have defined the Korean War as a civil war' ('Naejŏn' 2006). Ch'ŏngwadae, the Blue House, tried to calm the waters of the political storm by offering a greatly toned-down explanation: by the term 'civil war', Roh meant only 'a war within the same people' ('Naejŏn' 2006).

As these controversies attest, the historical origins and exact nature of the Korean War are still both touchy issues in South Korea. To be seen to endorse certain lines of interpretation of this war, the nature of which has long been a major point of contention among both domestic and overseas scholars, regularly invites condemnation on the grounds of pro-Communism. What is at stake in this act of defining the nature of the Korean War? To put the question differently, when the Blue House explains that the late President Rho was only referring to the Korean War as 'a war within the same people', what further meanings is the clarifying remark meant to exclude?

According to the conservative point of view, a civil war and a war of aggression are two different things; they cannot and must not be con-flated. To quote one conservative Korean scholar:

> To view the Korean War as a civil war means to see it as a war in which one people liberates its own under oppression. The reason why North Korea invaded South Korea is that it wanted to liberate the subjugated southern people. That is, it was a national liberation war . . . This kind of thinking glamorises and justifies North Korea's aggression. ('Migugi' 2020)

Viewed in this light, to regard the Korean War as a civil war implies that the historian wishes to 'exonerate the national traitors' who invaded their own people and wants to 'deny the right to patriotism and self-esteem' to those South Koreans who fought against the invasion. In a similar fashion, to see the Korean War in terms of civil conflict is to hold the UN military forces unjustly responsible for the fact that the civil war quickly turned into one with undeniably international dimensions. According to the rightist perspective, then, there was no civil war in Korea to begin with. Instead, 'Stalin used Kim Il-sung as an instrument for his grand scheme on the world' ('6.25-lŭl' 2017). From the same rightist perspective, to attempt to see the Korean War as a product of

224   *The Korean War Novel*

the Cold War – as President Moon does in his reference to 'a war that began as an offshoot of the larger Cold War conflict' ('Address' 2018) – is nothing more than a sly rhetorical gesture, 'a euphemism that is designed to protect the agents of the war' ('6.25-lŭl' 2017) by attributing responsibility for its outbreak to an indifferent global structure.

Another reason why the civil war perspective has ruffled many conservative South Koreans' feathers is that it is seen to challenge the legitimacy of the first South Korean government under the leadership of Syngman Rhee. Two years before the outbreak of the Korean War, the conservatives maintain, there were already two opposed governments established along the two sides of the thirty-eighth parallel: the South Korean government, which was established on 15 August 1948, and the North Korean government, which was established on 9 September 1948. For this reason, the use of the term 'civil war' in the Korean context not only fails to account for the presence of the two different states but also glosses over the fact that the government in South Korea was the only one that had been sanctioned by the UN.

Nonetheless, it is precisely the legitimacy of the South Korean government as the only UN-endorsed regime on the Korean peninsula with which the proponents of the civil war theory take issue. A comparison of the two Koreas during the first few years of the postliberation period is necessary to understand this point. The Communists who had been installed in power by the Soviet army in the wake of national liberation immediately purged the territory in the north of all pro-Japanese collaborators. As mentioned earlier, in March 1946, the Communists then implemented a radical programme of land reform in order to provide a solution to the major source of social conflict in the traditionally agricultural nation – the conflict between rural labourers and rural landowners. This programme was implemented within six months of national liberation. In stark contrast, despite the fact that the Constituent Assembly in the South had legislated a purge of pro-Japanese collaborators in September 1948, the bill to enact this measure was obstructed by President Rhee himself, who had formed an alliance with the rightist, moneyed class, many of whom had helped the Japanese during the colonial period. It was finally dropped in October 1949, when the Pro-Japanese Collaboration Inspection Committee was dismantled. This took place after some members of the special inspection force had been beaten up and then imprisoned by the National Police. For its part, the process of land tenancy reform was delayed until early 1950. Viewed in this light, North Korea would appear to have been far ahead of South Korea in reconstructing itself as a modern postcolonial nation. The aggressive reactions of South Korean rightists to the civil war theory

Conclusion   **225**

may be ascribed to the sorry truth that the legitimacy of the first South Korean government was politically compromised. It lagged behind its northern counterpart in terms of its political commitment to implementing a programme of modernisation and a process of decolonisation.

Above all, the weak claims to the legitimacy of the first South Korean government derive from the events surrounding the South Korean Constitutional Assembly election of 10 May 1948, the first democratic election held on the Korean peninsula. It was through the process of this general election that the National Assembly was constituted and Rhee was elected president in the National Assembly. Nonetheless, the political situation in South Korea, both before and after the election, was not one that might legitimately be called favourable to Rhee. As Robert T. Oliver and other historians have noted (Oliver 1954: 254, 262–3; D.-C. Kim 2000: 147–8), the political forces that participated in the UN-sponsored election on 10 May 1948 were limited to just two political parties, the National Association, which constituted the forces around Rhee, and the Korean Democratic Party. In contrast, Kim Koo and Kim Kyusik, the leadership of the provisional government, the political organisation that had guided the conservative nationalist forces from the time of the anti-trusteeship movement, chose to boycott the general election and instead attended the leadership conference in Pyongyang, which had representation from both South and North Korea. Yŏ Unhyŏng, the moderate left leader, who also sought to forge a unified government on the Korean peninsula, was assassinated by far-rightist terrorists in July 1947. With his major rival forces out of the way, Rhee mobilised the rightist youth corps, who threatened people at the polling stations into voting for his followers and other suitable conservative candidates.

Although Rhee was eventually nominated as president, the results of the 10 May election were not an overwhelming vote of endorsement. In total, 200 assemblymen were elected to the national forum, with Rhee's organisation garnering fifty-eight seats, the Korean Democratic Party mustering twenty-eight and as many as eighty-five independent candidates elected. The independents thus represented 42.5 per cent of the total number of congressmen. According to Park Tae-gyun (2005: 148), it was these independents, who constituted the 'Younger Group' at the Assembly, that soon passed a law to punish pro-Japanese collaborators and also submitted a resolution for the withdrawal of the US Army from South Korea. Rhee's response to this political predicament was to arrest the Younger Group, framing them as Communist agents. During his twelve-year dictatorship, this was to be a practice to which he often resorted (D.-C. Kim 2000: 83–4). These incidents, including the central event of a flawed general election, brought down on Rhee's government

226   *The Korean War Novel*

strong criticism from the UN Commission on Korea (T.-G. Park 2005: 148). As a result of these anti-democratic activities – together with the fact that most of the forces of the right and the left had boycotted the general election – the status of Rhee as the lawful first president of South Korea is called into question and his claim to being its Founding Father is undermined.

The dispute over the origins of the Korean War is neither simply a part of the internal politics of South Korea nor an issue solely limited to inter-Korean politics. It is, at the same time, an international issue that is still creating tensions and conflicts in the triangular relationship of South Korea, the US and China. The latest example is the backlash of Chinese fans against the Van Fleet Award Speech by the world-famous K-pop idols BTS. Since 1995, the Van Fleet Award has functioned as a means of honouring James Van Fleet, commander of the US Eighth Army, who fought in the Korean War, with the Korean Society offering the award annually to individuals and groups that have promoted US–South Korea relations. In 2020, on the occasion of the Korean War's seventieth anniversary, the award was offered to BTS as well as to a number of other individuals. During his online acceptance speech, RM, BTS's lead singer, stated that 'we will always remember the history of pain that our two nations shared together, and the sacrifices of countless men and women.' '[O]ur two nations' is a reference to South Korea and the United States. According to *The Global Times*, these remarks enraged many Chinese netizens, who bitterly resented that the speech ignored the pain of 'Chinese soldiers who sacrificed their lives in the war.' These same netizens also complained that 'the speech plays up to US netizens, but the[ir] country played the role of aggressor in the war' ('BTS Hurts' 2020). Based as they are on a limited historical understanding of the causes of the Korean War, these angry responses in turn befuddled and enraged South Koreans. Many of them retorted that without the Chinese intervention in the Korean War, Korea today would be a single united nation. These Koreans noted that 'the Chinese put the blame for their unlawful intervention onto South Koreans' ('Pangt'ansonyŏndan' 2020). A Korean newspaper editorial attributed the Chinese backlash to the untruthful history education offered in Chinese schools and sanctioned by the Chinese Communist Party ('Shame' 2020).

The line of thought of these Chinese netizens on the Korean War accords with the official view of the Chinese Communist Party. In his 23 October 2020 speech at a grand gathering in the Great Hall of People in Tiananmen Square to commemorate the seventieth anniversary of the Chinese intervention in the Korean War, President Xi Jinping confirmed the Party's official view on the war. Xi remarked:

The great war defied the invasion and expansion of imperialism and safe-guarded the security of New China; It also safeguarded the peaceful life of the Chinese people, stabilized the situation in the Korean Peninsula and upheld peace in Asia and the world; The great victory of the war will be forever etched in the history of the Chinese nation and the history of peace, development and progress of humankind. ('Xi' 2020)

As Xi's words indicate, the leadership of the People's Republic of China not only glosses over the issue of North Korean aggression but puts the entire blame for the war on the 'expansion of [American] imperialism'. In this light, the gap between the understanding of the causes of the Korean War on the part of China on the one hand and South Korea and the United States on the other appears to be as unbridgeable as it was seventy-five years ago. It remains capable of causing regular eruptions of antagonism among all the parties to the conflict.

Over the years, North Korea has staged numerous military provocations against South Korea, despite the armistice signed on 27 July 1953. North Korea's deadly acts of war include the 1958 hijacking of a South Korean airliner; the 1968 capture of the USS Pueblo, a US Navy intelligence vessel; the 1976 Ax Murder incident, which took the lives of two US Army officers in the demilitarised zone; the 2010 artillery bombardment of the South Korean island of Yŏnp'yŏng; and the 2010 sinking of the South Korean Navy ship Ch'ŏnan in the West Sea, which claimed the lives of forty-six crew members. What is more, since 2006, North Korea has carried out a series of tests of its nuclear warheads. North Korea's armed provocations and its testing of its nuclear capabilities are a clear indicator to the citizens of South Korea that the Korean War is not yet over.

T'aegŭkki rallies: A déjà vu?

If the failure to end the Cold War continues to be responsible for the confrontation and hostility between the two Koreas, it may also be deemed the explanation for many of the political conflicts within South Korea. The presence of the Cold War as an episteme in South Korean politics is unmistakably felt in contemporary political issues such as the ongoing controversy over the issue of South Korean National Foundation Day. What is more, the Cold War episteme was deeply involved with the controversy surrounding the impeachment of President Park Geun-hye who led South Korea from 2013 to 2017.

On 3 July 2008, the majority-conservative Grand National Party submitted to the National Assembly a motion to celebrate 15 August as National Foundation Day. For the conservative South Koreans, what this meant was a dual celebration of national liberation from Japanese rule in 1945 and the establishment of the government of South Korea in 1948. The opposition parties made a concerted effort to oppose the motion. These parties maintained that to entwine the celebration of national liberation with the establishment of the post-war South Korean government would be to authorise, in an indirect manner, the division of the Korean peninsula that had been imposed by the foreign powers. In the eyes of the official opposition, the system of the 'two Koreas' remains something that the Korean people should seek to dismantle politically rather than enshrine legally. For this reason, a vote in favour of this misguided motion would be tantamount to an abandonment of the national task of reunification.

The controversy over National Foundation Day recurred exactly ten years after the motion submitted by the Grand National Party had been thrown out. On this occasion, however, it was President Moon who sparked the controversy. On 14 August 2017, Moon referred to the year 2019 as the centennial for both the day of National Foundation and the Establishment of the Provisional Government. The explanation for Moon's position was that he was counting from the time of the 1 March 1919 Independence Movement. Moon's speech served to enrage a segment of conservative South Korean opinion that believed this position served to denigrate the memory of President Syngman Rhee and his government. In their eyes, making 1919, or attempting to make 1919, the year of South Korean foundation implicitly contests the legitimacy of President Rhee as Founding Father, a leader comparable in the eyes of conservatives to George Washington.

The Cold War episteme had been upheld for so long both by Rhee's regime and by the military dictatorships that followed that it has penetrated deeply into the minds of the citizenry. In this way, the anti-communist social order of South Korea has been reinforced. What is more, the ramifications of this phenomenon are not limited to domestic politics. Instead, its effects extend into the realm of international affairs, with the ultra-right-wing forces trying to gain the sympathy of the United States in its struggle for domestic power.

During the trial for impeachment of office of President Park Geun-hye, the connection between the realms of the domestic and the international was made clear. During the period of 26 October 2016 to 29 April 2017, over 16,000,000 people – almost one-third of the population of South Korea – came out, staging large-scale, nationwide candlelight protests, demanding the removal of President Park from power. President Park was strongly suspected of having allowed Ch'oe

Sunsil, her close confidante, to intervene in state affairs and to have personally benefitted by Choi's influence peddling. In order to counter the mass candlelight protests, the conservative pro-Park supporters also mobilised themselves.

As Kim Wang-bae, the Korean sociologist, has suggested, the pro-Park protesters are composed of a variety of far-right organisations. These include *Paksamo*, a group of Park supporters; the rightist leagues, including the Northwest Youth Corps, the Marine Veteran Association and, most importantly of all, the conservative and ultra-right religious associations (W.-B. Kim 2017: 21). What is notable about these far-right protesters is their use of flags at their protests. At many of their rallies, the conservative protesters wave the '*T'aegŭkki*', the Korean term for the South Korean national flag. This has earned them the nickname of '*T'aegŭkki* protesters'. At a certain point, however, these protesters started to fly two sets of national flags: the national flag of South Korea and the US Stars and Stripes. The conservatives foresaw that the forces of the left were set to take control of the country once Park stepped down, and Park's abdication might imply the beginning of a new civil war, requiring a second intervention by the forces of the United States. The far-right organisations actually placed their rallying call in the classified sections of certain conservative newspapers such as *The Chosunilbo* and *The Dong-A Ilbo*.

In one of the classified advertisements in *The Chosunilbo* of 28 February 2017, the Christian Veteran Association urged politically right-leaning people to join a political rally to celebrate the 1 March 1919 Independence Movement. Hailing the right-wing forces as 'patriotic citizens', the advertisement claims that their participation in the rally will honour and continue the spirit of the leading Korean nationalists who launched the 1 March 1919 Independence Movement. The same rallying call proposes three slogans:

> Let us purge the pro–North Korean leftists who endanger our national security; Let us consolidate our national security by reinforcing the US–Korean alliance; Let us contest the nuclear power of the North with a nuclear program of our own and, above all, let us wipe out the North's nuclear threat using the combined forces of the *T'aegŭkki* and the Stars and Stripes.' ('3.1chŏl' 2017: A6; author's translation)

An earlier proclamation made by another ultra-right-wing group, this one called National Action Campaign, reproduces the vilification of the left by the US during the Cold War, insisting that Koreans choose 'between [a liberal] South Korea and a communist reunification' ('2017nyŏn-ŭi' 2017: A31). Another rallying call advertised in *The Donga-A Ilbo* calls

Figure 7.1 Pastor Kang Ch'ungguk on his way to a T'aegŭkki rally carrying a cross with US and Korean national flags attached to it. (Source: © News&Joy)

on Korean citizens to defend President Park against impeachment, highlighting her ex officio services to the country, such as disbanding the 'pro–North Korean' United Progressive Party (2011–14), illegalising the 'left-leaning' Korean Teachers and Education Workers Union, preventing the dissolution of the ROK/US Combined Forces Command and correcting 'left-leaning' history textbooks ('Ch'immuk'amyŏn' 2017: A31). The far right in South Korea also praised Park's decision to shut down the Kaesŏng Industrial Complex. Since the time of previous President Kim Dae-jung, the Kaesŏng Industrial Complex had served as an example of economic cooperation between the two Koreas ('2wŏl 25il' 2017: A31). It signifies to the Koreans the symbol of the two Koreas' peaceful coexistence and cooperation to which President Kim Dae-jung's Sunshine Policy gave birth. This South-North détente, which had led a number of South Korean companies to move their production lines to Kaesŏng, where they hired North Korean labour, came to an end during Park's term in office.

The stigmatisation of the progressive movement is explained as the upshot of a number of interrelated conservative fears. The first fear is that of the progressive demand for the US Army's withdrawal from South Korea. Conservatives tend to see certain progressive elements of the liberal-left as pro–North Korean forces in disguise. They believe that

Figure 7.2 A T'aegŭkki rally sporting three sets of national flags. (Source: © News&Joy)

these disguised pro–North Korean forces wish to surrender South Korea to the North or to invite a second civil war for the same traitorous purposes. For these conservatives, Park's impeachment formed an integral part of this traitorous, pro-Communist plan. In Figure 7.1, Pastor Kang Ch'ungguk, whose ancestors are from the northern half of the Korean peninsula, may be seen carrying to one of the *T'aegŭkki* rallies a cross with the two national flags attached at the top. According to this Pastor: 'If [the candlelight protests] grow bigger, North Korea will invade again. *T'aegŭkki* rallies are fighting with Kim Jongun' ('Nomoksaga' 2017).

What made the development of this ideological confrontation even more intriguing is that at a certain point, some of the far-right protesters began waving three national flags at their rallies. A group known as the New Right Protestants began to carry the national flag of Israel as a third flag to the pro-Park, anti-left-wing rallies (Figure 7.2). According to one political commentator, the far-right pro-Park protesters were envious of the unconditional support Israel enjoys from its staunch ally, the United States. In the view of this political commentator, Park's supporters were thereby symbolically expressing their wish for South Korea to form a third partner in the special relationship that exists between the United States and Israel ('T'aegŭkki' 2019). Another commentator suggested that the three flags were an attempt to forge a 'global far-right alliance' with extremists in both the US and Israel. Anti-communism,

232 *The Korean War Novel*

from this perspective, forms one pillar of their tripartite war against Communism, homosexuality and Islam ('Han'gugŭi' 2017).

Although the global contest between NATO and the Eastern bloc ended with the collapse of the Soviet Union, South Koreans have continued to wage a more local version of the Cold War, in which the right-wing forces endeavour to deter the takeover of South Korea by those people they believe to be North Korean sympathisers. The Cold War has been institutionalised on the Korean peninsula, in whose continuance the conservative forces have vested interests. Even before the outbreak of the Korean War, major state apparatuses in the South have been geared towards making this global war 'our war'. Of course, this phenomenon of living the Cold War is not unique to South Korea but also found in a number of other parts of Asia. Chen Kuan-hsing's observation concerning Taiwan and the rest of Asia strikes a strong note of assent in the mind of this South Korean scholar when the Taiwanese scholar asserts: the 'Cold War effects have become embedded in local histories, and will not be just dissolved even if the Cold War were announced to have finished in reality' (Chen 2010: 118).

Bibliography

'Address by President Moon Jae-in of the Republic of Korea at the 72nd Session of the United Nations General Assembly' (2018), Cheongwadae, 26 September.

Agamben, Giorgio (1998), *Homo Sacer: Sovereign Power and Bare Life*, trans. Daniel Heller-Roazen, Stanford: Stanford University Press.

Ahn, Junghyo (1990), *Silver Stallion: A Novel of Korea*, New York: Soho.

__ (2012), 'Agijangsu chŏnsŏri toraonŭn sewŏl' [The Times for the Return of the Infant General], in Junghyo Ahn, *Ŭnma* [Silver Stallion], Paju: Nanam, pp. 5–19.

Althusser, Louis (1971), *Lenin and Philosophy and Other Essays*, trans. Ben Brewster, New York: Monthly Review.

Anderson, Benedict (1983), *Imagined Communities*, rev. ed., London: Verso.

'Author Choi In-hun Dead at 84: "The Square" Is Considered a Pivotal Piece of Korean Literature' (2018), *Korea JoongAng Daily*, 23 July <https://korea joongangdaily.joins.com/2018/07/23/books/Author-Choi-Inhun-dead-at-84-The-Square-is-considered-a-pivotal-piece-of-Korean-literature/3050986 .html> (last accessed 23 August 2021).

Baik, Crystal Mun-hye (2020), *Reencounters: On the Korean War and Diasporic Memory Critique*, Philadelphia: Temple University Press.

Bakhtin, Mikhail M. (1984), *Rabelais and His World*, trans. Hélène Iswolsky, Bloomington: Indiana University Press.

Baudrillard, Jean ([1981] 1994), *Simulacra and Simulation*, trans. Sheila Faria Glaser, Ann Arbor: University of Michigan Press.

Belletto, Steven (2015), 'The Korean War, the Cold War, and the American Novel', *American Literature*, 87.1, pp. 51–77.

Brooks, Charlotte (2000), 'In the Twilight Zone between Black and White: Japanese American Resettlement and Community in Chicago, 1942–1945', *The Journal of American History* 86.4, pp. 1655–87.

'BTS Hurts Feelings of Chinese Netizens and Fans during Speech on the Korean War' (2020), *The Global Times*, 11 October <https://www.globaltimes.cn/ content/1203151.shtml> (last accessed 15 June 2021).

Camus, Albert ([1951] 1984), *The Rebel*, trans. Anthony Bower, New York: Penguin.

234 *The Korean War Novel*

Caprio, Mark E. (2011), 'Neglected Questions on the "Forgotten War": South Korea and the United States on the Eve of the Korean War', *Asia-Pacific Journal 9.5* (31 January) web.

Chang, Chun'gap (2007), 'U.S. Military Government in Korea's Action against Jeju 4·3 Incident: Prelude to Violence and Genocide', *Jeonbuk History* 31, pp. 205–26 (in Korean).

Chang, David Cheng (2020a), *The Hijacked War: The Story of Chinese POWS in the Korean War*, Stanford: Stanford University Press.

___ (2020b), 'The Korean War Prisoners Who Chose Neutral Nations: An Introduction', *The Journal of American-East Asian Relations* 27, pp. 214–34.

Chen, Kuan-hsing (2010), *Asia as Method: Toward Deimperialization*, Durham: Duke University Press.

'Ch'immuk'amyŏn naraga chongbukseryŏgege nŏmŏganda' (Silence Would Help to Surrender the Nation to the Pro–North Korean Forces) (2017), *Dong-A Ilbo*, 2 February, A31.

'Cho Bong-am Cleared of Spy Charge in 52 Years' (2011), *The Korea Times*, 20 January <https://www.koreatimes.co.kr/www/news/nation/2011/01/113_80056.html> (last accessed 31 August 2021).

Cho, Tonghwan (1957), *Pan'gongŭi hwaetpul* [The Beacon of Anti-Communist Struggles], Seoul: Pomun'gak.

Choi, Chungmoo (1998), 'Nationalism and Construction of Gender in Korea', in Elaine H. Kim and Chungmoo Choi (eds), *Dangerous Women: Gender & Korean Nationalism*, New York: Routledge, pp. 9–32.

Choi, Don Mee (2016), *Hardly War*, Seattle: Wave Books.

Choi, Eun-Jin (2020), 'The Farm Tenancy Dispute after the Enforcement of the "Farm Law in Chosun" in the Mid-1930s', *The Journal of Korean History* 189, pp. 261–307 (in Korean).

Choi, In-hun ([1960] 1985), *The Square*, trans. Kevin O'Rourke, Devon: Spindlewood.

___ ([1960] 2010), *Kwangjang* [The Square], Seoul: Munhakkwajisŏngsa.

___ ([1960] 2014), *The Square*, trans. Seong-kon Kim, Champaign: Dalkey Archive Press.

Choi, Sang-Yong (2002), 'Trusteeship Debate and the Korean Cold War', in Bonnie B. C. Oh (ed.), *Korea under the American Military Government 1945–1948*, London: Praeger, pp. 13–39.

Choi, Susan (1998), *The Foreign Student*, New York: Harper Flamingo.

Choi, Yoon-gyeong (2014), 'A Study on Adaptation of Choi In-hun's "Guangjang"', *The Journal of Modern Literary Theory* 59, pp. 355–82 (in Korean).

Choi, Youngkeun (2018), 'A Study on the Relationship between Socialism and Protestantism in the 1920s Korean Society under the Japanese Colonial Rule', *Sinhaksasang* [Theological Thought] 181, pp. 289–329 (in Korean).

Chung, Hyeyurn (2013), 'Love across the Color Lines: The Occlusion of Racial Tension in Susan Choi's *The Foreign Student*', *American Fiction Studies* 20.2, pp. 55–70.

'Chungnibiran shidaeyŏk'aeng' [Neutralisation Goes against the Times] (1957), *Hankukilbo*, 4 March.

The Commission of International Association of Democratic Lawyers (1952), 'Report on U.S. Crimes in Korea,' 31 March <https://www.iadllaw.org/newsite/wp-content/uploads/2017/10/Crime_Reports_1.pdf> (last accessed 28 September 2023).

Courteaux, Olivier (2015), 'General de Gaulle and the Second World War: Constructing a French Narrative', in Natalia Starostina (ed.), *Between Memory and Mythology: The Construction of Memory of Modern Wars*, Newcastle upon Tyne: Cambridge Scholars Publishing, pp. 3–21.

Cumings, Bruce (1981), *The Origins of the Korean War Vol. 1: Liberation and the Emergence of Separate Regimes 1945–1947*, Princeton: Princeton University Press.

___ (1984), *The Two Koreas*, New York: Foreign Policy Association.

___ (1990), *The Origins of the Korean War Vol. 2: The Roaring of the Cataract 1947–1950*, Princeton: Princeton University Press.

___ (1995), *Divided Korea: United Future?* Headline Series 306, New York: Foreign Policy Association.

___ (1999), *Parallax Visions: Making Sense of American–East Asian Relations at the End of the Century*, Durham: Duke University Press.

___ (2010), *The Korean War: A History*, New York: Modern Library.

Dallin, David (1961), *Soviet Foreign Policy after Stalin*, New York: J. B. Lippincott Com.

Eckholm, Eric (2020), 'After an Attack, Chinese Won't Print Expatriate's Novel', *The New York Times*, 24 June <https://www.nytimes.com/2000/06/24/books/after-an-attack-chinese-won-t-print-expatriate-s-novel.html> (last accessed 1 July 2020).

Elliott, George P. (1964), 'A Moral Tale', *The New York Review of Books*, 20 February <https://www.nybooks.com/articles/1964/02/20/a-moral-tale-2/> (last accessed 2 June 2020).

Engels, Frederich (2008), 'On the History of Early Christianity', in Karl Marx and Friedrich Engels, *On Religion*, Mineola, NY: Dover Publications, pp. 316–47.

Foot, Rosemary (1985), *The Wrong War: American Policy and the Dimensions of the Korean Conflict, 1950–1953*, Ithaca: Cornell University Press.

___ (1990), *A Substitute for Victory: The Politics of Peacemaking at the Korean Armistice Talks*, Ithaca: Cornell University Press.

Foucault, Michel ([1966] 1973), *The Order of Things*, New York: Vintage Books.

Frank, Pat ([1951] 1953), *Hold Back the Night*, New York: Bantam Books.

Fugita, Stephen S. and David J. O'Brien (1991), *Japanese American Ethnicity: The Persistence of Community*, Seattle: University of Washington Press.

'Full Text of President Moon Jae-in's Speech at Swedish Parliament House' (2019), *Yonhap News*, 14 June <https://en.yna.co.kr/view/AEN20190614008500315> (last accessed 10 June 2021).

Fulton, Bruce (1992), '*Silver Stallion* by Ahn Junghyo', *The Journal of Korean Studies* 8, pp. 223–6.

'Future of Korea: Consultation with Nation on Neutralization Plan Urged' (1953), *The New York Times*, 4 October.

Galloway, David D. (1964), 'The Love Stance: Richard E. Kim's *The Martyred*', *Critique* 7.2, pp. 163–71.

236 *The Korean War Novel*

Gibson, Campbell and Kay Jung (2005), 'Historical Census Statistics on Population Totals by Race, 1790 to 1990, and by Hispanic Origin, 1970 to 1990, for Large Cities and Other Urban Places in the United States', *Working Paper No. 76*, Washington DC: U.S. Bureau of the Census, Population Division.

Go, In-hwan (2005), 'On *The Guest*: Hwang, Soek-young's Postcolonialism', *Journal of East Asian Studies* 39, pp. 281–98 (in Korean).

Gowman, Philip (2008), 'Sex, Modernity and the Korean War: A Review of Ahn Junghyo's *Silver Stallion*', *London Korean Links*, 9 January <https://londonkoreanlinks.net/2008/01/09/sex-modernity-and-the-korean-war/>(last accessed 24 August 2020).

Gunn, Simon (2006), *History and Cultural Theory*, Harlow: Pearson Longman.

Hahn, Monica (2013), 'The Gap between "Uprising" and "Massacre": A Review of the Sinchon Incident in Hwanghae Province', *Ihwa sahak yŏngu* [Ewha Historical Research] 46, pp. 97–137 (in Korean).

___ (2019), 'Socio-Economic Changes in North Korea and the Response of the Christian Community, 1945–1949: A Case Study of Sincheongun, Hwanghae Province', *Kyohoesa yŏngu* [Study of Church History] 54, pp. 145–83 (in Korean).

Hall, Stuart (1990), 'Cultural Identity and Diaspora', in Jonathan Rutherford (ed.), *Identity, Community, Culture, Difference*, London: Lawrence & Wishart, pp. 222–37.

Hammond, Andrew (2006), 'From Rhetoric to Rollback: Introductory Thoughts on Cold War Writing', in Andrew Hammond (ed.), *Cold War Literature: Writing the Global Conflict*, New York: Routledge, pp. 1–14.

'Han'gugŭi kŭgujuŭirŭl kwant'onghanŭn shingminji paeksŏngŭi muŭishik' [The Unconscious of the Colonised That Informs South Korean Right-Wing Extremism] (2017), *Hankyoreh*, 19 March <https://m.hani.co.kr/arti/society/society_general/787030.html#cb> (last accessed 25 June 2021).

Harden, Jacalyn D. (2003), *Double Cross: Japanese American in Black and White Chicago*, Minneapolis: University of Minnesota Press.

Harrington, John and Grant Suneson (2019), 'What Were the 13 Most Expensive Wars in U.S. History?' *USA Today*, 13 June <https://www.usatoday.com/story/money/2019/06/13/cost-of-war-13-most-expensive-wars-in-us-history/39556983/> (last accessed 19 June 2021).

Hernando, Almudena (2017), *The Fantasy of Individuality: On the Sociohistorical Construction of the Modern Subject*, trans. Pedro Fermin Maguire, Gewerbestrasse, Switzerland: Springer International.

Hirsch, Arnold R. (1995), 'Massive Resistance in the Urban North: Trumbull Park, Chicago, 1953–1966', *The Journal of American History* 82.2, pp. 522–50.

Hong, Christine (2012), 'Pyongyang Lost: Counterintelligence and Other Fictions of the Forgotten War', in Steven Belletto and Daniel Grausam (eds), *American Literature and Culture in an Age of Cold War: A Critical Reassessment*, Iowa City: University of Iowa Press, pp. 135–62.

___ (2020), *A Violent Peace: Race, U.S. Militarism, and Cultures of Democratization in Cold War Asia and the Pacific*, Stanford: Stanford University Press.

Hong, Yong-Pyo (2000), 'Han'guk chŏnjaengi nambuk kwan'gyee mich'in yŏnghyang' [The Influence of the Korean War on the Inter-Korean

Relationship], in Han'gukchŏnjaengyŏn'guhoe [Society for the Korean War Studies] (ed.), *Reappraisal of the Korean War in the Post-Cold War Era*, Seoul: Baiksanseodang, pp. 307–29.

Hughes, Theodore (2012), *Literature and Film in Cold War South Korea: Freedom's Frontier*, New York: Columbia University Press.

Hwang, Eundeog (2013), 'Diaspora and Cultural Translation: Focusing on Susan Choi's *The Foreign Student*', *Modern Fiction Studies* 20.1, pp. 151–74 (in Korean).

Hwang, Sok-yong ([2001] 2005), *The Guest*, trans. Kyung-Ja Chun and Maya West, New York: Seven Stories Press.

Hwang, Su-kyoung (2016), *Korea's Grievous War*, Philadelphia: University of Pennsylvania Press.

I, Manyŏl (2016), 'Pundan 70nyŏn, han'guk kidokkyoŭi sŏngch'algwa pansŏng' [National Division of Seventy Years, Critical Reflection on Korean Church], *Christianity and History in Korea* 44, pp. 5–25 (in Korean).

I, Tŏkchu (2008), 'Christian Nationalism and Socialism under Japanese Colonialism', *Theology and the World* 63, pp. 74–114 (in Korean).

Ijenŭn marhal su itta – manggagŭi chŏnjaeng: hwanghaedo shinch'ŏnsagŏn [Now It Can Be Told – The War of Oblivion: The Hwanghae Province Shinch'ŏn Incident] (2002), report, Munhwa Broadcasting Corporation.

Jameson, Fredric (1981), *The Political Unconscious: Narrative as a Socially Symbolic Act*, Ithaca: Cornell University Press.

___ (1988), 'Postmodernism and Consumer Society', in E. Ann Kaplan (ed.), *Postmodernism and Its Discontents: Theories, Practices*, London: Verso, pp. 13–29.

Jin, Daying (1993), 'Accounts of the Chinese People's Volunteers Prisoners of War: A Translation', *Graduate Student Theses, Dissertations, & Professional Papers*, University of Montana.

Jin, Ha (1990), *Between Silences: A Voice from China*, Chicago: University of Chicago Press.

___ (1999), *Waiting*, New York: Pantheon Books.

___ (2004), *War Trash*, New York: Vintage International.

___ (2008), *The Writer as Migrant*, Chicago: University of Chicago Press.

Jo, Jeong-rae ([1983–9] 2002), *T'aebaeksanmaek* [Taebaek Mountains], 10 vols, Seoul: Haenaem.

___ (1995), 'T'aebaeksanmaeg ch'angjakpogosŏ' [Writer's Report on T'aebaeksanmaek], *Chakkasegye* [Authors' World], pp. 96–124 (in Korean).

Joung, Ju-A (2014), 'The Age of Ideological Authenticity and Yi Mun-yol's Works of the 1980s', *Journal of Korean Literary History* 54, pp. 7–33 (in Korean).

Ju, Yeongbok (1993), *The 76 Prisoners of War*, Seoul: Taegwangch'ulp'ansa.

Jung, Byung-Joon (2012), 'North Korean Occupation of South Korea and the Change of Rural Society during the Korean War', *Journal of Korean Modern and Contemporary History* 62, pp. 33–77 (in Korean).

Kang, Ŭnchi (2001), 'Mikunŭi sinch'ŏn minkanin haksal puchŏnghan chŏk ŏpsta' [I Have Never Denied the US Army's Civilian Massacre in Shinch'on], *Bookmagazine Minjog21*, October, pp. 50–3.

Kee, Kwangseo (2012), 'People's Committee Elections in the South under North Korean Control during the Korean War', *Korean Unification Studies* 16.2, pp. 33–66 (in Korean).

238   The Korean War Novel

Kim, Chaeyong (2001), 'Naengjŏnjŏk pundan'gujo haech'eŭi sosŏlchŏk t'amgu – hwang sŏkyŏngŭi sonnim' [A Study of Dismantling the Cold War Division System in Hwang Sok-yong's *The Guest*], *Silcheon munhak* [Literature of Practice] (August), pp. 322–32 (in Korean).

Kim, Daniel Y. (2009), '"Bled In, Letter by Letter": Translation, Postmodernity, and the Subject of Korean War: History in Susan Choi's *The Foreign Student*', *American Literary History* 21.3, pp. 550–83.

___ (2020), *The Intimacies of Conflict: Cultural Memory and the Korean War*, New York: New York University Press.

Kim, Dong-Choon (2000), *The Unending Korean War: A Social History*, trans. Sung-ok Kim, Larkspur, CA: Tamal Vista Publications.

Kim, Haknoh (2022), 'Who Is Us? The People's Uprising of October 1946 as a Hegemony Struggle for the Formation of US', *Korean Political Science Review* 56.1, pp. 5–34 (in Korean).

Kim, Hun Joon (2014), *The Massacres at Mt. Halla: Sixty Years of Truth Seeking in South Korea*, Ithaca: Cornell University Press.

Kim, Hye-in (2016), 'History of Exile, Time of Refuge: Focused on Self-Narrative of Joo, Young-Bok Captive for Neutral Nation during Period of Korean War', *Sanghur Hakbo: The Journal of Korean Modern Literature* 48, pp. 49–88 (in Korean).

Kim, Hyunsook (1998), '*Yanggongju* as an Allegory of the Nation: Images of Working-Class Women in Popular and Radical Texts', in Elaine H. Kim and Chungmoo Choi (eds), *Dangerous Women: Gender & Korean Nationalism*, New York: Routledge, pp. 175–201.

Kim, Ilsu (2004), 'Taeguwa 10wŏl hangjaeng' [Taegu and October Uprising], *Kiŏkkwa chŏnmang* [Memory and Prospect] 8, pp. 145–57.

Kim, Jae Woong (2020), 'Pro-Japanese Group Liquidation and Land Reform in North Korea Seen through the Eyes of the Public', *The Journal of the Humanities for Unification* 81, pp. 235–74 (in Korean).

Kim, Jodi (2008), '"I'm Not Here, If This Doesn't Happen": The Korean War and Cold War Epistemologies in Susan Choi's *The Foreign Student* and Heinz Insu Fenkl's *Memories of My Ghost Brother*', *Journal of Asian American Studies* 11.3, pp. 279–302.

___ (2010), *Ends of Empire: Asian American Critique and the Cold War*, Minneapolis: University of Minnesota Press.

___ (2017), 'Settler Modernity's Spatial Exceptions: The US POW Camp, Metapolitical Authority, and Ha Jin's *War Trash*', *American Quarterly* 69.3, pp. 569–87.

Kim, Joo Ok (2022), *Warring Genealogies: Race, Kinship, and the Korean War*, Philadelphia: Temple University Press.

Kim, Kirsteen and Sebastian C. H. Kim (2018), 'The Christian Impact on the Shaping of the First Republic of Korea, 1945–48: Anti-Communism or Vision for a New Nation?', *Religion, State & Society* 46.4, pp. 402–17.

Kim, Kwangsik (1987), '8·15 chikhu han'guksahoewa migunjŏngŭi sŏnggyŏk' [The Nature of Korean Society and the US Military Government after 8·15], *Critical Review of History* 1, pp. 49–72 (in Korean).

Kim, Kyoung-Tae (2016), 'The Proliferation of the Tenancy Disputes and the Demands of Lowered Tenant Rental up to 40% in the First Half of the 1920s', *Sarim: The Historical Journal* 55, pp. 165–204 (in Korean).

Bibliography   239

Kim, Monica (2019), *The Interrogation Rooms of the Korean War: The Untold History*, Princeton: Princeton University Press.

Kim, Myŏng-in ([1990] 1991), 'Han hŏmujuŭijaŭi kil ch'atki' [A Nihilist's Search of a Path], in *Imunyŏllon* [Criticism on Yi Munyeol], Seoul: Saminhaeng, pp. 162–92.

Kim, Richard E. (1964). *The Martyred*, New York: Penguin.

___ (1985), *Irŏbŏrin shiganŭl ch'ajasŏ* [In Search of Lost Time], Seoul: Sŏmundang.

Kim, Seung-Tae (2006), 'Pro-Japanese Collaboration of the Korean Protestant Churches: Degeneration and Reorganization of Denominations in the Late Japanese Colonial Period', *Christianity and History in Korea* 24, pp. 5–65 (in Korean).

Kim, Song-chil (1993), *Yŏksa ap'esŏ: han sahakchaŭi 6.25 ilgi* [In Front of History: A Historian's Diary of 6·25], Seoul: Ch'angjakkwa pip'yŏngsa.

Kim, Sŏnho (2020), *Chosŏninmin'gun: puk'an muryŏgŭi hyŏngsŏnggwa yuil ch'ejeŭi kiwŏn* [Korean People's Army: The Making of the North Korean Army and the Origin of the Kim Il-Sung's Regime], Seoul: Hanyang University Press.

Kim, Wang-bae (2017), 'Language, Emotion and Collective Behavior: The Case of Anti-impeachment Rally of President Park, Geun-hye', *Korean Journal of Cultural Sociology* 25, pp. 7–59 (in Korean).

Kim, Wook Dong (2007), *Richard E. Kim: His Life and Work*, Seoul: Seoul National University Press (in Korean).

'Kimwŏnbong iŏ sŭt'ok'ollŭm yŏnsŏlkkaji' [Going from Bad to Worse: From Kim-wŏn-pong Speech to Stockholm Speech] (2019), *JoongAng Daily*, 20 June <https://news.joins.com/article/23501516> (last accessed 10 June 2021).

Kindig, Jessie (2021), 'The Violent Embrace', *Boston Review: A Political and Literary Forum*, 5 April <https://www.bostonreview.net/articles/the-violent-embrace> (last accessed 24 August 2021).

Kitano, Harry H. L. (1981), 'Asian-Americans: The Chinese, Japanese, Koreans, Pilipinos, and Southeast Asians', *AAPSS* 454, pp. 125–38.

Ko, Young-Eun (2016), 'A Study of Anti-communism Ideology in Korean Churches', *Theology and Praxis* 52, pp. 867–93 (in Korean).

Koh, Boo Eung and Eun Jin Na (2008), 'The Construction of a Transnational Space in Susan Choi's *The Foreign Student*', *American Fiction Studies* 15.1, pp. 29–52 (in Korean).

'Kongsanseryŏk chungnipchuŭi iyong' [Communist Forces Exploit Neutralization] (1957), *Hankukilbo*, 6 March.

The Korea Institute of Military History (KIMH) (1997), *The Korean War Vol. 1*, intro. Allan R. Millett, Lincoln: University of Nebraska Press.

'Korean Rejects Senator's Plan' (1960), *The New York Times*, 23 October.

Kurashige, Lon (2002), *Japanese American Celebration and Conflict: A History of Ethnic Identity and Festival, 1934–1990*, Los Angeles: University of California Press.

Kwon, Boduerae (2012), 'The Vision of Neutralism 1945–1968: Asia beyond the Cold War Regime, or Notes on Choi In-hoon's Fictions', *Sanghur Hakbo: The Journal of Korean Modern Literature* 34, pp. 261–313 (in Korean).

Kwon, Heonik (2010), *The Other Cold War*, New York: Columbia University Press.

LaFeber, Walter (1992), 'An End to Which Cold War?' in Michael J. Hogan (ed.), *The End of the Cold War: Its Meaning and Implications*, New York: Cambridge University Press, pp. 13–20.

Lait, Jack and Lee Mortimer (1950), *Chicago Confidential*, New York: Dell.

Lee, Byeong-ju ([1981, 1985] 2006), *Chirisan* [Mount Chiri], rev., 7 vols, Paju: Hangilsa.

Lee, Chong-sik (1963), 'Land Reform, Collectivisation and the Peasants in North Korea', *The China Quarterly* 14, pp. 65–81.

___ (1964), 'Korean Partition and Unification', *Journal of International Affairs* 18.2, pp. 221–33.

Lee, Eun Seon (2018), '6.25 War and WCC and Korean Church', *Korea Reformed Theology* 58, pp. 213–53 (in Korean).

Lee, Gyu-tae (2006), 'The Activities of Committee for the Preparation of Korean Independence (CPKI) and Groping for Unification of Korea', *Journal of Korean Modern and Contemporary History*, 36 (2006), pp. 7–48 (in Korean).

Lee, Hyung Kyu (2020), 'A Sociological Study of Religious Violence in the Korean War', *Asia Journal of Religion and Society*, 8.2, pp. 91–127 (in Korean).

Lee, Im-Ha (2010), 'The Execution of Communist Collaboration during the Korean War', *Sarim: The Historical Journal* 36, pp. 101–40 (in Korean).

Lee, James Kyung-Jin (2021), 'Richard Eun-kook Kim', in Victor Bascara and Josephine Nock-Hee Park (eds), *Asian American Literature in Transition, 1930–1965*, Cambridge: Cambridge University Press, pp. 332–51.

Lee, Jongsoo James (2006), *The Partition of Korea after World War II: A Global History*, New York: Macmillan.

Lee, Kihan (2003), '*The Martyred* Revisited: Challenging the Parameters of Asian American Literature', *Journal of American Studies* 35.3 pp. 160–77.

Lee, Shin-Cheol (2004), 'Civilian Massacres Perpetrated in the Northern Areas of the Korean Peninsula during the Korean War', *Quarterly Review of Korean History* 54, pp. 131–70 (in Korean).

Lee, Sun-woo (2013), 'The Characteristics and Arrangement of the Prisoners of War Who Chose to Go to Neutral Countries during the Korean War', *Yŏksawa hyŏnshil* [History and Reality] 90, pp. 317–58 (in Korean).

Lee, Youkyung (2018), 'South Korea's Moon Becomes Kim Jong Un's Top Spokesman at UN', *Bloomberg*, 26 September <https://www.bloom berg.com/news/articles/2018-09-26/south-korea-s-moon-becomes-kim-jong -un-s-top-spokesman-at-un> (last accessed 11 June 2021).

'Letter from Filipov (Stalin) to Soviet Ambassador in Prague, Conveying Message to CSSR Leader Klement Gottwald' (1950), History and Public Policy Program Digital Archive, Russian State Archive of Socio-Political History (RGASPI), fond 558, opis 11, delo 62, listy 71–72. Reprinted in Andrei Ledovskii, 'Stalin, Mao Tsedunh I Koreiskaia Voina 1950–1953 godov', *Novaia I Noveishaia Istoriia* no. 5 (September–October 2005), 79–113, trans. Gary Goldberg, 27 August <https://digitalarchive.wilson-center.org/document/112225> (last accessed 23 September 2023).

Bibliography 241

'Letter, Syngman Rhee to Dr. Robert T. Oliver [Soviet Translation]' (1949), History and Public Policy Program Digital Archive, CWIHP Archive, trans. Gary Goldberg, 30 September <https://digitalarchive.wilsoncenter.org /document/119385> (last accessed 20 August 2021).

Lim, Jie-Hyun (2010), 'Victimhood Nationalism in Contested Memories: National Mourning and Global Accountability', in Aleida Assmann and Sebastian Conrad (eds), *Memory in a Global Age: Discourses, Practices and Trajectories*, London: Macmillan, pp. 138–62.

MacDonald, Callum (1991), '"So Terrible a Liberation" – The UN Occupation of North Korea', *Critical Asian Studies* 23.2, pp. 3–19.

Macherey, Pierre (1980), *A Theory of Literary Production*, trans. Geoffrey Wall, London: Routledge.

Marx, Karl ([1932] 1978), *The German Ideology: Part I*, in Robert C. Tucker (ed.), *The Marx-Engels Reader*, 2nd ed., New York: Norton, pp. 146–200.

___ ([1867] 1990), *Capital Volume I*, intro. Ernest Mandel, trans. Ben Fowkes, New York: Penguin.

Masuda, Hajimu (2015), *Cold War Crucible: The Korean Conflict and the Postwar World*, Cambridge, MA: Harvard University Press.

McIntyre, Alasdair (1984), 'The Virtues, the Unity of a Human Life, and the Concept of a Tradition', in Michael J. Sandel (ed.), *Liberalism and Its Critics*, Oxford: Basil Blackwell, pp. 125–48.

Michener, James A. ([1953] 1973), *The Bridges at Toko-ri*, New York: Fawcett Books.

'Migugi hanbando naejŏnggansŏbŭl wihae ch'ulbyŏnghaessŏtta' [The US Sent Out Its Troops to Intervene in Korea's Internal Affairs] (2020), *Monthly Chosun*, July <https://monthly.chosun.com/client/news/viw.asp?nNews Numb=202007100045> (last accessed 13 June 2021).

Millett, Alan (2004), 'The Korean People: Missing in Action in the Misunderstood War, 1945–1954', in William Stueck (ed.), *The Korean War in World History*, Lexington: University Press of Kentucky, p. 13–60.

Min, Kyung Kil (1997), 'The Korean War and the Repatriation of P.O.W.', *Seoul International Law Journal* 4.1, pp. 1–15 (in Korean).

Mitgang, Herbert (1990), 'Books of the Times; Korean's Novel Is Anti-war but Not Anti-American', *The New York Times*, 21 February.

'"Naejŏn p'yohyŏnŭn chwap'ajŏk shigak" han'gukchŏnjaeng chŏnmun'gadŭl chijŏk' ['The Term Civil War Is a Leftist Marker', Korean War Experts Say] (2006), *JoongAng Daily*, 21 November <https://news.joins.com/article /2513462> (last accessed 13 June 2021).

Nessly, William (2018), 'Plotting Colonial Independence: Intra-Asian Conflict in the Novels of Richard Kim', *MELUS* 43.2, pp. 53–77.

'A "Neutralized" Korea: Some Advantages to U.S. Discerned, but Its Achievement Is Held Unlikely' (1953), *The New York Times*, 1 October.

'Nomoksaga shipchaga tŭlgo chip'oeganŭn iyu' [Why an Old Pastor Goes to a T'aegŭkki Rally Bearing a Cross] (2017), *Newsjoy*, 24 February <https:// www.newsnjoy.or.kr/news/articleView.html?idxno=209137> (last accessed 8 September 2021).

Oh, Bonnie B. C. (2002), 'Introduction: The Setting', in Bonnie B. C. Oh (ed.), *Korea under the American Military Government 1945–1948*, London: Praeger, pp. 1–11.

242 *The Korean War Novel*

Oliver, Robert T. (1954), *Syngman Rhee: The Man behind the Myth*, New York: Dodd, Mead & Com.

Paik, Nak-chung (2021), 'On "Eradicating the Vestiges of Pro-Japanese Collaborators"', trans. Myoungsook Park and Phillip Maher, *The Asia-Pacific Journal*, 19.21.4.

Pak, Inchan (2009), 'The Pitfalls of Literary Globalization: Korea's Self Othering in Ahn Junghyo's *Silver Stallion*', *The New Korean Journal of English Language and Literature* 5.1, pp. 213–31.

Pak, Jacqueline (2006), 'Cradle of the Covenant: Ahn Changho and the Christian Roots of the Korean Constitution', in Robert E. Buswell Jr. and Timothy S. Lee (eds), *Christianity in Korea*, Honolulu: University of Hawai'i Press, pp. 116–48.

Pak, Yŏngryul and Chinhŭi Pak (2001), 'Shinch'ŏn haksarŭn kidokkyowa sahoejuŭi taeribŭi sanmul' [Shinch'ŏn Massacre Is a Product of the Antagonism between Christianity and Socialism], *Wŏlganmal* [Monthly Word] (July), pp. 162–7.

Palaver, Wolfgang (1995). 'Schmitt's Critique of Liberalism', *Telos* 102, pp. 43–71.

'Pangt'ansonyŏndan (BTS) paenp'ŭllit'ŭsang susang sogame chung net'ijŭn punnohan iyu' [Reasons for Chinese Netizens' Anger at BTS's Van Fleet Award Speech] (2020), *Topstarnews*, 12 October <https://www.topstarnews.net> (last accessed 15 June 2021).

Parikh, Crystal (2009), 'Writing the Borderline Subject of War in Susan Choi's *The Foreign Student*', *Southern Quarterly* 46.3, pp.7–68.

Park, Bo-Kyoung (2019), 'Korean Church during the Korean War: Missiological Reflection on War and Peace', *The Institute for Korean Christianity Culture* 11, pp. 1–30 (in Korean).

Park, Chung-shin (2003), *Protestantism and Politics in Korea*, Seattle: University of Washington Press.

Park, Joohyun and Jungkyu Suh (2009), 'The Subaltern Speaks: *Silver Stallion* as the Rhetorical Space for *Yanggongju*', *Comparative Literature* 49, pp. 261–80.

Park, Josephine Nock-Hee (2016), *Cold War Friendships: Korea, Vietnam, and Asian American Literature*, New York: Oxford University Press.

Park, Myung-Lim ([1996] 2016), *Han'guk chŏnjaengŭi palbalgwa kiwŏn 2* [The Korean War: The Outbreak and Its Origins 2], Paju: Nanam.

___ ([1996] 2017), *Han'guk chŏnjaengŭi palbalgwa kiwŏn 1* [The Korean War: The Outbreak and Its Origins 1], Paju: Nanam.

Park, Tae-gyun (2005), *The Korean War*, Seoul: Ch'aekkwa hamkke (in Korean).

Park, Wan-suh ([1992] 2009), *Who Ate Up All the Shinga?* trans. Young-nan Yu and Stephen J. Epstein, New York: Columbia University Press.

'Puk sŏnjŏnmaech'e yŏnil mun taet'ongnyŏng parŏn pinan ... haegoehan chujang' [North Korean Propaganda Media Criticizes Again President Moon's North European Speech ... Absurd Claim'] (2019), *Newsis*, 29 June <https://newsis.com/common/?id=NISX20190629_0000695853&method=> (last accessed 11 June 2021).

Raeder, Linda C. (1998), 'Liberalism and the Common Good: A Hayekian Perspective on Communitarianism', *Independent Review* 98.4, pp. 519–35.

Rau, Petra (2013), *Our Nazis: Representations of Fascism in Contemporary Literature and Film*, Edinburgh: Edinburgh University Press.

Rees, David (1964), *Korea: The Limited War*, New York: St Martin's Press.

'Remembering Emmett Till' (n.d.), United States Civil Rights Trail <https://civilrightstrail.com/experience/sumner/> (last accessed 29 October 2023).

Rhee, Jooyeon (2016), 'Against Nihilism of Suffering and Death: Richard E. Kim and His Works', *Cross-Currents* 5.1, pp. 63–84.

Ricoeur, Paul (1970), *Freud and Philosophy: An Essay on Interpretation*, trans. Denis Savage, London: Yale University Press.

Rightmyer, Jack (2004), 'On Becoming Learned: A Profile of Ha Jin', *Poets & Writers* 32.5, pp. 44–50.

Ryu, Tae-ha (2005), 'A War Historical Significance through the Re-Illumination on the Sincheon 10·13 Anti-Communism Movement', *Kunsa* [Military History] 54, pp. 179–216 (in Korean).

Ryu, Youngju (2015), 'Truth or Reconciliation?: *The Guest* and the Massacre That Never Ends', *Positions: Asia Critique* 23.4, pp. 633–63.

Sandel, Michael J. (1984), 'Justice and the Good', in Michael J. Sandel (ed.), *Liberalism and Its Critics*, Oxford: Basil Blackwell, pp. 159–76.

'Shame on Chinese Fans' (2020), *Korea JoongAng Daily*, 14 October <https://koreajoongangdaily.joins.com/2020/10/14/opinion/editorials/BTS-The-Van-Fleet-Award/20201014192312357.html> (last accessed 16 June 2021).

Shin, Yong-Ha (1989), 'The Revolutionary Movement of the Tonghak Peasant Army of 1894: Seen Vis-a-Vis the French Revolution', *Korea Journal* 29.10, pp. 28–33.

Stone, I. F. ([1952] 1971), *The Hidden History of the Korean War*, New York: Monthly Review Press.

Stueck, William (1995), 'The United States, the Soviet Union, and the Division of Korea: A Comparative Approach', *The Journal of American–East Asian Relations* 4.1, pp. 1–27.

___ ([1995] 1997), *The Korean War: An International History*, Princeton: Princeton University Press.

___ (2002), *Rethinking the Korean War: A New Diplomatic and Strategic History*, Princeton: Princeton University Press.

Su, Lezhou (2012), *Narrative of Modern Chinese Masculinity in Ha Jin's Fiction*, Electronic Theses and Dissertations, University of Louisville.

Suh, Joong-seok (1998), 'The National Unification Movement around the Liberation', *Journal of Korean Independence Movement Studies* 12, pp. 355–70 (in Korean).

Sun, Mira (2018), 'The Modality and the Symbol of the Reform in Donghak and the Declaration in K. Marx', *Semiotic Inquiry* 57, pp. 155–76 (in Korean).

'T'aegŭkki pudaenŭn wae isŭrael kukkirŭl tŭrŏssŭlkka' [Why T'aegŭkki Protesters Waved Israel's National Flags] (2019), *P'irench'eŭi shikt'ak* [Dining Table of Firenze], 19 July <https://firenzedt.com/3542> (last accessed 25 June 2021).

Tsu, Jing (2010), *Sound and Script in Chinese Diaspora*. Cambridge, MA: Harvard University Press.

Valdés, Mario J. (1966), 'Faith and Despair: A Comparative Study of a Narrative Theme', *Hispania* 49.3, pp. 373–80.

Walsh, Chad (1964), 'Another War Raged Within', *The New York Times Book Review*, 16 February.

Watson, Jini Kim (2014), 'A Not-Yet-Postcolonial Peninsula: Rewriting Spaces of Violence, Division and Diaspora', *The Cambridge Journal of Postcolonial Literary Inquiry* 1.1, pp. 69–87.

___ (2021), *Cold War Reckonings: Authoritarianism and the Genres of Decolonization*, New York: Fordham University Press.

Weathersby, Kathryn (1993), 'The Soviet Role in the Early Phase of the Korean War: New Documentary Evidence', *The Journal of American–East Asian Relations* 2.4, pp. 425–58.

___ (1995), 'New Russian Archival Materials, Old American Debates, and the Korean War', *Problems of Post-Communism* 42.5, pp. 25–33.

Westad, Odd Arne (2007), *The Global Cold War: Third World Interventions and the Making of Our Times*, New York: Cambridge University Press.

White, Hayden (1973), *Metahistory: The Historical Imagination in Nineteenth-Century Europe*, Baltimore: Johns Hopkins University Press.

Wong, Sau-ling Cynthia ([1993] 2001), *Reading Asian American Literature: From Necessity to Extravagance*, Princeton: Princeton University Press.

'Xi Delivers Speech on War to Resist US Aggression and Aid Korea' (2020), *China Daily*, 23 October <https://www.chinadaily.com.cn/a/202010/23/WS5f923acaa31024ad0ba80812.html> (last accessed 15 June 2021).

Xiang, Sunny (2018), 'Race, Tone, and Ha Jin's "Documentary Manner"', *Comparative Literature* 70.1, pp. 72–92.

___ (2020), *Tonal Intelligence: The Aesthetics of Asian Inscrutability during the Long Cold War*, New York: Columbia University Press.

Xie, Xinqiu (2012), '*War Trash*: War Memoir as "False Document"', *Amerasia Journal* 38.2, pp. 35–42.

Xu, Tong (2018), 'Visualization of the Korean War and the US Army in Chinese and Korean Novels', *Hanminjongmunhwayŏn'gu* [The Review of Korean Cultural Studies] 64, pp. 67–90 (in Korean).

Yang, Hyunah (1998), 'Re-Membering the Korean Military Comfort Women: Nationalism, Sexuality, and Silencing', in Elaine H. Kim and Chungmoo Choi (eds), *Dangerous Women: Gender & Korean Nationalism*, New York: Routledge, pp. 123–39.

Yi, Munyeol (1992), *Shidaewaŭi purhwa* [Discontent with the Times], Seoul: Chayumunhaksa.

Yoo, Hyon Joo (2012), 'The Incurable Feminine: Women without a Country', in Naoki Sakai and Hyon Joo Yoo (eds), *The Trans-Pacific Imagination: Rethinking Boundary, Culture and Society*, Singapore: World Scientific Publishing, pp. 167–88.

Yoo, Theodore Jun (2020), *The Koreas: The Birth of Two Nations Divided*, Oakland, CA: University of California Press, ebook.

Yun, Chŏngran (2013), 'Han'gukchŏnjaeng hyujŏnhoedam pandaewa han'gukkyohoe' [Opposition to the Armistice of the Korean War and the Korean Church], *Han'guk kidokkyo yŏksa yŏn'gu soshik* [Korean Church History Center Newsletter] 102, pp. 19–24.

Zhang, Zeshi ([2000] 2009), *Chunggukkun p'oroŭi 6·25 ch'amjŏn'gi* [A Chinese POW's Memoir of the Korean War], trans. Chunsik Son, Seoul: Institute for Military History, Ministry of Korean Military Defense.

'2wŏl 25il taet'ongnyŏng ch'wiim 4chunyŏn kungmin ch'onggwŏlgiŭi nal' [25 February, Four Years from Park's Presidential Inauguration, the Day of Nationwide Rallies] (2017), *Dong-A Ilbo*, 24 February, A31.

'3.1chŏl t'aegŭkki chip'oee ch'onggwŏlgihapshida [Let's Stand up at the T'aegŭkki Rally of 1 March] (2017), *Chosunilbo*, 28 February, A6.

'6.25-lŭl naejŏnŭro pon saram: sŭt'allin, mot'aektong, kimilsŏng, munjaein' [Those Who Saw 6.25 as a Civil War: Stalin, Mao, Kim Il-sung, and Moon Jae-in] (2017), *Chogabje.com*, 19 October <https://www.chogabje.com /board/view.asp?C_IDX=75136&C_CC=AZ> (last accessed 13 June 2021).

'2017nyŏnŭi sŏnt'aek: taehanmin'guginya, kongsanhwanya' [The Choice of 2017: South Korea or Communist Reunification?] (2017), *Chosunilbo*, 3 January, A31.

Index

Anderson, B., 200
anti-communism, 15, 28, 30, 46–7, 50, 104, 162, 170–1, 175–6, 207, 213, 220, 229, 231–2
  anti-communist persecution, 24, 25, 26, 27–8, 29, 34, 50–3, 56, 61, 72–4, 104, 119, 120–5, 133, 146, 156, 180, 190–1
  anti-communist state-building, 8–11, 12–13, 161–3, 170–1, 208, 216, 228
  communist containment, 4, 5, 91, 94, 145

Baudrillard, J., 93
Belletto, S., 24, 35, 213
biopolitics, 80–1, 115
Bridges at Toko-ri, The (J. A. Michener), 23
Brooks, C., 108, 109, 110

Caprio, M., 19
Chang, D. C., 120, 123, 125–6, 136, 140, 148n, 175
Chinese Civil War, 116, 118, 120, 144–5
Chirisan (Mount Chiri, Lee Byeong-ju), 217–18, 219
Choi, S.-Y., 100
Chosŏn Democratic Party, 49, 184, 197
Cold War, 4–5, 15, 19, 33, 74, 103, 136, 175–6, 184, 212, 224
  anti-Cold War project, 25, 26–7, 29, 33, 34, 35–8, 91–2, 93,

116, 121, 122–3, 146, 150–1, 152–3, 161–3, 169–72, 170–1, 172, 175, 202, 203, 207, 214, 215–16, 221
  as epistemology, 1, 6, 7, 26, 29, 162, 227, 228
  as legacy, 3–4, 111–13, 176–7, 220–2, 227–32
  as our war, 2, 28, 30, 208–9, 221, 232
  as US-centred framework, 2, 23–4, 35, 38, 104, 111, 213
  post-Cold War neutralism, 169–72
  propaganda, 26, 36–7, 60, 66–7, 122–3, 136, 145
  regional, 7–12, 15, 28, 30, 96–100, 153, 188–9, 207–9
  US-led, 25, 29, 56, 60, 91, 116, 161–2, 163, 215
CPKI, 8, 9, 10, 48, 98, 189
Cumings, B., 5, 8, 9, 10, 13, 14, 16–17, 37, 39, 47, 48, 49, 51, 66, 94, 99, 102, 103, 113, 116, 143, 189, 193, 194, 197–8

Dallin, D., 16
decolonisation, 4, 9, 15, 16, 17, 25–6, 29, 30, 98, 103, 104, 111–12, 212, 225
division (system), 2, 7, 27–8, 30, 96, 104, 182, 184, 208–9, 214–15, 220, 228

Engels, F., 207

Filipov letter, 16
Foot, R., 26, 133, 145
Foreign Student, The (Susan Choi)
   anti-trusteeship campaign, 100–1
   chronological errors, 104–5, 108–10
   Cold War as lifeline for
      collaborators,104
   corroborating the Cold War
      perspective, 111–12
   elision of postcolonial dimension,
      96–105, 112–13
   elision of US racism, 105–6
   historical amnesia, 110
   Orientalism as ideological
      compensation, 106–7, 108
   panethnic solidarity, 108
   retro-styling, 93, 108–10
   Taegu Uprising, 102, 103
Foucault, M., 6

General Assembly election, 9, 14, 99,
   145, 225–6
Guest, The (Hwang Sok-yong)
   alliance of Christianity and
      communism, 187–8, 189–90
   Christian landowners as
      collaborators, 192–4, 196–7
   Christians as agents of the Cold
      War, 207–9
   class war disguised as a Cold War,
      183–4
   class war within a religious war,
      184–6, 188–9, 190–200, 204
   commonality between Marxism
      and Christianity, 206–7
   communal responsibility, 206
   critique of materialistic Christians,
      206–7
   historical reduction, 184–5,
      188–9
   inter-Korean reconciliation, 207
   land reform as Christian practice,
      206–7
   land reform as postcolonial justice,
      191–5, 197–200
   meaning of the guest, 181–2
   opposition to armistice, 209–10
   role of US army, 202–3
   see also Shinch'ŏn Uprising

guilt-by-association persecution, 25,
   61, 67, 73, 219

Hahn, M., 184, 196–7, 201
Hernando, A., 74–5
Hodge, J., 8, 9, 10, 11, 12, 87,
   96–100, 101–2, 103, 104–5,
   112
Hold Back the Night (Pat Frank),
   23–4
homo sacer, 72, 73, 84, 159, 175
Hong, C., 15, 29, 30, 33, 35, 77,
   212, 214

I, M., 208
ideological branding, 25, 73
impeachment of Park Geun-hye, 228
   far-right supporters, 229
   implications of flag waving, 231–2
   pro-Park rallying calls, 229–30

Jameson, F., 93, 118, 147
Jeju (Cheju) Uprising 10, 11, 92,
   96–100, 102

Kim, D. C., 14–15, 19, 51, 52, 62,
   63, 66–7, 73, 163
Kim, D. Y., 25, 29, 91–2, 94, 106–7,
   108, 146, 182, 183, 208, 213
Kim, J., 1, 6, 19, 25, 91–2, 103, 115,
   212–13
Kim, M., 10, 11, 87, 98, 105, 135,
   145, 169, 174, 175
Korean Democratic Party, 8–9, 9–10,
   17, 225
Korean nationalists, 8, 9, 10, 48–9
   Christian nationalists, 48–9, 181,
      183–4, 186, 190–1, 195–6, 197,
      198–9, 204–5
   Kim, Koo (Ku), 9, 100, 101, 112,
      170–1, 225
Korean War
   armistice talk, 15, 22, 26, 28, 126,
      133, 144, 209–10, 227
   as a civil war, 1, 2, 12, 13–14, 15,
      16–17, 18, 24–5, 29, 33, 36–8,
      63, 65–7, 92, 93–5, 102, 103,
      111, 116, 184, 213, 221–4
   as a complex war, 18–19, 184

248 *The Korean War Novel*

Korean War (*cont.*)
  as a proxy or international war, 1,
    12, 16, 17, 24, 25, 36, 42, 48,
    189, 221
  as a regional Cold War, 223–4
  Chinese perspective on, 226–7
  conservative perspective on, 221–2,
    223–5
  Stalin's approval of, 18
  moral war, 26, 56, 120, 136–7,
    144–6
  unfolding of, 20–2
  US air bombing, 39–40, 41, 56, 60,
    67–8, 69, 86, 119, 213, 214, 216
KPR, 8, 9–10, 11, 98
Kurashige, L., 109
Kwon, B., 170–1, 172
Kwon, H., 1, 6, 73, 74

LaFeber, W., 5
land reform, 17, 49, 51, 62, 99, 183,
    190–4, 198, 199, 207, 224
Lee, G.-T., 8, 10, 98
Lee, S.-C., 39, 51, 52
Lee, S.-W., 175, 176
legitimacy of the First Republic of
    South Korea, 12, 224–6, 228

MacDonald, C., 44–5, 47, 51, 53
Macherey, P., 3, 34, 57, 60, 104
Manchurian Candidate, The (Richard
    Cordon), 24
Martyred, The (Richard E. Kim)
  eclipsing of war crimes, 38–40,
    43–7, 56
  existentialism, 55, 56
  figuration of war crimes, 41–2,
    50–3
  proxy struggle between Christianity
    and Communism, 42, 48, 50–3
  religious persecution, 34, 37, 52–3,
    56
  religious persecution as diversion,
    41, 56
Marx, K., 130, 164, 207

Nambugun (Southern Partisan Army,
    I T'ae), 219
National Foundation Day, 227–8

national liberation 7–8, 17, 63, 87,
    94, 150, 199–200, 218, 223,
    228
  aftermaths of, 8–15, 16–17, 25,
    48–9, 91, 93, 96–105, 111–12,
    162–4, 170–1, 189–90, 192,
    194, 196–8, 207–8, 218, 224–5
Nessly, W., 33, 35–6, 38, 213
neutralisation of Korea, 27, 172, 176,
    218
Northwest Youth Corps *see* rightist
    youth corps

Oh, B. B. C., 8–9, 98, 163
Oliver, R. T., 13, 14, 225
Orientalism, 25, 26, 30, 59, 106,
    107, 108, 110, 115

Parikh, C., 91, 107, 108
Park, J. N.-H., 23, 29, 33, 56, 92, 94,
    106, 108, 213
Park, M.-L., 9, 12
partisan fiction, 28, 216–21
peace initiative by Moon Jae-in, 221
  conservative response to, 221–2,
    223
  North's response to, 222
People's Committee, 8, 9, 10, 48, 49,
    62–3, 99, 101, 186, 190, 195–6
postcolonial conflict, 11, 16, 25, 27,
    37, 93, 97, 98–9, 111–13,
    191–5
  reverse, 27, 104, 184, 216
postliberation Korean politics *see*
    national liberation
post-war narrative (Olivier
    Courteaux), 60

Rau, P., 2
Rawls, J., 135
Rees, D., 16
repatriation, 22, 26, 125–8, 132–3,
    136–7, 140, 143, 144–5, 173,
    178n
  non-, 126, 138, 171
  screening, 27, 119, 121, 127, 131,
    138, 149, 150, 169, 173, 216
  (non-)voluntary, 22, 26, 133, 140,
    145, 150, 220

Index   249

reunification, 7, 12, 14, 19, 27, 28, 176, 207–10, 212, 216, 218, 219, 220, 228
rewriting of (hi)story, 1, 2, 27, 33–4, 56–7, 61, 83, 145–6, 185
rice collection, 102
Ricoeur, P., 3
rightist youth corps, 10–11, 24, 33–4, 42, 46–7, 50, 51–3, 64, 98, 111, 185, 186, 190, 200, 225, 229
right-wing Christians, 27–8, 42, 48–50, 52, 163, 181, 184–6, 188–92, 195, 202, 205, 207–10, 216
right-wing terrorism, 10, 11, 27, 46, 50, 51, 99, 103, 119, 120, 121–2, 123, 125, 126, 131, 146, 155, 156, 159, 225
Ryu, T-H., 184–5, 202
Ryu, Y., 182, 183

Shinch'ŏn Uprising
  as a postcolonial class struggle, 182–4 190–5, 196–9, 204
  as a religious conflict, 183, 184–7, 188–9
  civilian massacre, 200–1, 204–5
  contested by Commission of International Association of Democratic Lawyers, 202–3
  historical facts of, 184–5, 187–8, 189–91, 196–7, 198
  MBC's investigation of, 203
  North Korea's propaganda of, 201
  two-hour-stay theory of, 201–2
Silver Stallion (Ahn Junghyo)
  ambivalence to the diseased Other, 80–5
  birth of a new female subject, 74–8, 89
  clash between Confucianism and individualism, 68, 86–7, 89
  critique of foreign forces' intervention, 60–1, 63, 65–6, 67, 72, 76–7
  eclipsing of class struggle, 60, 63, 72
  female bonding, 74–5

ostracism as metaphor of anti-communist persecution, 25, 61, 73–4
patriarchal anxiety, 68–70, 86, 88
war against patriarchy, 78–80, 86–7
xenophobia, 70–1
Square, The (Choi In-Hun)
  coffin as a metaphor of Cold War Korea, 152–3
  corruption of public square, 154–5, 156–9, 166–7
  critique of rival Korean regimes, 152–64, 168, 169, 215–16
  differences of editions, 152–3, 167, 168, 171, 173, 177n, 216
  failure in ideological becoming, 155–6
  fate of real-life non-repatriates, 174–6, 178n
  Korean neutrality, 169–72, 176
  love relationship as a shelter, 150, 164–7
  meaning of the protagonist's suicide, 172–4, 176
  neocolonial dependence of the South, 161–3, 169–71
  political sabotage, 168, 169
  sham revolution, 158–9, 163–4, 169
Stone, I. F., 14, 19
Stueck, W., 7, 8, 19, 20–1
Sunshine Policy, 112, 230
Surrendered, The (Chang-rae Lee), 22–3

T'aebaeksanmaek (Taebaek Mountains, Jo Jeong-rae), 219–20
T'aegŭkki protesters, 28, 210, 228–32
Tonghak Movement, 187
Truman, H. S., 7, 14, 19, 20, 25, 122

US military government see Hodge. J.

victimhood nationalism, 2, 37, 150

250 *The Korean War Novel*

Waiting (Ha Jin), 114–15
war crimes, 27, 34
  eclipsing of, 52, 56
  KPA's, 24, 34–5, 39, 48, 51, 216
  rightist youth corps', 10–11, 24,
    33, 46–7, 48, 50–3, 111, 225
  ROKA's, 44, 47, 51–2, 56, 92, 95,
    111, 213–14
  US Armed Forces', 3, 24, 33, 38–9,
    41, 44–6, 52, 56, 60–1, 63,
    67–8, 71, 131, 142, 180–1, 201,
    202, 203, 215–16
  see also right-wing terrorism;
    Shinch'ŏn Uprising
War Trash (Ha Jin)
  capitalist thinking, 130–1, 133–5
  claim on objectivity, 116, 117–18,
    119, 128, 135, 146–7
  collective struggle, 127–8, 131–5,
    137–43, 147
  comparison with Jin Daying, 144
  comparison with Zhang Zheshi,
    26, 116, 118–20, 121, 123, 131,
    138–9, 143–4
  documentary style, 116, 119, 121,
    128
  eclipsing international dimension,
    140

  history of Chinese Civil War, 118,
    120
  liberal individualism, 26, 116,
    133–5, 137–40, 146–7
  mechanical egalitarianism, 129–30,
    133, 134
  plagiarism, 118, 147n
  pro-Communist terrorism, 121,
    123–4
  psychological profiling, 140–3
  withholding of back stories, 120–1,
    124–6
  writer's mission, 115, 117
Watson, J. K., 29, 183
Weathersby, K., 18–19
Westad, O. A., 4, 5
White, H., 117–18, 147
Wong, S.-L., 3

Xiang, S., 116, 143
Xie, X., 115, 143

Yang, H., 69–70, 71
Yongbingtuan gushi (Huang Lu), 44
Yŏngungshidae (The Age of Heroes,
  Yi Munyeol), 218–19
Yoo, H. J., 80
Yoo, T. J., 8, 10, 215